THE FÜHRER LED
BUT WE OVERTOOK HIM

Author on fiftieth anniversary of VE Day.

The Führer Led
But We Overtook Him

by

PHIL DURHAM

with a Foreword

by

Admiral of the Fleet Sir Julian Oswald GCB

The Pentland Press
Edinburgh – Cambridge – Durham – USA

First published in 1996 by
The Pentland Press Ltd
1 Hutton Close
South Church
Bishop Auckland
Durham

ISBN 1-85821-365-7

Typeset by Carnegie Publishing, 18 Maynard St, Preston
Printed and bound by Bookcraft, Bath

Contents

	Illustrations	vii
	Maps	ix
	Foreword	xi
Chapter 1	Mediterranean Peace	1
Chapter 2	Arctic Winter	7
Chapter 3	The Battle For Narvik	15
Chapter 4	Frenchmen, Friends or Foes	31
Chapter 5	Blitzed Portsmouth Technical Courses	40
Chapter 6	Standing by a New Ship	50
Chapter 7	To Sea In *Laforey*	54
Chapter 8	The Capture of Diego Suarez	65
Chapter 9	Eastern Fleet	78
Chapter 10	Operation Pedestal	83
Chapter 11	On Patrol in a German U-boat	90
Chapter 12	Working up in *Stoic*	117
Chapter 13	Eastward Bound in *Stoic*	131
Chapter 14	First Malacca Strait Patrol	146
Chapter 15	Special Operation Off Sumatra	156
Chapter 16	A Chase Off Penang	163
Chapter 17	The Captain's Trilby Hat	172
Chapter 18	In The Java Sea	179
Chapter 19	Sunda Strait	189
Chapter 20	By U-boat to Westminster	196
	Glossary	208

Illustrations

Author on fiftieth anniversary of VE Day. . . . . frontispiece

Barham's 48-foot Scott Payne picket boat, powered by three 100-HP petrol engines. 3

HMA/S Trawler *Beryl* patrolling off the boom, Alexandria, October 1939. 5

Norfolk: severe Arctic weather on Northern Patrol, February 1940. . . . 13

Result of *Echo*'s fishing by depth charge during campaign to recapture Narvik, May 1940. 20

Laforey, newly commissioned in Scapa Flow, August 1941. 55

Ark Royal torpedoed by *U81* off Gibraltar, 13 November 1941. 58

Watching *Laforey*'s Courier Bay bombardment, Madagascar, May 1942. . 69

Captured tug *Count Benyowski* at Diego Suarez, Madagascar, May 1942. . 73

Laforey refuelling at sea from *Indomitable* before Pedestal Malta convoy, August 1942. 81

'Sam' Marriott who commanded *Graph, Stoic* and *U776* 106

A trot of S-class submarines alongside their depot ship. (From a painting by Tom Dowling.) 110

The crew of *Graph* (ex *U570*) alongside their depot ship, February 1943. 114

Stoic's crest (I stand fast) 127

Stoic's crew on return from the Far East, February 1945. 193

'Joe' Perowne, 'Sam' Marriott and the author on *Stoic*'s return, February 1945. 199

Sailing the captured *U776* up to Westminister Pier, May 1945. 201

Sceptre, commanded by the author, and *Taciturn* leaving Portland for exercises, May 1946. 206

Illustrations

Maps

Movements of HMS *Echo* in Norwegian waters 18
Capture of Diego Suarez, Madagascar 66
Malacca Strait 147
Java Sea 180

Foreword

1995 WAS A SPECIAL YEAR FOR ANNIVERSARIES, for looking back and for remembering. For the non-participants in the Second World War, those who were still in short trousers or playing with dolls, and who have subsequently lived through the frosty peace of the Cold War, it is increasingly difficult to comprehend the pain, misery, degradation, discomfort, suffering and eventual relief of those who fought, and finally emerged victorious from, the worst war in history.

First hand accounts, such as *The Führer Led But We Overtook Him*, written from the bottom up as it were, which tells us, through the eyes and ears of witnesses, how people reacted, of their hopes, fears, sufferings, successes, fallibilities, strengths and particularly of their humour – naval humour *is* rather special – while largely omitting the already over discussed and disputatious grand strategy and political aspects of the struggle, refresh our understanding of what was really like for those at the very tip of the spear.

To many young (and no so young) readers it will seem almost incredible that, as a Midshipman, the author saw active service in a Battleship, an Anti-Submarine Trawler (of which he was Second-in-Command), a County Class Cruiser, a Destroyer and a Battlecruiser. One could be forgiven for thinking that he had fought a pretty full war in surface ships before he got into his beloved submarines! But submarines were his goal and he served in them with success and distinction. His fascinating story, including the explanation as to why he served in two former German U-Boats is all here in the pages which follow.

The pluck shown by Phil Durham in war is matched in his subsequent life ashore where he refused to let serious physical disability deter him from leading a full, active, successful and happy public and family life. We can see the very special qualities which made this possible shining through this enthralling tale of one very exceptional young man's war at sea.

Remembrance Day 1995
Julian Oswald

CHAPTER I

Mediterranean Peace

WARSHIPS OF THE MEDITERRANEAN FLEET lay moored in the shimmering midday heat of Alexandria Harbour when the Second World War broke out on 3rd September 1939. Just after Neville Chamberlain's sad, flat-toned broadcast, a signal addressed "All concerned at home and abroad" was distributed; it read "Commence hostilities at once with Germany. Time of origin 1117." The day before, on conclusion of the Fleet Regatta, Admiral Layton, who flew his flag in *Barham*, had talked of life at sea in war and advised us of the importance of taking regular exercise, by which he did not refer to weight lifting, glass by glass.

For a junior midshipman in the battleship *Barham*, flagship of the 1st Battle Squadron, little changed. All polished surfaces, such as the ends of gun barrels and brass work, were painted over and, quite uselessly, the gunroom snotties were set to work to copy silhouettes of all the German heavy ships in indian ink to be pasted on the doors of the heads. The 2100 penance of the fleet flashing exercise still took place. Morse letters, numbers and symbols winked from the duty ship's yard arm at twelve words a minute. The better the performance the less often pairs of snotties, one reading and one writing down, had to rouse themselves up on deck after dinner: poor performance could disrupt evening shore leave and social activities.

Every evening, except Sundays, the gunroom dressed for dinner. On Sundays plain clothes were worn for supper which was followed by a film show under the quarterdeck awning and the 15-inch guns of Y turret. In the cool of the evening, in between reels, it was peaceful to watch the life of a fleet in harbour. Lights of other ships mirrored by their reflections were all around: cruisers to the North inside the breakwater; destroyers berthed both in trots at anchor and alongside their depot ships; submarines lying alongside *Maidstone*, their depot ship, and Empire flying boats, civilian versions of the Sunderlands, which maintained a regular, if slow, service to South Africa, lit up at their moorings beside which Ras el Tin Lighthouse flashed. To and fro steamed the boat traffic of the Fleet, their red, green and white steaming lights reflected in the murky harbour water, each boat commanded by a white helmeted midshipman wearing a dirk, a small sword the size of a bayonet, on his hip. It was a dancing prospect of busy activity, peaceful but full of life, with only the dark coal wharves and the odd silhouette of a felucca sail eclipsing the lights of Alexandria beyond.

In the previous two months the Mediterranean Fleet had prepared for war. The battleships *Warspite, Malaya* and *Barham* had each been docked in Malta for repairs, bottom scraping and painting. A week-long exercise in the waters between Greece, Crete, Cyprus and Egypt saw mock battles between red and green fleets; *Barham* carried out full calibre firing from both the 15-inch turrets and the port and starboard batteries of 6-inch guns. Great flakes of soot fluttered down, griming the scrubbed teak quarterdeck after each salvo; more work for the squads of seamen despatched at 0630 each weekday to scrub decks with brooms and then to squeegee off the dirty water from the teak, which dried from brown to a light silvery sand colour as the sun and temperature rose.

Once a week, lines of men on all fours would sand and holystone (a form of pumice) the well wetted decks: the kneeling men (hence the holy) slowly moved forward in line abrading off every mark which could mar the light golden grain of the teak which then dried golden white. With over 1,000 men needed to man a battleship's weapons and keep it steaming at action stations, such labour intensive activities were needed to keep crews occupied, as were such drills, practices, harbour exercises and maintenance work as could be devised.

While *Barham* was docked in Malta, I had taken over as midshipman of the first picket boat, a beautiful sleek black-enamelled 45-foot Scott Payne boat powered by three 100-horsepower petrol engines controlled by bendix levers. At about 10 knots the hard-chined bow would lift and the 3-ton boat would skim the waves at 23 knots. The fingertip engine controls, three propellers and twin rudders, allowed great handling finesse. The boat could move sideways between obstructions fore and aft, a valuable asset when leaving a short jetty, as in Alexandria when over a dozen boats would be berthed to await officers coming off shore at 1800 in time to bathe and change for dinner. As skill increased, these high octane petrol-thirsty boats were a joy to manoeuvre and provided an early opportunity to practise the art of shiphandling.

A draft of naval reserves newly called up had arrived in Alexandria a fortnight before war was declared to bring crews up to a war time complement. Extra shells and cordite were embarked, the shells fused, war routine exercised and darken ship practised. Still sea exercises involved lines of warships manoeuvring in company, streaming fog buoys for the ship astern to follow, maintaining station three cables apart and behaving as if a repeat of the battle of Jutland, or indeed Trafalgar, was likely. Yet the days of these great old battleships, vast

Barham's 48-foot Scott Payne picket boat, powered by three 100-HP petrol engines.

armoured gunforts, pachyderms of the ocean, unmanoeverable, wet at sea and capable of only just over 20 knots when all twenty four boilers were at full steam, were drawing to a close. They were quite unable to catch the fast modern German heavy ships built far more recently. When the enemy's attempt to cut Britain's food supplies became more effective, the old battleships were found an escort job as protection to more important convoys against attacks by German surface raiders and also as floating gun batteries for bombardment or to cover a landing. Life in the gunroom seemed a little unreal and most of the midshipmen hoped to be drafted to a smaller, more active ship.

It was, therefore, a relief to be told, together with the other four members of our group in *Barham*, each to join an anti-submarine trawler as second in command.

How Kipling would have relished the names of the five A/S trawlers based in Alexandria: *Amber, Beryl, Coral, Jade* and *Moonstone*, converted fishing trawlers with a 4-inch gun mounted on a platform forward, fish holds turned into primitive crew accommodation, a depth charge rail aft and a depth charge thrower on each quarter. Coal-burning and slow, each was commanded by an Asdic bosun, a warrant officer specialised in what is now called Sonar. Later

Moonstone was to capture intact an Italian submarine in the Red Sea, while *Beryl*, to which I was sent, sank at least one U-boat while patrolling the entrance to Grand Harbour during the Malta siege.

When *Beryl* sailed with *Jade*, I discovered that these trawlers, being deep drafted aft, turned chunkily with full rudder and had hardly any swing once the helm returned amidship. Our job was to patrol the buoy-supported anti-submarine wire boom about a mile to seaward of the entrance to the harbour through the breakwater. We were to relieve *Moonstone* and *Coral* after we had exercised with a submarine. *Jade* then took over Borgha's Pass entrance while *Beryl* patrolled the Great Pass. To deter a U-boat attempting to get through the boom in her wake before the gate could be closed, any merchant ship entering harbour was followed. The gates being shut from sunset to sunrise, at night the trawlers would lie at buoys close to the boom, pinging to try to detect any marauding U-boat.

The first night was dark with a nasty sharp sea running, with only the southern horizon lit by the distant glow of Alexandria's lights. When at last we found our buoy it was occupied by an Egyptian customs patrol boat which we eventually persuaded to let go to allow us to secure. Bringing to a buoy an underpowered unmanoeverable 400-ton trawler rising and falling six feet is not easy. I was sent to the bow to supervise lowering a buoy jumper to get a line on the buoy. Each time we lost steerage way the bow fell away, defying even the most catlike buoy jumper. When at last he did eventually drop on to the black, slippery buoy, the hook rope jangled so jerkily taut that he was unable to reeve the 2½-inch wire through the ring and had to be hauled back aboard by the lifeline round his waist. Somewhat shamefully, the assistance of the Egyptian launch was needed to reeve the wire through the ring and back inboard. After nearly three hours' frustration a hot, overcooked supper was demolished and the Egyptians tied up astern.

The wind was rising and, despite every half-hour freshening the nip of the wire where it passed through the fairlead, there was a risk of its parting so an anchor and engine room watch was closed up. Some time after midnight, on watch on the bridge I heard a shout from the bow that the wire had parted. Putting on port helm, I rang "ahead" on the engine room telegraph, called the Captain and set course for the gate in the boom. We had travelled some distance before anyone remembered that we were towing the Egyptians astern. They seemed sound asleep and it was some time before we heard a hubbub of excited voices, their engine fired and we cast them off, soon to disappear into the night in sound but no longer in sight. *Beryl* began a rolling patrol two miles to seaward of the boom before the skipper returned to his bunk, leaving me once more

HMA/S Trawler *Beryl* patrolling off the boom, Alexandria, October 1939.

alone on watch. This was much better than life in an overcrowded battleship gunroom. It was clear that discipline did not depend on shining white uniforms and salutes. The helmsman wore none too clean overalls while the Asdic operator sported a scarlet soccer shirt. It was quite impossible to remain unsooted in these coal burning trawlers and soon, like everyone else, I was rigged in shirt, shorts and gym shoes, all topped by an old tweed fishing hat to earn me my nickname as the Poacher.

A few days of peaceful patrolling were broken by an alarm. A float-fitted Swordfish aircraft from *Arethusa* reported a possible submarine sighting. Joined by our sister ships, the trawlers patrolled in line abreast pinging away on our Asdics. Soon one of the others hoisted a contact flag and dropped a pattern of depth charges. Then we gained contact and went in to attack. A depth charge exploding in fairly shallow water close astern of a trawler pounding along at its full 10 knots lifts the whole ship about a foot with a savage jerk and clatter and she seems to hesitate before moving forward again. Next day a destroyer put a diving party down only to discover the remains of an old wreck whose peaceful rest had been so savagely disturbed.

A fortnight of happy and untrammelled life followed this excitement. There was real pleasure and satisfaction for an 18-year-old midshipman to be entrusted with the safety of a ship on watch alone, and to navigate and signal with a hand held Aldis flashing lamp morse orders to neutral merchant shops to lie off the port till daybreak, all much more satisfactory than that evening fleet flashing exercise in harbour. It was so enjoyable that it seemed too good to last and so it proved.

While at sea a signal arrived ordering the trawler midshipmen to join *Suffolk*, a County Class cruiser fresh from the China station, sailing shortly for Gibraltar. *Barham*'s picket boat, driven by the snotty who had taken over from me and loaded with my kit, came out to meet us and transferred me and my worldly goods to *Suffolk* as she left harbour. It was back to uniform and gunroom life once more. Four days later, at Gibraltar, two of us were transferred to *Norfolk*, another County Class cruiser also being recalled to UK waters. Within three weeks of leaving Alexandria, white uniform abandoned, she would be close to the Arctic circle.

CHAPTER 2

Arctic Winter

AFTER GIVING WEEKEND LEAVE, *Norfolk* sailed from Devonport to Scapa, entering the Flow in a blinding snowstorm. Tin trunks of tropical rig and white uniforms were stowed deep below in the baggage room, while balaclava helmets, woollen gloves and even a few sweaters were issued to those likely to be exposed in the open to the elements. Already knitting needles were clicking away making warm clothing for the forces and, 1939/40 being a particularly severe winter, every garment arriving aboard was eagerly sought and worn.

With fuel and food topped up, *Norfolk* sailed to a billet north-west of the Faroes on Northern Patrol. This was maintained by a handful of cruisers and armed merchant cruisers trying to prevent German warships, raiders and supply ships entering or leaving the Atlantic and to blockade the northern entrance to the North Sea. Merchant ships were boarded and doubtful vessels sent under a boarding party for cargo inspection to Kirkwall contraband control. Conditions in County Class cruisers designed for the tropics, better fitted with fans than electric fires, were unpleasant, but for those in armed merchant cruisers, most of them converted liners from the Far Eastern run now mounting four single 6-inch guns, they were far nastier. We sometimes sat down for meals in the mess wearing duffle coats and gloves, but their vast saloons were impossible to heat. We had just arrived in our billet when *Rawalpindi*'s report that she was in action against German heavy ships was received.

Our captain turned *Norfolk* south and increased speed to 30 knots to close her position several hours' steaming away: the turbine sound rose to a high pitched scream and the hull juddered to the thump of the propellers. Some hours later we were ordered west by the Admiralty to Bill Bailey's Bank and speed was reduced to save fuel. That night a bright moon gave good visibility between the frequent sleet showers which would blot out the horizon and leave us temporarily blinded - no radar then.

Further south the cruisers, *Newcastle* and *Delhi*, had seen the loom of the flashes of the action over the horizon and later sighted the floating wreckage from *Rawalpindi*, whose commanding officer, Captain Kennedy, was posthumously awarded a VC for his courageous handling of his ship against hopeless odds. The enemy escaped.

After it grew light and dawn action stations had fallen out, *Norfolk* fruitlessly patrolled her area all day. Again at dusk we closed up at action stations to spend an uncomfortable night at instant readiness. When, in the middle watch, a dark shape was sighted, all guns were loaded and trained to bear on it. The Yeoman of Signals was ordered to flash the challenge letters, there was a momentary pause before the correct reply flashed back from a fellow patrolling cruiser. Huddled in gun control position or turret or beside torpedo tube, the weather was foul and cold, making even a fitful sleep difficult to snatch. These were the few times that the stokers in their hot steamy engine and boiler rooms had the best of it.

The remaining cruisers were next sent to join a patrol in sight of each other between Norway and the Faroes, sadly all in vain with the enemy already safely back in harbour. We returned to Scapa to fuel and provision before setting forth again into the teeth of a full northerly gale, to be buffeted by a sharp, bad-tempered sea to the east of Orkney. Finally, to avoid damage, the 10,000-ton cruiser had to heave to, steaming about 6 knots to maintain steerage way head to sea.

After my watch in the lookout position above the bridge under the range finder of the main armament director, and some welcome hot lunch, I had climbed into my comfortable hammock slung in the midshipmen's chest flat right aft above the rattling steering engine. In rough weather a hammock slung in a passage way and swinging to and fro like a pendulum offered stability and relief from the bucketing of the ship denied those who slept in bunks. Still not fully asleep, I felt a dull thud and heard a distant bang; a moment later the aircraft alarm sounded and each occupied hammock disgorged its occupant to wriggle into sea boots, grab a duffle coat and dash to his anti-aircraft station.

A large explosion 200 yards on the port beam, followed by a second in our wake, had raised two poplars of blackened water. No source of the explosions was evident and eventually cruising stations were resumed. It was only later that a British direction-finding report of a U-boat transmitting east of Orkney was followed by a German propaganda report from Lord Haw-Haw that the U-boat had sunk a County Class cruiser. Churchill, in his war history, tells of the Admiralty's anxiety till all the cruisers in the area were accounted for.

Gunter Prien who had sunk *Royal Oak* in the Flow was the U-boat commanding officer concerned. After later serving in a captured U-boat I found his feat in coming to periscope depth to fire in such conditions remarkable. Premature firing of magnetic torpedo heads was a familiar problem to both Germany and Britain then and later.

Soon after this, *Norfolk* needed to dock in Harland & Wolfe's yard in Belfast because a leak in a fresh water tank had allowed salt water to pollute boiler fuel. Repairs complete, and after celebrating Christmas a day early, *Norfolk* unsteadily sailed out of Belfast Lough Arctic-bound. Life followed a routine where, apart from watchkeeping four hours on eight hours off, action stations closed up daily at dawn when gunnery control drill, turrets following director, and exercising breakdown and fire parties occupied the hour till it was light. In the forenoon hands cleaned ship and midshipmen not on watch were instructed by schoolie. Then, apart from not infrequent alarms and excursions, the rest of our time was free. During the dog watches some of us would gather in a cabin and listen to classical music on a radiogram, read plays and debate, important mental stimulation and relaxation in a time of war.

After an uneventful patrol, *Norfolk* entered the Tail of the Bank to observe a sunken French destroyer which had fired one of her own torpedoes to explode forward in the crew's mess deck with sad loss of life. Only her bridge, masts and the top of her funnel were to be seen above the waters of the Clyde. No sooner had fuel and food been replenished than we were off round the Mull of Kintyre, up the Minch and through the Pentland Firth to Rosyth where a cruiser striking force was gathering. What we were to strike never became apparent, for the force never sailed and *Norfolk* was next sent to a patrol billet in the Denmark Strait between Iceland and Greenland.

Fortunately, as it grew colder and colder, I had been promoted from an action station in the after gun control position, an exposed windswept platform on the main mast to be used should the main director be destroyed, to the job of spotting officer in the main director, an enclosed armour plated box containing the main range finder. The spotting officer had to observe through binoculars the splashes of a bursting salvo and correct the settings up or down to straddle the target. At long range, there would be two more salvos in the air before the first arrived so, sometimes, the settings of these wasted salvos would have to be deducted before a proper correction was made to achieve a hit. This was my action station.

In cruising watches, I was one of the three midshipmen doing four hours each in charge of the lookouts in the air defence position above the bridge and around the director mounting. This windy, open platform had three pairs of binoculars each side, mounted on brackets with swivelling seats for lookouts. Each lookout was given a sixty degree sector to sweep continually with his glasses, while the midshipman and leading seaman were there to supervise, identify anything sighted and then to report to the bridge by telephone. The platform was four paces wide and in the long bleak Arctic nights the leading hand and I used to tramp up and down, left right, left right, turn, for hours on end, trying to keep warm and alert.

Part of the Northern Patrol's duties was to board and investigate neutral ships and, if doubtful of their destination or cargo, to send them with a boarding party to the Contraband Control station in Kirkwall. A dirty, cold stormy North Atlantic night with a rolling swell topped by foaming seas at two-thirty in the morning is not the happiest time to be despatched as midshipman of the boarding party, as happened to me on this patrol.

The sea boat, a cutter, had been called away to cross the quarter mile gap to the rolling merchant ship lit in the beam of the port searchlight. Oilskinned men shinned up the scrambling net into the open boat hanging from the davits. The art of launching a sea boat is to lower her to just above the crest of a wave and let go as the next crest arrives. This time the coxswain misjudged and slipped the one-ton boat with its full crew of fourteen and an additional boarding patrol of ten into a trough. With an almighty splash, the boat dropped six feet and filled with ice-cold water, leaving the crew to pull clear of the ship's sides as the rest of us baled for dear life, forgetting our bone-shaken bruises. As the cutter pulled away, sight was lost both of *Norfolk* and the merchant ship in the trough of each wave. It seemed an age before the boat's exhausted crew reached the calmer water in the lee of the cargo ship.

Up a Jacobs ladder dropped over her side scrambled and climbed the boarding party leaving the crew to bale the rest of the water from the cutter. The boarding officer and I, revolvers loaded and ready, led the party and were escorted by the Swedish captain to his most luxurious cabin. Travelling to Kirkwall in this comfort would be a vast improvement on life in *Norfolk*. It was not to be. The Captain produced papers, including a certificate from the British Consul in Baltimore, confirming that SS *Karlholm* of Kalundsburg had an approved and inspected cargo. It was back to the cutter for a pitching pull back to *Norfolk* with members of our boarding party relieving on the oars some of the exhausted boat crew, one of whom had fainted.

Hooking on to a heavy, swinging wooden block when rising and falling several feet is not easy and, once the boat was attached each end, the sudden jerk of the heavily laden boat carried away the fore guy of the davits. Once more the cutter was slipped to heave and thump against the cruiser's side till a jury replacement guy had been fitted to the davits. Trying to hook on once more, the bowman lost the tops of three fingers in the forward block. At last all was secure and we were hoisted clear of the angry sea. Another crewman passed out but fortunately rolled down the scrambling net into the scuppers and not over the side.

Back in Scapa Flow in mid February *Norfolk*, after finishing refuelling but before the ship was fully reprovisioned, was ordered to sail immediately to the support of the flotilla leader, *Cossack*, which was about to enter a Norwegian fjord to board a German blockade runner. While we were still pounding NE of the Orkneys, *Cossack* reported her successful boarding of *Altmark* and the rescue of her South Atlantic prisoners, so we were despatched straight on up to the northernmost patrol area of all, on the edge of the pack ice between Iceland and Greenland in the Denmark Strait. On the way, in fair weather off the Faroes, a trawler was sighted so, *Norfolk* having sailed short of fresh food, a cutter was slipped to pull across with rum and cigarettes and return laden to the gunwales with freshly caught cod and haddock. The average housewife would hardly recognise the superb flavour and firm flesh of fresh cod straight from the sea: the whole ship's company feasted on it for several meals.

West of Iceland, above the horizon, lit for a few minutes by the recently risen and already setting sun, two pink ethereal, snowy Icelandic mountains floated only to fade again as if they had never been. We steamed past a lifeboat and four rafts surrounded by floating wreckage; there was no sign of life and, being in a U-boat danger area, we could not stop to investigate two very dead seaman awash in one of the rafts. The temperature continued to drop till, when at last the edge of the pack ice came in sight, it steadied at about twenty-two degrees of frost, with the extra chill effect of high winds lowering it so much that spray thrown up by the bow was beginning to freeze by the time it reached the lookout position seventy feet above water level, stinging the face before pattering on deck. Gradually, parts of the deck became coated by up to three feet in ice and snow, while the rigging wires formed cores to a foot diameter of ice; the extra top weight of all this ice increased the rolling of the ship, and County Class cruisers with twenty feet of freeboard were never backward rolling performers at the best of times. Walruses blew their moustaches in the sea and, as we steered along the pack ice, the Greenland plateau came in sight.

By now it had become so cold that lookouts were only keeping quarter-hour watches. They were mostly 17-year-old boy seamen and were apt to pass out if left much longer. The snotties being still expected to maintain a four hour watch moaned, but we were both a little older and far better kitted up. Our rig might be begged, borrowed or stolen laddered silk stockings next to the skin under long under-pants, vest, seamen's blue jumper, polo-necked sweater, tucked into uniform trousers, under a reefer. Over the trousers were pulled stockings made of unwashed greasy wool pulled up over the trousers before thrusting feet down into leather sea boots and, finally overall, woollen gloves and duffle coat. Everyone was shaped like a rotund sweater-loaded umpire in a country cricket match after the sun suddenly came out, but we did manage to keep ourselves warm. Rapid movement in such a rig was not possible but, combined with a mid-watch cup of kai (thick steaming mouth and stomach searing ship's slab cocoa), it kept the cold at bay, despite the discomfort we had to accept when the icicles, which often formed on upper eyelashes, made blinking most painful.

One rare calm afternoon in the dim Arctic winter, I was given permission to crunch along the snow and ice coated forecastle to the jackstaff right forward and there to try to take photographs of our snow cruiser looking aft. To work the camera, I was forced to remove a glove. After one or two shots, the camera shutter began to freeze so that it had to be pushed across manually, as was possible with a 4.5 Zeiss Ikon. By the time the film had all been exposed, before returning below deck to the gunroom, my right hand had been ungloved for nearly quarter of an hour. Soon it started to swell, then to ache, and then became agonizingly painful. Almost crying, I made for sick bay, where they put it under a heat lamp; the aching eventually ceased, but three fingers had lost all feeling and so they remained, white and dead looking, for several weeks, while layers of skin peeled away one after another as feeling slowly returned. A mess mate stuck a pin in a finger and even stubbed a cigarette end out on one without my feeling anything; nevertheless, when one of my snapshots appeared in *The Times*, it seemed worth it.

Norfolk returned east from Greenland along the ice till, just north-west of Iceland, the wind blew up from gale to hurricane, with jagged roaring foam-streaked white-topped breakers, superimposed on and often combining with the swell, riding down and crashing about the ship. As we lay head to sea and hove to, a monster wave buried the bow deep out of sight and smashed its way aft to flatten the ¾-inch steel breakwater which protruded a foot high to protect the bridge structure further aft. The weakened bulkhead below the breakwater bent, allowing the deck to sag, so that water started to seep through and flood the mess below, which required continuous bailing out.

Later, the starboard quadruple torpedo mounting, which, when trained over the side protruded about two feet outside the hull twenty feet above the water line, was lifted bodily on end, torpedoes and all, by a solid sea which had wrenched away its base-plate. In order to try to secure the reared up torpedoes in their tube, for fear of the havoc their six tons would cause if they broke completely adrift, *Norfolk*, risking a broach-to, was successfully turned at speed stern on to the wind and sea. While men were trying to rope the tubes secure, a sizzling white-capped wave smashed down on the quarter-deck and raced forward; we had been pooped. The hands working on the tubes were washed chest deep along the waist deck on their lifelines till they could grab something solid and hang on. They gyrated along supported by air-filled oilskins looking like crinolined skittles till the lifelines jerked taut.

Norfolk: severe Arctic weather on Northern Patrol, February 1940.

Eventually, once the mounting had been roped to a stay and a davit, all decks cleared and watertight doors clamped shut again, *Norfolk* attempted to turn back head to sea. Whilst almost beam on, a mighty wave crashed into the port side of our 10,000-ton cruiser, heeling it over to a forty degree angle to starboard and bodily skidding it sideways. The ship hung perilously over at that angle for what seemed an age before slowly righting itself and rolling back into another thumping shuddering breaker and eventually turning back head to sea. When *Norfolk*'s bridge was down in the trough of a wave, the crest of the next wave hid the horizon even up there, seventy feet above normal sea level.

For two more days, unable to do anything but keep steerage way and remain head to sea, *Norfolk* lay helplessly hove to. When at last the storm moderated to a mere gale and it became possible to return on deck, chaos reigned. The Walrus flying boat had disappeared from the catapult amidships; no one had heard or seen it go. A one ton steel washdeck locker had been carried across from its moorings on the port side of the forecastle screen forward over to the starboard side and then more than fifty feet aft till it finished up jack-knifed under a cutter, which itself had been wrenched out of its cradle and turned sideways to rest across it. Another boat was wrecked with the whole of its side torn bodily away.

Below decks, hammocks were floating, broken crockery was tinkling from side to side in the dirty salt water slopping about and it seemed as if everything movable or smashable had been moved or smashed. It was a sorry ship, its decks still ice covered, that returned on a sunny March morning to the Tail of the Bank in Greenock to patch up and repair its damage; even the paint on the ship's side had flaked away to reveal large patches of red lead.

A signal was waiting drafting me and another midshipman to destroyers. My draft was to be *Echo*, which was completing a refit in Henry Robb's Yard in Leith. Despite the pasting we had just suffered, I was sad to leave *Norfolk*, which was a happy ship. My lasting memory of that first winter of the war in the North was of greyness: grey paint, grey seas, grey skies, grey clouds, grey dawns and grey dusks - a monochromatic world with variations of shade and tone but never of colour.

CHAPTER 3

The Battle For Narvik

WHEN I EVENTUALLY FOUND *Echo*, a 1,350-ton destroyer mounting four 4.7-inch guns and two sets of four torpedo tubes, in the basin of Leith Docks, she looked very unready for sea: a gun was missing forward; the wireless aerials lay on deck; two men were erecting a steel searchlight platform amidships, while the ship's side was a patchwork of streaks of red lead, recently painted dark grey and areas of bright, newly chipped bare steel. A generator, throbbing on the jetty, was supplying power for a general clatter of chipping hammers, riveters and drills, while vivid blue arc-striking flashes spurted occasionally from one of several electric welders working on deck.

The quartermaster at the gangway led me to the wardroom, which was a typical standard between-the-wars destroyer wardroom stretching from side to side of the ship under the after superstructure. Curtained off on one side of the central door was a mahogany table and chairs, with a hatch through to the pantry; on the other side, separated by a curtain, was an anthracite-burning stove surrounded by a club fender, three leather armchairs and a padded seat the length of the ship's side. The two scuttles each side to let in daylight were framed by bright chintzy curtains and the new cream enamel still smelt fresh.

The First Lieutenant, a bluff, cheerful and friendly bearded figure made me welcome, and told me what my duties would be before packing me off on leave where I heard on the news of the bomb damage and casualties suffered by *Norfolk* in Scapa Flow.

On return from leave, I visited *Norfolk* in Fairfield's Yard, Glasgow where she was under repair. The 500-lb bomb had passed through the midshipmen's chest flat where all of us had slung our hammocks to sleep, and then exploded in a fuel tank below; three of my former messmates had been killed and another wounded in the explosion. *Norfolk*'s Commander, a large man of extensive vocabulary, was taking a bath in his bathroom in the flat next door. A member of the repair party a few minutes later became aware of muffled sounds escaping from the Commander's bathroom: the upside down bath emitted a series of low rumbles and, when it was lifted, a purple-faced naked but quite undamaged officer emerged.

During April, while Norway was invaded and the first and second Narvik battles were fought, *Echo* had been towed under the Forth Bridge to Rosyth Dockyard to complete her refit with all haste. One day the battle cruiser *Renown* came in for repair after receiving two 11-inch shell hits below decks and a third, which failed to explode, clean through one leg of her tripod foremast, leaving a thin rib of metal either side. She had been in action against German heavy ships off Narvik in severe weather and low visibility. I struck up a friendship with the midshipman of *Orzel*, a Polish submarine which had given a good account of itself on Baltic patrol in the midst of the German invasion and was later to be lost patrolling in the same area.

April was well advanced before the refit was sufficiently complete to allow *Echo*, fully ammunitioned, stored and provisioned, but with several dockyard maties finishing off odd jobs still on board, to sail and escort a tanker to Scapa. No time could be spared to work the ship up after the refit and, as soon as fuel was topped up in the Flow, the workmen left. Admiral Diesen, Commander in Chief of the Norwegian Navy, accompanied by two of his staff, was piped on board, and we sailed north to catch up a 13-knot convoy of troopships, consisting of *Colombie* as Commodore, three other French liners, *Ville d'Alger, Chenonceau* and *Mexique,* which had sailed earlier from Brest, and two British liners, *Empress of Australia* and *Monarch of Bermuda.* As the convoy steamed north, sailing in two columns and escorted by four British destroyers and the French destroyer, *Épervier*, signals were constantly intercepted telling of ship sinkings and damage suffered while attempting to evacuate troops from Namsos. The convoy of loaded transports, cruisers and destroyers, steaming west from Namsos to clear the coast as fast as possible, crossed our convoy's wake close astern in twilight.

Back in the Arctic Circle two days later, the distant snowy Lofoten Island peaks, rose-tinted by the low sun, came into sight as the British liners left us to sail up the Vest Fjord inside the islands and reinforce troops trying to reach Narvik while the remainder sailed on, bound for Tromsö, 100 miles further north. We fixed the ship by bearings taken of the tall, erect white finger of Andenes Lighthouse, of which I would later take many periscope bearings. The sun was warm as we led our convoy between sheer 4,000 foot snowy mountains tumbling precipitously to the water's edge into Malangen Fjord, with destroyers closed up at action stations due to uncertainty of the situation ashore.

In a wide part of the fjord, the troopships and remaining destroyers anchored, while *Echo* embarked a Polish general, a French colonel and the Commandant of *Épervier* before steering through the narrows to berth at a jetty in Tromsö, where we sadly bade farewell to the charming but anxious Admiral Diesen and his staff. The General had explained that the Polish troops of the Highland Brigade, known as Carpathian Chasseurs, embarked in *Chenonceau* and *Mexique* accompanied by a great number of mules, were desperately short of water. They'd been at sea for fourteen days since leaving Brest and now had almost empty tanks. On his arrival, the British Consul promised to arrange water supplies and to charter suitable boats to ferry troops ashore; the Mayor of Tromsö, accompanying him, agreed to assist in this; there were many other visitors and we tried to keep everyone happy, but it seemed that no one knew about us or where we were to go or what we were supposed to be doing. The looming mountains interfered with reliable wireless communication.

Our captain eventually agreed with the Polish general, who was equally without any orders, that the troops would be landed further south at Maalself as soon as the thirsty and obstreperous mules had been watered. *Echo* set forth to have a look at the proposed landing place, only to be met by a small Norwegian gunboat *Thorodd* which hailed us and informed us that we could not possibly land troops there, but that at Lysbotten in Lys Fjord the men could "landed be".

Off once more around the fjords till, returning within sight of the anchored transports, one of them flashed a morse message that army orders to land at Harstad had been received. After frantic chart searching, Harstad on the island of Hinnoy, 100 miles steaming further south, was found. Then, at long last, while the reliability of the Army's orders was being discussed on the bridge, a signal from Admiralty was deciphered ordering the whole convoy to proceed to sea and await orders. The convoy was duly shepherded back out to sea where our Australian Captain, who had been up for thirty-six hours without sleep, took to his bunk.

A day later another signal was received ordering the convoy to arrive at Harstad at nine in the evening, reporting on which day we would be there. So the army orders were correct. It being too late to make it that day, we steamed our convoy north for the night, reaching a latitude north of Nord Kap, the northernmost point of Europe. As the convoy steamed back south next morning, *Ark Royal*, flying off aircraft, accompanied by a cruiser and three destroyers appeared over the horizon. Promptly at 9 pm we entered Harstad Harbour, which was to be our base for the next month. It is a deep, well sheltered anchorage ten miles in from the coast with two entrances separated by a line of rocks and low islands.

At anchor in the harbour, among several destroyers, tankers and supply ships, was the cruiser *Effingham*. She flew the flag of Admiral the Lord Cork & Orrery, loved and feared in the Service as Ginger Boyle who, it appeared, was Flag Officer, Narvik. He it was who had upset some mothers of Dartmouth cadets at a prizegiving three years earlier with his speech in which he told us that we

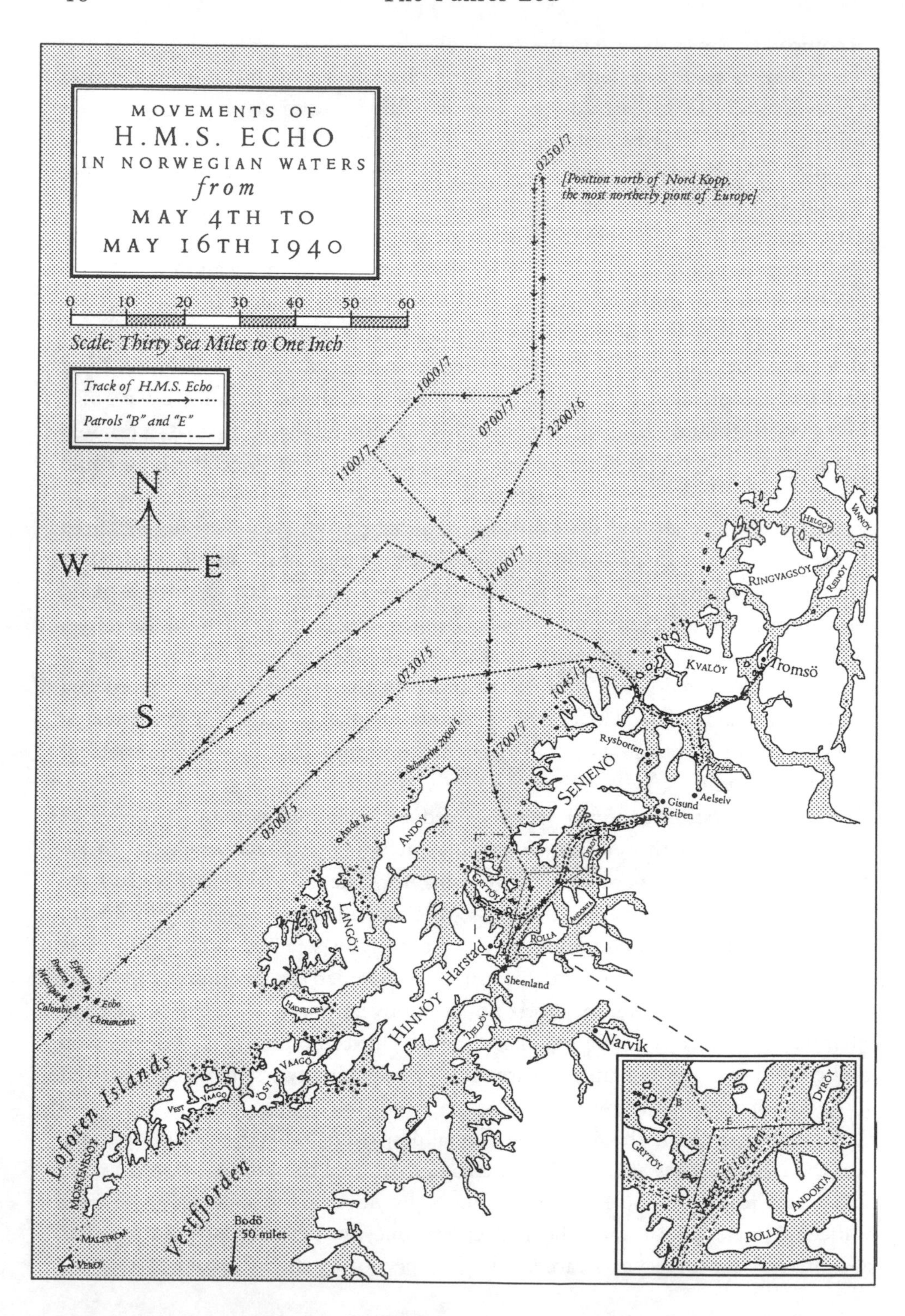
MOVEMENTS OF
H.M.S. ECHO
IN NORWEGIAN WATERS
from
MAY 4TH TO
MAY 16TH 1940
0 10 20 30 40 50 60
Scale: Thirty Sea Miles to One Inch
Track of H.M.S. Echo
Patrols "B" and "E"
N
W
E
S
0250/7
[Position north of Nord Kopp, the most northerly piont of Europe]
1000/7
0700/7
2200/6
1100/7
1400/7
0730/5
1045/5
1700/7
0500/5
Submarine 2000/6
Anda Is.
ANDÖY
LANGÖY
HADSELÖEN
HINNÖY
Harstad
Sheenland
TJELDÖY
Narvik
ÖST VAAGÖ
VEST VAAGÖ
Lofoten Islands
MOSKENESÖY
MALSTRÖM
VERÖY
Vestfjorden
Bodö 50 miles
GRYTÖY
ROLLA
ANDORTA
DYRÖY
SENJENÖ
Rysborten
Gisund
Reiben
Aelselv
KVALÖY
Tromsö
RINGVAGSÖY
REINÖY
HELGÖY
VANNÖY
Echo
Vaagsfjorden
B
E

were not in the Royal Navy to show the flag, or see the world, or for any other purpose but to fight and that we had better all realise that it would not be long before we were doing so.

The fog of war, wireless interference, as well as often unknown wavelengths used by different nations and services, made it a little less surprising that a convoy should arrive at the wrong place or remain in doubt of what to do and without orders for several days, entirely dependent on the initiative of those on the spot. The Admiralty, in attempting to control both evacuations and landings up and down the Norwegian coast and also the movement of numerous ships in the North Sea trying to support shore operations as the panzers rumbled down through the Low Countries, had not managed to inform our convoy or escort of the base at Harstad, never mind that Flag Officer Narvik flew his flag there as part of a combined HQ. There, contact had to be maintained with British, French, Norwegian and Polish troops, with the RAF and Fleet Air Arm and with merchant ships of many nationalities. It later appeared no love was lost between the Admiral and General Mackesy, a recipe for the muddle and chaos that ensued.

Soon after *Echo* entered Harstad Harbour, the first air raid began. Raids continued daily, several times a day, for weeks on end and, as it remained light all night, there was no respite; the wireless office was constantly informing the bridge of OEAB (I am being bombed) signals received from ships under way in the network of fjords outside the harbour. Often it was a single aircraft on reconnaissance high up, which would drop a stick of bombs before leaving. Only if one of the anti-aircraft cruisers, *Coventry, Curlew, Cairo* or *Calypso*, were in harbour could fire be opened on these high flying bombers. With most destroyers' main armament being quite unable to fire at aircraft, the crew would remain under cover during air raids, apart from machine-gun crews who could never find a plane low enough to fire at.

Soon ships ceased anchoring in harbour but instead kept slowly steaming up and down, often just drifting, but always ready to give a burst ahead on the engines if necessary. One night *Echo* was among four destroyers, two each side, being filled up with oil fuel alongside a tanker which was happily steaming round the harbour towing them all with her during an air raid. In one raid, the cruiser *Southampton,* lying stopped close on our beam, failed to sight an attacking bomber till the last moment; she sounded her siren and went ahead on both engines in the nick of time to avoid a direct hit on the stern; sadly a man on her quarterdeck was killed and several others injured by bomb splinters from the exploding bomb close in her wake. Near misses like this were common and an occasional hit inevitably damaged or sank its target. Most bridge watchkeepers suffered "Narvik neck" from time to time from too much looking up and sky scanning.

Result of *Echo*'s fishing by depth charge during campaign to recapture Narvik, May 1940.

As supplies of fresh food were short throughout the Narvik campaign, destroyers were allowed to drop a depth charge every few days and then to lower a boat to collect the stunned fish which were mostly cod and haddock but also included a startling bright-red fish whose edibility was in doubt till, remarkably, a cigarette card was found picturing the Norway Haddock and pronouncing it good eating. Often the depth charge would provide enough fish to half fill a whaler.

Two patrol lines had been set up to cover the sea entrances to the Vaagsfjord and Harstad in an endeavour to detect any U-boat attempting to enter. While pinging up and down one of these, our wireless office intercepted a signal from an *Ark Royal* Swordfish aircraft reporting sighting a surfaced submarine in Dyroysund on the inland sea route to Tromsö, half an hour's steaming north of our position. Instructing our opposite number, *Brazen*, to move and cover an escape route to seaward, *Echo* steamed off to Dyroy, dropping a depth charge on a very doubtful Asdic contact en route. In the narrow fjord a whaler was lowered to seek information ashore. Finding no English speakers, the RNVR sub who had landed with me discovered a phone in the village post office and eventually contacted the local English speaking pastor who soon arrived on a motor cycle. He could tell us nothing but we returned with 190 eggs bought with a pound note, an egg for each member of the crew for supper.

After further fruitless searching, *Echo* returned and a small boat rowed out from the opposite shore. In broken English the local policeman said a submarine had been seen earlier. Once more we lowered the whaler, including in the complement the canteen manager and wardroom messman this time. While they were buying sixty dozen eggs and much other fresh food, a red-jumpered youth told us in idiomatic English that a black painted submarine flying a Norwegian flag had steamed past steering south early that morning. Abandoning the chase, but better victualled, we resumed our patrol, to be informed by *Wishart,* who had relieved *Brazen*, that a signal reporting the submarine's proposed passage had been distributed in Harstad Harbour the day before. The airwaves were too cluttered by fighting in Holland, Belgium and the North Sea to justify transmitting the signal on the air.

Returning to Harstad two days later *Wolverine* entered harbour, with several hundred survivors of a bombed transport full of Irish Guardsmen, over 200 men and three-quarters of their officers having lost their lives. Fuelled once more, *Echo* joined a tribal class destroyer, *Matabele,* to act as escort to the cruiser *Effingham* accompanied by the AA cruisers *Coventry* and *Cairo*. Our task force set off under overcast skies steering for the open sea at a rattling 22 knots just as yet another air raid on Harstad began. Bren carriers and trucks were lashed down on *Effingham*'s quarterdeck, surrounded by khaki clad figures; she flashed that a thousand South Wales Borderers were aboard to be landed at Bodö, 130 miles south of Harstad, reinforcing a Guards battalion who were getting the worst of an attempt to halt the German advance from the south. The only chart of the entrance to Bodö on board was small scale and somewhat inadequate. When the party arrived off the port at suppertime, *Effingham* signalled that she proposed, for fear of mines, to use a narrow alternative route rather than the main channel, while *Cairo* and *Coventry* were to remain stopped outside to give air cover.

I was at the back of *Echo*'s bridge with the navigator's notebook noting all orders issued, and recording times against them, and overheard an anxious discussion between Captain and Navigator about the rock-strewn route chosen by *Effingham*; despite speed having been slightly reduced, it looked a chancy course to follow with only our small scale chart. The Captain's orders were curt and staccato, as they always became when he was anxious or under stress. *Effingham* signalled *Echo* to close to one and a half cables abeam of *Matabele*, but we had already edged in much closer than that. Watching *Matabele* on the port aft side of the bridge, I saw her give a faint shudder, heel over slightly and all her aerials and rigging started to jump and quiver; she had grounded on the rocky bottom but had scraped over.

We both sounded on our siren and flashed to *Effingham* the morse letter U, the emergency signal for "You are running into danger" but it was far too late;

the same rock, like a tin opener, ripped a jagged hole the length of *Effingham*'s hull. She started to list, almost stopped and was making huge clouds of black smoke, with steam soon surging from the safety valves on the funnel and later also escaping from a scuttle on her starboard side. We stopped engines, as had *Matabele,* whose port screw was damaged and unusable.

While *Matabele* slowly manoeuvred astern on her remaining propeller to rejoin *Coventry* and *Cairo* outside and investigate her damage, I was ordered down from the bridge to muster the whaler's crew and stand by to be lowered. Instead of this, however, in order to simplify disembarking men, our Captain accepted the risk of *Effingham* rolling over on top of us and came alongside the starboard side towards which she was listing. *Effingham*, having manned all her boats, lowered a cutter and cast overboard all Carley life rafts, had settled much lower in the water and was clearly in danger of sinking.

Troops were ordered to abandon kit bags and cross over with their rifles immediately we were secured; quite unaware of the magnitude of the disaster and that *Effingham*, apart from her list, was several feet deeper in the water, the soldiers showed extreme reluctance to abandon their kits; maybe they were misled by the quiet calm of *Effingham*'s crew, closed up at action stations and patiently awaiting orders. After several very sharp commands, men began to climb over the guard rails on to our forecastle and then to move aft down to the waist beside the funnels and torpedo tubes where, from our vantage point in the whaler above, the leading hand and I packed them in as tight as they could go.

All this time our ship was gently towing *Effingham* towards a possible beaching island. Once the Norwegian large scale chart of the area, of which *Effingham* carried the only copy available, was passed over, navigation became easier and we grounded her on the rocky islet. Then, despite the overload of our small ship by 1,000 extra troops aboard, a decision was taken to risk embarking one watch of *Effingham's* crew as well.

Our overloaded ark, having had the greatest difficulty in swinging the stern clear of *Effingham* without jamming our bow under her overhanging side, managed to shuffle uncertainly, steering sluggishly and taking on a large list with even the minimum of helm, till we could bump into *Coventry's* side to disembark survivors; then, like a different ship with manoeuvrability restored, we steamed back to the stricken cruiser. There, apart from a small salvage party, the remainder of *Effingham*'s officers and crew, with all the loose gear they managed to salvage, climbed across to *Echo*. Sacks of confidential books were swung over, then a rating nursing the ship's cat was helped across and finally we piped her haggard and drawn Captain aboard. On our return later following a Captain's conference in *Cairo, Effingham* was being attended by a Norwegian merchant ship, surrounded by puffers, unloading the Army's kit, supplies and vehicles for Bodö as hard as they could go.

Remarkably, there had been no casualties in *Effingham*. This was due to quick thinking and initiative on the part of the RNVR sub-lieutenant (E) in charge of boiler rooms, who saw the rock pass down the centre of his boiler room and immediately shut the main steam bulkhead valve and ordered the shutting off of the fuel pumps and all oil fuel to the sprayers. Before abandoning the boiler room, he had also ordered an ejector started so that, as the sea water rose in the dark steam-filled compartment, the steam was vented outboard.

Two Skuas circled overhead and effectively chased away a twin-engined shadower who arrived during the middle watch to see what was afoot. As soon as there was room for *Echo* to come alongside, *Effingham*'s salvage party, assisted by our working party, started to transfer as much of the food as possible, including the contents of the bread and meat screens on deck, and also binoculars, sextants, chronometers, all the essential gun locks from 6-inch, 4-inch, pom-pom and multiple machine-guns, some officers' baggage and much other loose equipment before we departed for Harstad, only to be recalled a couple of hours later to return and torpedo *Effingham*. All this time her wretched Captain had been on our bridge, his hair having turned from grey to white during the night, and now he had to watch his command torpedoed. The single torpedo from the forward tubes seemed to take an age to reach its target. Then there was a flash, a loud thumping bang in her engine room and a splash rose twice the height of her masts before spreading so that she was completely hidden by spray. Disappointingly, when the spray settled, she had not completely sunk, but she was beyond salvage. We returned to Harstad using a short cut, compared with passing outside the islands, through the Vestfjord and the Tjelsundet, which is a narrow winding channel exceptionally well marked with navigational aids and lights. Though no wider in parts than 100 yards, navigation was not too difficult and even ocean liners used it safely.

On arrival in port, the Captain, Commander and Navigator of *Effingham* were whisked off in a motor boat to join a Polish transport sailing at once for Britain. We kitted up the rest of the salvage party as best we could and, in return, they left us a salvaged silver challenge cup and Hitler, their ship's cat, complete with a small black moustache just like his namesake.

After twenty-four hours' peace on A/S patrol we returned to Harstad in the midst of a rather fuller scale air raid than usual. As we entered, an oil tank ashore was bombed to blaze and spew out vast clouds of dense black smoke which drifted across the harbour, slowly rising and darkening the sky. The hillside opposite, where trees had earlier been set alight by baskets of incendiary bombs, was shrouded in a grey haze beneath the black cloud. One small tanker had already been sunk and several other ships damaged.

Ships were firing and bombs exploding all over the harbour in Wagnerian crescendoes of sound. Then, before we had even reached our berth, as suddenly as the raid had begun, it ended; the bombers flew away; all guns ceased fire and all that broke the silence was the ripple of waves, the crackle of burning timber and the faint hiss of escaping steam from a damaged tanker. *Delight*, our sister ship, lost her motor boat and a member of its crew in a direct hit as they lay alongside the pier inshore waiting to collect bags of mail. She and *Echo* were soon ordered back to sea to meet a convoy, which turned out to be a bedraggled collection of very rusty old ships. Three were detached to be escorted into harbour by *Delight*, while we were left out at sea to steam around with two tankers, a small tramp and a rusty salt-caked Norwegian coaster looking ready to fall apart and sink at the first puff of breeze.

For five restful, blissful, sunbathing days we zigzagged in front of our 8-knot flock, reasonably safe from bombing. When we approached the land on return to Harstad, the barren snow-covered landscape had been transformed into green fjord shores dotted with vivid coloured patches where flowers in bloom below the snow cover had been revealed. The colours seemed to complement the brightly painted wooden shoreside houses.

After refuelling in harbour from the tanker, *British Governor*, we had hardly let go wires before all the warships in harbour whooped an alarm on sirens and went ahead on their engines to circle and steam to and fro in a sharp downpour of bombs, two of which exploded beside the fleet tanker, *Oleander,* lifting her bodily to subside in a rapidly spreading oil slick with steam escaping amidships. Even as the raid continued, *British Governor* manoeuvred alongside her to pump out her damaged tanks. Amongst the ships firing outside the harbour *Curlew,* vainly trying to protect a number of anchored supply ships, was sunk with direct bomb hits fore and aft of her bridge. As her sister ship, *Cairo*, had been severely damaged since our trip to Bodö a week earlier, only *Coventry* was left operational out of four AA cruisers. This could not continue very long. However, some help was at hand: that afternoon twelve Hurricanes flown from *Ark Royal* at sea landed on a strip of flat land close to *Curlew*'s grave.

Next day, *Echo* and *Delight* were ordered back down the Tjelsundet to Narvik, where the fight to capture the town and its vital iron ore terminal was nearing success. We passed the beached hull of a German destroyer sunk in the first battle for Narvik and sighted the scattered township. Wispy smoke rose from trees round the railway sidings full of open ore trucks on the hill above. We watched three Heinkels successively break formation for each to drop a string of twelve bombs on Polish troop positions west of the town. Through binoculars, the formation of falling bombs could be clearly seen till they exploded in a line of spouts on the rocky ground. There was a rattle of machine-gun fire, a very loud bang when an ammunition lighter was hit, then, to cheers, a Hurricane appeared. In attacking and shooting down the bomber responsible it, also, was hit, caught fire and plummeted into the fjord. The baled-out pilot landed close to a destroyer which rescued him.

Close beside us the sole surviving AA cruiser, *Coventry,* was hidden by five large bomb bursts, only to emerge, apparently undamaged as it cleared the curtain of smoke and water. We seemed to have escaped the Harstad frying pan to enter the Narvik fire.

During the night of 29th May, Narvik was recaptured and a limp Norwegian flag flew once more from the hospital flagstaff on the bluff above the town. I was lowered in the whaler to land a naval fieldgun's crew from *Southampton* to man a captured German gun. Scattered among the bare rocks and dwarf birch trees was a litter of corpses, ammunition boxes and debris left from the day before's fighting. Soon after our whaler was hoisted aboard, *Echo* was off again in answer to a signal to rendezvous with the Foreign Legion and offer bombardment assistance. From the fjord shore opposite the retreating enemy a motor boat put out to deliver a beribboned French general with English speaking staff officer and wireless operator. The Legion, in an effort to harass and drive back the Germans on the railway line to Sweden, which hugged the 400 foot contour of the steep, sometimes sheer, pine girt mountain, was spread above and advancing along it. This rugged terrain offered numerous ideal rearguard bastions from which our help was needed to drive out small parties of troops holding up the Allied advance.

After studying the map, the First Lieutenant climbed back into the director above the bridge. Our first instruction was to try to block off the far end of one of the many tunnels along the line. Having to fire ten degrees up at a target high above sea level never seemed to have been considered for low angle 4.7-inch naval guns. It was a matter of trial and error, so the gunnery officer decided to fire single-gun ranging shots. The flash, puff of yellow smoke and dusty cloud of rock fragments from an exploding high explosive shell were most difficult to spot, so it was decided to fire uncorrected salvos to give a spread out line of shells. The crack of each bursting salvo of four shells left rumbling echoes bouncing to and fro, gradually weakening till silence descended again. Eventually, one shell burst on the masonry supporting the far side of the tunnel, while the following salvo using the same settings brought the whole end down.

When the dust cleared we could see it was completely blocked. Because our complement of ammunition was three semi-armour-piercing shells to every high explosive shell, we fired one experimental salvo of SAP and found that despite a less bright flash we could see where they landed. We ceased fire.

The portable wireless on the bridge crackled with Gallic excitement. It appeared that the Germans had entered the far end of our tunnel and the Legionnaires awaited their re-emergence with interest. To the west a large formation of highflying Dorniers was blanketing the hill above Narvik and the town with incendiary bombs interspersed with high explosives. A thundering boom further along the railway thumped the air. A steam engine, gathering momentum, rolled over and over down from the line, uprooting trees and discarding chunks of steel till, sizzling, it splashed and half sank into the fjord below.

As the enemy withdrew along the line, *Echo* was called on for several more bombardments. Twice we were actually aiming at a squad of grey coated men crossing patches of frozen snow and once converged a four shell salvo amongst them. Black craters, abandoned equipment and several bodies pock marked the white backdrop. Eventually, after *Echo* had fired over 100 HE and 250 SAP shells, the enemy moved out of sight towards the Swedish border and we were recalled to Narvik. There a puffer came alongside to collect the wireless operator and to deliver the British Consul, for whom we sent a cipher reporting the loss of the consulate's confidential books.

Yet again, we were recalled to bombard a vigorous counter attack by German troops which had forced the advancing Foreign Legion and Poles back into gun range once more. This time our fire was spotted by the naval liaison officer on the French general's staff high up on the opposite shore where he could observe shell bursts out of our sight. The Allied forces halted the counter attack and resumed their advance and we were finally allowed to cease fire and sponge out guns. A signal from the shore "Your shooting was much admired by battalion commander and was effective in keeping the Boche down" was received after securing.

We sailed west till Narvik, with smoke still rising from its smouldering houses, and its harbour, blocked by the masts and funnels of thirty-five separate wrecks, was lost from view. A high flying escort of three Junker 88s was sighted. Speed was increased to 30 knots and we began to weave along and across the fjord in a series of figures of eight and circles, each alternation being followed by the vapour trails in the sky above.

The first stick of bombs exploded harmlessly between us and a trawler zigzagging nearby. Nearly a quarter of an hour, and several circles later, the second bomber's offering raised brown waters in our wake; one more to go. The sub on the bridge was ordered to keep close watch on the third Junkers through his binoculars and, just after full starboard helm had been ordered and *Echo* shuddering at full speed listed to port, he shouted that bombs were dropping. The Captain ordered a reverse of helm; perhaps quarter of a minute later two large bombs burst on the starboard quarter exactly where we would have been but for the helm alteration. Bomb splinters tinkled on deck: the closest yet.

Later in the day, now in company with *Delight* and *Arrow*, who had been ordered to return with us and evacuate troops from Bodö where they had been fighting a rearguard action to delay German troops advancing from the south, several more ineffective bombing attacks were made on us.

Using the main channel well south of the rock topped by the wreck of *Effingham* now lying on her side, we stopped at midnight off Bodö Harbour. Still in grey daylight, *Delight* and *Arrow*, after turning in the narrow channel outside, backed alongside the stone jetty near which blazed two circular oil tanks. Beyond, all that remained of the town of Bodö were standing stone chimneys, derelict, blackened fingers like the remains of a fire gutted stone forest pointing skyward. The wooden houses were no more. Over the brow of the hill straggled tired and listless groups of soldiers to embark in the waiting destroyers. Isolated flames licked in the ruins.

Once *Arrow* had embarked her complement of 500 men and pulled out from the jetty, we replaced her. The arriving soldiers, bundles of exhaustion, unshaven and haggard, dragged one foot after the other as if in a dream. Once aboard, cocooned in their khaki greatcoats against the chill night air, many dropped asleep on the open deck. An officer ordered a squad to get rid of a Bren carrier and a lorry parked on the jetty. It was easy to shove the short-wheel-based carrier over the end of the jetty where it oscillated on its belly till a final heave dropped it with a mighty splash in to the sea. This was not possible with the lorry; instead a jerry can of petrol was poured over it and set alight where it stood. Blazing fiercely, a fantastic pyrotechnic display erupted from its canopy as everyone ducked. "Ah yes," remarked the officer, "of course, that's where we stored the explosives."

A party of men bearing Bren guns, who had gathered in the shelter of a ruined warehouse, now crossed to embark, followed finally by Brigadier Colin Gubbins who had commanded the brigade. As he made his way along the waist to the bridge, huddled men leapt smartly to attention as he passed. Despite being outnumbered and suffering severe losses as they withdrew, this was clearly a proud, disciplined and efficient fighting machine even in defeat; it was most impressive. The men, who had not eaten for two days, were given corned beef and ships biscuits, all we could spare, and sent below decks because the destroyer, almost empty of fuel, was top heavy. The whole evacuation had taken barely an hour before we slipped to join our consorts and clear the coast at slow speed due to lack of fuel.

The cloud base was well below the mountain tops and no air attack hindered the landing of our evacuees, mostly territorials of Scots and Irish Guards and South Wales Borderers. We were still unaware that the Dunkirk evacuation now in progress had made the holding of northern Norway no longer possible.

Between 3rd and 9th June, when 24,000 men and most of their equipment were evacuated, the low cloud ceiling shrouded the intense marine activity. Yet only the day before it started a sudden scream of Stuka dive bombers had descended on *Echo* out of the low sun. The alarm had sounded and as I dashed forward along the port waist, I just had time to drop flat beside the torpedo tubes as the last bomb exploded in the water alongside, splattering a tinkle of splinters to ricochet off the funnel around me. I rapidly dropped with burned fingers the souvenir fragment I tried to pick up. By the time I'd climbed the ladder to the bridge the attack was over and the planes involved had already vanished over the mountains. For the week of the evacuation half a dozen destroyers ferried men to the convoy of liners lying in the narrow fjords. The Hurricanes from Skaanland had all succeeded in landing back on *Glorious*, despite a lack of arrester gear. The ferry, *Royal Ulsterman*, signalled that she had forty bags of mail for us, the first news from home for five weeks. We sent a boat over to collect it.

The evacuation had been planned in two convoys. While Group I loaded, the transports in Group II kept well out to sea to avoid air attack. When *Lancashire, Georgic, Franconia, Monarch of Bermuda,* several cargo ships with lorries, guns and stores, and the cruiser, *Vindictive,* sailed we were amongst five destroyers escorting them, two of us changing convoys to lead back seven liners to evacuate the remaining troops and material. *Echo* was despatched back to Narvik to collect the rearguard of the Foreign Legion. Bowed down under large packs, the Legionnaries climbed clumsily aboard from puffers; most had acquired cameras, watches and other loot, announcing with evident satisfaction, *"tout le temps, l'ennemi allaient au pas gymnastique"*. By the end of the week, evacuation complete, six destroyers ahead led the convoy of *Oronsay, Ormonde, Duchess of York, Arandora Star,* and the ferries, *Royal Ulsterman, Ulster Monarch,* and *Ulster Prince* followed by two cruisers, out past Andelsnes Lighthouse for the last time. The ocean to the west of Norway was dotted by groups of ships.

As the convoy steamed south we sighted *Ark Royal* flying off aircraft, escorted by three destroyers, the battleship *Valiant* with an escort of four Tribal Class destroyers and finally the battle cruiser *Repulse,* which eventually joined our convoy. Unknown to us, *Scharnhorst* and *Gneisnau* were at sea south of us and had sunk the carrier *Glorious,* overloaded with evacuated Hurricanes as well as her own complement of aircraft, and both her escorts, *Ardent* and *Acasta.* Group 1 convoy heard the guns but remained undiscovered. Later the two German battleships had steamed past the hospital ship *Atlantis*, leaving her unmolested; it was only after she had met *Valiant* that it was known that they were at sea. No wireless report from *Glorious* and her escorts was received and it was only after three days, when survivors were rescued, that their sinking became known. Our Service of Thanksgiving for the Divine Providence that protected the safe evacuation of 24,000 men and most of their equipment had every justification.

Leaving the convoy to refuel in Scapa, *Echo* rejoined it off Cape Wrath to pass through the Minch and anchor safely at the Tail of the Bank after an unmolested passage. At midnight on 12th June, for the first time in six weeks, *Echo*, lying at anchor, was without an officer of the watch on the bridge. We had steamed an average of 272 miles a day to travel 12,000 miles.

Echo's boiler hours were double those normal between boiler cleaning. This cleaning of water tube boilers normally took three days and on the mainland allowed a short leave break. We were unlucky, so after an abortive trip to sea to rescue survivors of the torpedoed armed merchant cruiser *Scotstown* and another to escort well into the Atlantic the carrier *Furious*, accompanied for protection by the cruiser *Devonshire*, bound for Halifax to collect American fighter planes for Britain's use, we entered Scapa to lie alongside the depot ship *Woolwich.* No chance of leave here.

That night, as boiler cleaning began, the wardroom mess in bow ties dined together for the first time in seven weeks to play liar dice and get contentedly drunk. We landed empty ammunition boxes, stocked up 4.7-inch shells and cordite to replace those fired at Narvik and, to keep our crew occupied and take their minds off missed leave, painted the ship.

Destroyers were in such short supply that, after only four days in harbour, we were sent to steam east in calm weather at 30 knots escorting the cruiser, *Newcastle*, to search for a German destroyer reported by an aircraft off the south coast of Norway. Sighting the coast and finding nothing, we were back in Scapa Flow in under twenty four hours, only to be sent off for gunnery practice at a tug-towed target and, to exercise the newly fitted Oerlikon gun, at an aircraft towed sleeve and then to search fruitlessly for a reported U-boat.

On return to harbour, orders for Midshipman Durham to join the battle cruiser, *Renown*, due at Scapa in two days arrived. Fortunately we sailed once more before *Renown* arrived and, after escorting a liner down the Minch in thick fog till off Arran, we were despatched back into the Atlantic to search for survivors of the torpedoed *Arandora Star*.

On a bright calm summer evening, in the reported position, lifeboats were sighted ahead. Reaching them we steamed into clarts of floating, black, viscous oil, with small pieces of cork, wooden barrels and spars and numerous life-jackets, many of them supporting lifeless bodies. About a dozen lifeboats were tied together with no sign of life. The two destroyers who had arrived earlier to rescue survivors were rewarded by meals cooked by some of London's most celebrated chefs. *Arandora Star* was carrying Italian and German internees bound for Canada when the very U-boat which had sunk *Royal Oak* and fired torpedoes at us in *Norfolk*, commanded by the ace Gunter Prien, sighted and sank her. Many of the dead had broken their necks either in the explosion or by jumping over the side from a height with an insecure life-jacket. We left the eerie and derelict scene and, sadly, on arrival off Greenock, Midshipman Durham set forth to join the Jellicoe Special train to Thurso and thence in the smoky, 50-year-old ferry, *St. Ninian*, to Lyness where *Renown*'s drifter awaited him and mail. Once more I was reporting to an officer of the watch, "Come aboard to join, Sir".

CHAPTER 4

Frenchmen, Friends or Foes

FINDING ONESELF SENIOR MIDSHIPMAN in a gunroom containing five sub-lieutenants and thirty snotties in a 32,000-ton battle cruiser was indeed a different world from being sole midshipman in a 1,345-ton destroyer. In place of four single, low angle 4.7-inch guns there were now six 15-inch and twenty 4.5-inch anti-aircraft high-angle guns in five twin turrets each side. *Renown* was flagship of the Battle Cruiser Squadron, *Repulse* was our consort, the third battle cruiser, *Hood,* being attached elsewhere.

All my sea time having been involved with guns and gunnery, here I was given torpedo duties. *Renown* had fixed above-water torpedo tubes firing on either beam, which would require an alteration of the ship's course to aim at an enemy. All I had to do was to peer over a simple sight on the bridge and give a firing order when the bearing of the target came on. Two days after joining we steamed up and down within Scapa Flow carrying out, first an anti-aircraft practice shoot, and then a torpedo firing, the first and last while I was aboard. Fortunately, the tin fish ran straight and under the target at which I had ordered their despatch.

Now there was scope for sport and taking exercise. Apart from daily PT in the mornings, in harbour or at sea on most afternoons there were ferocious games of deck hockey. Played with a rope grummet and flat sticks, teams endeavoured to hack the grummet across the opposing team's line. Kicking was forbidden but cannons off ventilators, turrets and other obstructions quite permissible. There were Sunday film shows under the quarterdeck awning and in one newsreel before the main picture I watched *Echo* being bombed in Harstad Harbour, it looked far more alarming and dramatic on film.

A week was spent in the torpedo shop assisting during the annual overhaul of a torpedo, which had to be taken apart and stripped down. After overhaul, the small engine on a wooden bench was tested by dry running under compressed air. I had the old trick played on me of being told to steady it so that it did not jump off the bench. As soon as air is turned on the engine reverberates so that bench and sucker holding on are danced around the parting shop, with every bone reverberating and tooth chattering. A torpedo engine develops the enormous power needed to drive it at 45 knots, propelled by a combination of burning fuel and superheated steam, all compacted in about 9 inches of the 21-inch diameter torpedo.

To find the way around a large warship involves constant exploratory visits so as to be able to find, say, the main switchboard, the plumbers' shop, B magazine or the artificers' mess and it was a fortnight before I felt reasonably confident of not getting lost. In that time we had sailed with the Home Fleet in response to a report, which proved a false alarm, that *Gneisnau* was about to leave Trondheim. On return to Scapa there was a great stir of activity aboard while twenty spare barrels and numerous boxes of other gun and machinery spares were embarked, anti-typhoid inoculations given and tropical gear hoisted from baggage rooms deep below. Rumours were rife till, on 10th August, *Hood*, flying the flag of Vice-Admiral Sir James Somerville, entered Scapa Flow. Our Admiral and his staff, soon to be lost in action, joined *Hood* while theirs crossed to us. Then *Renown* accompanied by the cruiser, *Sheffield*, with a destroyer escort sailed west and then south to rendezvous with the carrier, *Ark Royal*, up from Gibraltar.

"Blues" were replaced by "Whites" and the three ships which were to form the regular basis of Force H entered Gibraltar Harbour. Berthed at what was to become our normal berth alongside the South Mole, there was soon to be a frenzy of activity on the quarterdeck as Flag Officer Gibraltar called on our Admiral, who later returned the call, and the captains of all the other ships in harbour called on our Captain. The Commander, Officer of the Watch and Quartermaster had to rush frenziedly to and fro to salute and pipe aboard arriving and departing captains, some by boat on the port side, others over the gangway from the jetty to starboard.

When night fell and the chaos subsided, the ships of the fleet were darkened as usual but, because there was no disguising the bulky mass of the Rock, there was no black-out ashore; every ship movement was, in any case, reported to the Germans by their observers in Algeciras three miles on the far side of Gibraltar Bay. To welcome our arrival, two Italian attempts were made that night to bomb us. The first raider dropped three bombs which exploded harmlessly to the south of the harbour. A searchlight picked it up, lost and then found it again. Every army anti-aircraft gun opened fire, other searchlights joined in but none of the shell bursts seemed close enough to cause damage.

Renown's gunnery officer pleaded to be allowed to open fire and, despite instructions to conserve ammunition, was granted five, but only five, salvos from the starboard battery of ten guns. As the crack of the fourth salvo fired, the third burst around the SM82 bomber blowing off its tail. While most of the searchlights followed the tailless plane falling like an autumn leaf, one individualist kept his beam on the tail till it splashed into the bay. Next day our motor boat went out to collect part of the floating green-painted wooden wing from which the three fasces were cut out and retained as a war trophy, an auspicious start to *Renown*'s time at Gibraltar.

The water being warm enough for bathing, we adopted a new, early morning routine. The crew went to PT on the quarterdeck at six-thirty and, still hot and sweating from bending and stretching, were then piped to bathe in the harbour before breakfast. Most nights there was an aircraft alarm, but these solitary bombers caused more annoyance than damage.

Early in September, Force H sailed west to meet the battleship *Valiant* and the carrier, *Illustrious*. As the fleet returned to Gibraltar, planes from *Ark Royal* and *Illustrious* exercised together, finishing up with a concerted Swordfish torpedo bombing attack on the fleet, which was defended by twelve Fulmar fighters. The ensuing mock aerial battles overhead made entertaining viewing. As soon as the escorts to the enlarged fleet had topped up with fuel in Gibraltar Harbour, the convoy set sail into the Mediterranean. There were the usual alarms from the destroyer escort investigating asdic contacts, when the heavy ships would turn away from the suspected danger, while destroyers carried out depth charge attacks.

At noon on the first day out, all *Renown*'s 100 officers mustered in the wardroom where one of Admiral Somerville's staff explained that Operation HATS was to pass *Valiant* and *Illustrious* through the central Mediterranean to Admiral Cunningham's base in Alexandria. This was the first attempt to send through big ships since Italy had joined in the war.

Several feints were designed to confuse the enemy. The fleet would first steer north as if going to bombard Toulon, Genoa or Spetzia. After dark, it would turn back, but two destroyers would continue north and, beyond the Balearic Islands, transmit on wireless as if still northbound with the fleet. While they did this, the fleet south of Sardinia would send Swordfish air strikes from the two carriers against Elmas Aerodrome near Cagliari, the capital. When they returned aboard their carriers, the whole fleet would steam back west for three hours, as if returning to Gibraltar, before once more turning east. That evening, off Tunis Bay, the force would split up, *Illustrious, Valiant* and the AA cruisers, *Coventry* and *Calcutta*, with their destroyer screen, carrying on to Alexandria while the rest returned to Gibraltar. The ship's company was later given a less detailed lecture on the plan. It was such endeavours to keep everyone informed that contributed to *Renown* being such a very happy and efficient ship.

The plan for HATS was followed; two reconnaissance planes were shot down by Skuas south of Majorca; a large force of bombers was despatched, fruitlessly to attack the supposed fleet after the destroyer's wireless transmission; the air strike on Elmas left at 3 am and, after direct hits on hangars, barracks and planes on the runway, all landed back in time for breakfast without loss. The fleet remained closed up at action stations all day, but the large formation of aircraft which approached at dusk failed to attack and, after the fleets split up, a second dawn attack was made on Elmas before Force H, without a single casualty, next morning reached the Rock shrouded in a swirling, levanter cloud. Would that later "club runs" to the central Mediterranean could have been so simple and safe.

Our next experiences were to be far less successful and this time our problem was to be Vichy France not the Axis powers. A destroyer, *Hotspur,* on patrol in the Straits, reported that three cruisers of the *Georges Layques* class, escorted by three destroyers, were in sight steaming out of the Mediterranean. *Renown* prepared for sea but did not sail and even signalled *Bon Voyage* without acknowledgement. Rumours were rife on board. Our Admiral was reported to be furious at not being allowed to intercept. Eventually, we sailed in the evening but the French warships were well on their way to Dakar, the naval base on the north-west African coast. Off Casablanca next morning, *Vidette,* a destroyer in our escort, sighted a darkened ship, challenged it and opened her searchlight shutters to identify a French destroyer. When no reply was made to her challenge, she opened fire. The enemy made smoke and withdrew in her own smoke screen. There seemed to be no clear orders. Were we to intercept or not? *Bon voyage* or a salvo of shells?

A French Glen Martin bomber shadowed Force H. That night three destroyers were sighted, one identified as *La Fantastique*. We seemed to be in a fantastic muddle without guidance from our political masters. Months earlier, the French fleet in Oran had sadly been sunk and French warships in Alexandria demobilised. After two days steaming hither and thither, the fleet returned to Gibraltar. Over the next indecisive week we sailed and returned twice. Meanwhile, a British fleet accompanied by General de Gaulle and a Free French landing force were repulsed in their attack on Dakar, a battleship, *Resolution,* being torpedoed.

Renown, the only heavy ship in Gibraltar Harbour at 7 am on 24th September, came to anti-aircraft alert when a French aircraft flew low outside the Mole and away before any anti-aircraft fire could be aimed at it. At midday, without any alarm or detection of air activity by the very primitive radar of the time, a stick of bombs burst down Gibraltar Bay, straddling an A/S trawler on patrol. A further stick raised a cloud of red dust at Europa Point: the French were attacking their ex-allies.

Over the next three hours the raid continued and *Renown* alone had fired

1,200 rounds of 4.5-inch shells. I was standing in the port waist when the attack began and, as the bugle sounded anti-aircraft stations, I made my way to the armoured conning position where, through the slits in the armour, I could watch some of the action. The corrugated iron roof of the shed on the Mole alongside slowly fell apart from the continuous blast of the starboard guns only yards away. A stick of thirteen carefully counted bomb bursts advanced towards our stern, one after another. After number seven hit the shed alongside, number eight burst in the water close alongside and the rest raised columns of smoke and spray inside the harbour. Whilst I was looking towards the town, a string of bomb bursts under the Rock Hotel ended with total destruction of the dockyard canteen.

As this raid continued, two unperturbed Spaniards in a rowing boat outside the harbour were leaning over the side collecting fish killed or stunned by the bombs. The worst damage was caused by two bigger bombs which burst one on the land between the dry docks, and the other on a naval store from which I watched a heavy steel girder rise slowly on end before somersaulting down with a dusty clatter fifty yards from the ruin of the building of which it had been a part.

A call came down from the bridge for a volunteer to drive the motor dinghy moored under the stern across to Admiral Dudley North's headquarters in the dockyard. Volunteering and descending to the stern, shaken by ten 4.5-inch guns firing just over the top, I found another snotty waiting with the message.

The motor boat had been wrecked by bomb number eight but, despite a collapsed and partly burned canopy on the dinghy, the engine fired with the help of the boat's stoker and we crossed the harbour with our message. My colleague racing up to the jetty, across it and down into the Admiral's air raid shelter, delivered the message. Meanwhile, *Renown* was slipping wires to sail so, crossing back, we stopped under the crane and, in a lull in the firing, were hoisted, only to find that there was a hole in our jolly boat's stern where a shell splinter had entered just above the waterline. As *Renown* passed to sea through the gap between the Moles, we were cheered by a number of tin-hatted soldiers who were blissfully unaware that our departure had halved the anti-aircraft defence of the Rock.

That night, the BBC claimed thirty bombers had dropped 150 bombs and Vichy Radio that 120 bombers had carried out the attack. The same night a destroyer in the Strait challenged four French destroyers, both sides opened fire before the Frenchmen withdrew *à toute vitesse*. Next day, the Rock suffered more damage and a trawler alongside was sunk by a further 300 French bombs.

After five days cruising off Cape Finisterre, *Renown* returned to Gibraltar, only to leave again soon after, when it was announced on the ship's loudspeakers that two French destroyers in Spanish territorial waters were passing through the Strait at high speed. An order was passed that guns were to remain trained fore and aft and later, after sighting the peak of Santa Maria in the Azores low over the horizon lit by the rising sun, we returned to Gibraltar to fuel the destroyers on the screen, before setting off once more, shadowed by a French Glen Martin bomber.

At sea between Madeira and the Canaries, a V & W destroyer up from Freetown in Sierra Leone joined the screen and, as she took up position, *Wishart* made black smoke. In reply to FOH's signal "Why?" she signalled, "My boiler hours are 200 overdue for cleaning and the extra burst of speed was too much for them". The destroyers were grossly overworked, and were often never long enough in harbour to cool down boilers and carry out very desirable maintenance. So life continued: out to sea; back to Gibraltar; another alarm and off again.

Renown, as a large capital ship and flagship, mustered both C of E and RC padres who, in an ecumenical spirit in advance of its time, shared morning prayers, use of the chapel and much else besides. Father Thomas Gilbey, a Benedictine monk who had been a chaplain in Cambridge University, had a liberal outlook and shared with our Admiral a remarkable capacity to get on with young people and to understand their problems. For the Gunroom he had set up a debating society, The Complete Wranglers, which met fortnightly in his cabin. With his tongue in his cheek he had instituted an exaggerated ceremonial obeisance to "The Thing", a dragon-backed kimono which was always worn by the Chairman of the evening session. None of us had read G.K. Chesterton's essay "The Thing" or appreciated the religious implication of intoning, "O Thing, live for ever!" The heated debates were a welcome relief from the routine of that lowest form of life, a midshipman in a warship's gunroom.

As undeclared and, to our regret, one-sided war with Vichy France subsided, there was excitement when, at the end of October, Italian frogmen based on a merchant ship in Algeciras across the Bay, attempted unsuccessfully to attack the heavy ships of Force H. Then, early in November, a German raider was reported in the Atlantic and Force H sailed to protect two convoys steaming close together, later to be joined by a third. We acted as nursemaid to almost a hundred assorted merchant ships and tankers. No raider appeared and a signal awaited our return to harbour that Midshipmen Norman and Durham were to be examined in Seamanship aboard *Ark Royal* in November.

Over the last four months the schoolie had been lecturing on many of the subjects to be examined and detailed Ship Construction Plans had been drawn. The day of the exam broke. Dressed in best laundered white uniforms we crossed by boat to *Ark Royal* where midshipmen from other ships to be examined had gathered. The Captain's day cabin was a most luxurious and spacious room, occupying the whole of the carrier's stern high above the waterline. Large windows followed the circle of the stern, and pale green walls added a cool effect to the furnishings of the chairs with white loose covers edged with blue piping arranged round a circular, polished mahogany table. One could face aft to the North African mountains or look out at the dockyard to starboard or at Algeciras across the Bay to port. Three four-striped captains carried out examinations.

We spent the day waiting anxiously and fidgeting in between calls from various members of the Board. From the Certificate issued, it appears we were examined in Rigging, Anchor Work, Rule of the Road at Sea, Officer of the Watch Duties, Organisation, General Seamanship, Signals (oral, morse, semaphore and buzzer) and Ship Construction while our Midshipman's Journal was examined and marked. Somewhat exaggeratedly, it also certified we had qualified in Navigational Observations, Astronomical Navigation, Boats and Signals and only from lack of opportunity had failed to qualify in the Junior Officers Air Course and the Anti Gas Course. Quite exhausted by these endeavours we returned to our gunrooms for cold beer and unwise quantities of Fino la Ina, Creme de Menthe Frappé and after dinner liqueurs. Next day I was gratified to earn four months' seniority with 935 marks out of 1,000 and a First Class Certificate in Seamanship.

It would be a great sadness to leave one of the happiest of happy ships in which I served. Under our beloved Jimmy or Slim, one of the least distant of Flag Officers, we were supremely confident in ourselves and in the leadership we enjoyed. In most flagships, the Admiral was a distant, rather awe-inspiring figure but not in *Renown*. We knew him and he gave every appearance of knowing us.

Thus it was that Norman and I had the temerity to invite the Admiral through his Flag Lieutenant to our farewell party to which both the Wardroom and the warrant officers' Messes had been invited. As such parties are occasions of fairly rowdy horseplay we enquired whether he would object were he involved. The reply was that he'd be happy to come and, as long as we'd invited his staff who could protect him, we were welcome to do our worst.

Accordingly the evening ended with Sir James, some of his staff and most of the gunroom officers deprived of their nether garments. The fleet Gunnery Officer, Commander Holmes, a tough, black bearded character, had, however, defied all our efforts. Several of us managed to bear him, struggling furiously, to the deck but were still losing the battle when to our aid came, of all people, the Admiral himself and, with his help, success was achieved.

When the Cunard liner, *Franconia,* entered harbour, Norman and I were transferred with our kit to her for passage in a forthcoming convoy back to the UK. Soon after, Force H sailed out into the Mediterranean with a convoy. On their return a few days later we found out they had been in action inconclusively at extreme range. Neither side suffered casualties or damage and a far more powerful Italian fleet, headed by two modern battleships, fled south of Sardinia from *Renown* and *Sheffield, Ark Royal* being absent. Our convoy sailed, reaching the Tail of the Bank without incident.

It was four months later that I heard from Father Gilbey in a letter about *Renown's* activities. He wrote:

> From time to time I converse affably with the Admiral on signal pads; he believes in yoking all the forces at his disposal, and asks for prayers for a fog to come up or the wind to veer. Anyway, every operation produces its crop of backchat.

When we turned from Genoa I wrote:

> When Genoa town was last in the wars,
> Bombarded quite stiffly by *Louis Quatorze,*
> The canisters fired by that *grand monarque*
> Lacked heavenly bearing from men on the Ark.
> Undoubtedly he did not cut such a dash
> As "Sheffield", "Malaya", "Renown" and Force 'ash.

He immediately retorted:

> My word what a chap was that *Louis Quatorze*
> Surrounded by Cardinals, courtiers and w——s
> By my troth and alack and likewise O marry
> What a change for the worse is Fred Orange Harry:
> No longer the whites of his enemy's eye
> 'Fore he looses his broadside doth he seek to espy.
> He merely says "Martin, where the hell are we now?"
> And Martin replies (though he's guessing, I trow)
> "The lighthouse bears three two O and distant ten miles.
> No - you won't see it yet Sir - and not for some whiles
> But I'll bet my old sextant, deck watch and hard head
> It's as certainly there as the Chaplain's in bed!"
> "Well if you're damn sure, we'll now open fire,
> Though there is just one question I'd like to enquire,
> How the hell can you aim if the bull you can't see?

I'm a plain old torpedoman, its a mystery to me"
"Oh that, Sir's quite easy", says bugwhiskered Holmes,
"I've looked it all up in the gunnery tomes.
There's a thing called tumtum and tumtum the sky
Meets the sea - yes, horizon, Sir - but I always try
To avoid using long words when I've got to explain
And get something into a Flag Officer's brain"
(Oh lucky, Oh fortunate *Louis Quatorze*
Surrounded by Cardinals, courtiers and w——s.)

Father Gilbey finished up by reporting one or two meetings of the Complete Wranglers, saying that, though it started with more of a flourish it hadn't shown the regular constancy of the Wardroom Debating Society known as the Platitudinarians.

It was my last direct news of Force H till later my destroyer was sent out to Gibraltar and I was happy to find myself back under Admiral Somerville's command once again.

CHAPTER 5

Blitzed Portsmouth Technical Courses

HMS *VERNON*, THE TORPEDO AND ELECTRICAL SCHOOL, held my group's first course. It was a large rambling establishment of old stone and wooden buildings spread out between the dockyard and old Portsmouth. As we learned on the day after joining from Christmas leave, two underground rooms in telephone-touch with Dockyard ARP Headquarters controlled its air raid precautions. On the roof of the three storey, brick rating-accommodation block in the centre of the establishment was a machine-gun, its sole offensive armament. Each building had its own fire party and each area headquarters controlled its own repair party and small fire brigade, equipped with a trailer pump and hoses. Our group of fourteen acting sub-lieutenants was split in two watches and, within each watch, one manned the machine-gun with the rest assigned to different fire parties. Till then Portsmouth had been spared the concentrated night raids that London had suffered; this was fortunate because for sub-lieutenants a peacetime year's technical courses had been telescoped into three months, a very concentrated training programme.

After our first day's delving into the anatomy of a Mark IX torpedo, a friend and I set off for supper and a film in Southsea as relaxation from air bottles, servomotors, starting valves and cold runs. Later, while comfortably settled in the cinema circle, the sirens sounded and the normal wartime notice was projected on the screen informing the audience that anyone wishing to might leave for a nearby shelter but that the show would continue. A few minutes later there were sounds of gunfire and the odd, isolated thump shook the floor. We were wondering if this could all be gunfire when suddenly the lights went out, leaving hero and heroine abandoned in tender embrace. By torchlight the cinema manager announced that the programme would resume once power was restored. Feeling our way to the foyer, my friend's torch lit a door marked "Private"; on opening it and climbing a winding stair, we discovered another door leading to the cinema roof and emerged on a flat platform over the entrance. The whole dome of the sky glowed salmon pink and numerous fires flickered like fireworks below. It seemed as if much of the town was ablaze. Apart from a concentrated fire in the town centre, the whole horizon was dotted with bright silvery dots of spluttering incandescence among the burning houses. There were flashes of gunfire whose cracks punctuated the oscillating hum of background noise. Sweeping searchlight beams lit occasional barrage balloons but seemed to find no enemy bombers on which to focus. Surely this could not be a normal light raid?

There was a whistle and then a bomb exploded further up the street followed by a rumble of falling masonry. Then a clattering sound overhead became closer, louder, faster like an approaching train. We leapt into the doorway just as two aluminium canisters came through the roof and started to splutter molten magnesium. We had heard the sound of our first basket of incendiary bombs descending. Out in the street, on the roofs of houses opposite and on the church next door, many others were alight. Finding a bucket of sand, we clambered over the rafters to tackle our two incendiaries. Sand soon put one out but the other seemed more persistent while the blows we dealt it with our gas mask cases merely served to spread the flames. No one else seemed aware of our activities so, while my friend continued to fight and contain the blaze, I descended and shouted to the audience that the roof was on fire and they'd better move under the shelter of the balcony in case it fell. The cinema manager, until then quite unaware of the fire, now appeared bearing more sand buckets with which we managed to extinguish the bomb and, with a bucket of water, dowse the flames beginning to lick from the smouldering rafters.

Out in the street, firemen were hosing the next door church roof; too late, it fell with a rumbling crash as we were leaving to make our way back to *Vernon* two miles away. At the far end of one road on our route was a row of burning houses. Miserable little piles of furniture, clothes and personal possessions in the street seemed all that had been saved, as their unfortunate occupants watched their homes burn down. There was nothing to be done to help as we passed till, nearing the Guildhall, we reached another burning house. A tearful woman dashed out, grabbed my friend and screamed, "Get Granma out. She's in the shelter and won't come out". Rushing through the blazing house into the back garden he discovered the corrugated iron shelter already roofed with burning debris. Inside was Granma.

"I've come to save you."

"I'm safe," replied Granma, "they told me to stay here and I'd be safe."

The sight of Sub-Lieutenant Horneold-Strickland emerging from the blazing house with a spluttering, screaming, kicking indignant old lady over his shoulder was unforgettable.

We beat a hasty retreat, still laughing as we flattened on the road when a bomb burst nearby scattering tinkling splinters. Eventually, after passing the burned out shell of the theatre close to the Guildhall and making a detour round a blazing gas main in the centre of a bomb crater, we returned to *Vernon's* wardroom, a semi-circular building round what had been an ornamental garden, now a bomb crater. The bomb had broken all the wardroom windows and pockmarked the masonry but left the building intact.

Still with no electricity, but well lit by the rosy sky outside, we attacked a veal and ham pie on the mess table. It tasted gritty and we were looking for something else when a warrant officer came in with a torch to warn us that the food was full of glass splinters from the shattered windows. *Vernon* had escaped the raid lightly, but the power station just outside the south wall had been gutted and only by luck had Portsmouth Cathedral close by been left unscathed. The city was left without electricity.

Next morning, at breakfast, it was announced that our classroom was now roofless and we were to use a hut in the grammar school nearby. This had been damaged; unheated and with glassless windows it lay open to the January elements as we studied in our greatcoats. The old gunner who was our lecturer had trouble with his Hs and he and we had some difficulty with Ohm's Law and Holmes' lights.

We awaited the night with foreboding. Without electricity, with low gas pressure, inadequate water supplies, hydrants too far apart, a shortage of hoses and firemen still damping down the night before's ruins, Portsmouth was in no state to face a repetition. There was heavy cloud and a strong wind as darkness fell and half an hour later the sirens wailed forth. Small groups of figures gathered round *Vernon's* buildings. Soon the low beating drone of aircraft became audible. This was it. Several guns opened fire but nothing more happened and soon the All-Clear sounded and everyone went to supper. Despite two more alarms, we were left in peace. We were then granted several days in which to re-organise and improve arrangements before the next major raid.

In that raid, Portsmouth harbour station, between *Vernon* and the Dockyard, where trains met the Isle of Wight ferries, was totally destroyed by fire and, using this as a target, the area of the Hard was hit by many high explosive bombs. One plane gliding low dropped a flare which the machine-gun on D Block of *Vernon* managed to put out. However, there were also large well established fires about the shopping centre of the town. From our roof we could see the flames blowing out sideways from the tower of the Guildhall.

Because of the shortage of water, a call came to lay a hosepipe from Portsmouth Harbour, through *Vernon* to the Guildhall a mile inland. I was sent with a squad to manhandle a trailer pump halfway there to maintain the pressure from the harbour side trailer pump and then to lay hoses on to the Guildhall. When all was connected up and both pumps pumping the resulting supply of sea water helped save the buildings surrounding the now burned out shell of the gutted Guildhall.

Eventually, after staggering into bed dirty but too tired to wash, I was rudely awakened by the owner of a car parked in the same garage as George, my old BSA motor bicycle, to be told that the garage had burned down, his car was wrecked and I'd better look for George, a typical sub-lieutenant's course motor bike passed on from one to another. Sadly, when I went to search I discovered the garage roof had fallen on a number of burned out and barely recognisable cars and motor bicycles. Nothing salvageable was left and I could not even find George's skeleton in the shambles. Despondently, I returned to breakfast in deep mourning for RV3717 only to hear we'd lost our second classroom burned down in the night. We were now to travel to the Rechabites' Hall in Cosham by bus. When we got there it was undamaged and, even more important, warm.

Part of our course, which was to be in the Torpedo Attack Teacher had been cancelled, it having been demolished by a bomb the night before. Half asleep we began to learn about the use of low power electricity in circuits. Our brains also seemed to be in low power, including that of our instructor. On our return from lunch, the afternoon's studies were cancelled and we all went to catch up on lost sleep. That night's raid was light and after a further bus trip to Cosham we were told the bus could not be spared and we'd have to make our own travel arrangements in future. If only George were still available. Then, amazingly, I heard a rumour that one or two motor bikes had been pulled out of the blazing garage on the Hard. Hardly daring to hope, I found the side street mentioned and there, rusty, with the battery burned out, was George. After a couple of hours' work with a borrowed battery, I managed to get the engine running once more.

By packing five into each of our two cars and with pillion passengers on each of two motor cycles, owned by members of our group, our fourteen were ready to travel to Cosham using our own transport. The convoy set off at nine next morning, skirting the dockyard wall past Brickwood's Brewery, fortunately still intact and brewing, to be halted by the policeman on duty at the busy crossroad opposite the main dockyard gate.

George, with kick start and clutch worn out, stalled as did one of the bangers of cars. A line of buses, lorries and cars drew up behind. While the Ford party were cranking to restart their engine, our line of traffic was called on. Running as fast as possible, as I slapped the lever into first gear, the usual starting procedure, my pillion passenger just managed to catch up and leap aboard. The old Ford refused to fire and the constable had to join in pushing it out of the way to release the hooting traffic jam.

We all eventually reached the Rechabites' Hall and for the rest of our torpedo course the policeman watched out for our cavalcade at nine o'clock and held up all other traffic to let us through. He was not going to risk any repetition.

After several less severe night air raids, it was clear that, while we were abysmally ignorant of the finer points of torpedoes or electricity, the training staff at *Vernon*, fully aware of this, had already decided that such efficient fire fighters should not go unrewarded. We were all advised to be sure to attend revision the day before the exam was due. At this revision, the entire exam paper due next day was re-lectured, question by question, point by point, so that next day we were not unprepared. At the end of each of the five courses, Seamanship, completed as midshipmen, Torpedo, Gunnery, Signals and Navigation either First, Second or Third Class Certificates were awarded and the results determined the time to be served before putting up a second stripe as lieutenants. Our Torpedo results were a record; all received Firsts, maybe just as a reward for assisting the survival of several of *Vernon*'s old buildings.

Next, came a five week Gunnery Course at Whale Island, north of the dockyard. This famous gunnery school prided itself on smartness, strict discipline, drill, and doing everything by numbers and "at the rush". Whaley regarded the *Vernon* ethos as "Save it till Monday and then do it in overalls in your own time." Accommodation not being immediately available in *Excellent*, we were to stay in *Vernon* travelling to and fro by lorry. The ground was white with frost as we climbed down at the wardroom door.

Our class instructor met us with, "Where are your gaiters?"

We looked blank.

"Surely you've been issued with gaiters?"

We replied that we did not think *Vernon* was well up on gaiters, to be told a signal would be sent at once to ask them to be supplied that night on our return and meanwhile the field training office would lend us some.

Duly gaitered up, we returned.

"Officer in charge of class fall class in and double down to the parade ground."

Unsure of who was in charge, someone came forward and ordered us to fall in, turn right and double march. We reached the parade ground, a large gravel area where various squads were marching to and fro, and fell out.

Our instructor arrived, pointed out our doubling was dreadful, that we had not picked up our dressing on falling in, and that the order, "Turning right, dismiss," meant all turn right not twelve turn right and two left. We were informed we were not in *Vernon* now and my next door neighbour quietly whispered, "More's the pity." We were handed rifles, bayonets and belts and a tough old gunner's mate started to teach us the elements of drill, all by numbers.

We learned to order, slope, shoulder and present arms, to fix and unfix bayonets, how to carry rifles and much else, all by numbers and strictly in accordance with the drill book. We studied taking a pace forward, wheeling and left face, all by numbers, and learned the duties of right and left hand markers when fixing bayonets, one-and-two-and-three. We doubled away to the mess for lunch, doubled back again and continued with the dreary rifle drill. Finally, someone forgot which rank he was in, took two paces forward at the wrong moment, running into the man in front and dropping his rifle.

We failed to conceal our mirth.

With a ferocious scowl, our instructor ordered us to port arms, which entails the right arm parallel to the ground grasping a rifle with the elbow tucked to the side, very uncomfortable for any length of time.

"Double march," rang out the order. We left the parade ground and wheeled on to the road which circles the island. After a minute or two, the arms began to sag.

"Keep your arms out straight."

Soon the pace slackened.

"When I say double march, I mean double march."

My next door neighbour whispered he'd rather gathered that.

"Silence in the ranks."

We passed the mess on the far side of the perimeter from the parade ground.

"Keep the pace going."

At long last, at long, long last, we again reached the parade ground, halted, ordered arms and were allowed to stand easy.

"That was to point out field training is serious. You'll save yourselves a lot of trouble by not forgetting it."

The taming process had begun.

Next morning, wearing new yellow-green gaiters issued in *Vernon* we again climbed out of our lorry.

"Why haven't your gaiters been cleaned?"

We suggested it was perhaps because they were brand new.

"In *Excellent* gaiters are cleaned with green blanco."

Then a messenger handed him a signal. It was addressed R Group of Sub-Lieutenants *Vernon*, copy to *Excellent*, from C in C Portsmouth congratulating us on our unique Torpedo examination result.

He snorted, "You seem to have got on well in *Vernon*. I assure you we in *Excellent* are less generous in issuing First Class Certificates. You've got to work hard, be smart and well disciplined and, on present showing, you'll be lucky to even get Thirds. Carry on to divisions."

In a mid February raid, while we were still in *Excellent,* two sub-lieutenants in the course following ours were killed by a direct bomb hit on *Vernon's* South Area Headquarters. Whale Island, clear of the centre of Portsmouth and north of the dockyard, had suffered little air raid damage till then. The one excitement in this raid was when a shell from one of Whaley's 4-inch guns shot down *Excellent*'s sole barrage balloon. The thin piano wire descended with a sizzling rip and acting as a glorified cheese cutter, buried itself a foot underground. Then, just before our gunnery course ended on 9th March, a bright moonlit night, a raid concentrating on the dockyard as main target began.

In the usual way, the sirens wailed after dinner, followed by isolated gunfire and the explosion of the odd bomb. Soon, however, a large formation of bombers attacked, with hits on the dockyard putting the telephone out of action. A volunteer able to read morse was sought so I offered and was sent to a top floor cabin with an Aldis lamp. After flashing to the dockyard tower and receiving an acknowledgement I had a grandstand view of the developing raid.

A stick of bombs exploded near the pier and barrage balloon mooring as the guns on the lawn blazed away for all they were worth. Then a plane gliding low below the balloon barrage switched off its engine. I heard a whistle of air rushing past it and, at about 250 feet, four bombs in quick succession were dropped. There was a roar and a flash and, amid the shriek of falling bombs, craters opened up between two guns on a corner of the lawn, on the warrant officers' mess, and in the road outside the petty officers' mess. All I heard of the bomb hitting the WO's mess was the rumble of falling masonry as the gable blew out. A shout rang out for ambulances. One officer was saved by a door from the collapsed gable end while his companion alongside was killed.

Silence descended as the dust rose, and rescue parties arrived to dig in the ruins. Telephone contact restored, I was relieved and able to go down to see if more help was needed. As I approached, the whine of a bomb put me flat on my face before it exploded in the mud close to the bridge to the mainland. By this time everyone instinctively would fling themselves prone at the sound of a descending bomb. After several more bombs on the island the raid petered out, leaving fire, rescue, and first aid parties at work and the rest of us to turn in. Most nights there seemed to be alerts and raids till, after our three days of gunnery exams, the results were known and only three of our fourteen were awarded Firsts.

We were to stay on the island for our three week signal course, a more peaceful affair with one light moment. In daily signal manoeuvres on the parade ground, each sub-lieutenant represented a ship. "George 9" (a speed of 9 knots) was quick march while "George 18" represented moving at the double. All the turning signals for ships in formation were exercised with columns of ships turning any given number of degrees together, in succession, or leaders together and the remainder in succession. In due course, the flagship of the day lost control and, forgetting the signal for stop engines, the fleet steaming at high speed towards the senior staff watching the manoeuvres faced disaster. As they prepared to flee in disarray, he though of a solution and wheeled us ninety degrees to port together (left turn). Alas, dangerous rocks in the shape of an air raid shelter lay ahead into which the fleet piled in confusion. The Admiral was ordered to strike his flag in ignominy and his replacement, with a better memory, salvaged the fleet to navigate it safely into harbour at last. Fortunately, signalmen take life more calmly than gunnery officers and a prolonged cruise round the island was not demanded.

Following that exam, we moved to our final course in the Navigation School, *Dryad*. This was sited just inside the dockyard wall where, if the wind was right, tempting smells from Brickwood's Brewery wafted through the windows. The front facade of the building had collapsed into a deep bomb crater, leaving a lavatory indecently exposed. Next door, Admiral Bubbles James, Flag Officer Portsmouth (nicknamed from Millais' famous child portrait of him) flew his flag. In the classrooms by the courtyard inside we delved into the mysteries of tides, heavenly bodies (sadly only celestial) and the art of correcting a magnetic compass. While roof air raid duties were allocated, life seemed far less restricted than in Whale Island.

One night, on a run ashore with a friend and two girls to the Jokers Club in Southsea, the usual nightly sirens sounded. The guns on Southsea Common opened up and bombs started to drop all around. There was one just down the street, another hit a house in a nearby side turning and several went off fruitlessly in an already devastated area. The needle kept jumping off the record on the gramophone and dancing ended abruptly when a closer bomb rocked the building with its blast. The bartender shut his bar. With our fair companions, we joined a trickle of people leaving through the Cut Loaf Restaurant below to the street. Incendiary bombs were hissing on the roof of a building opposite and on the road. Someone was moving on the roof so, after checking that the incendiaries guttering on the road were unlikely to cause damage, we continued to the Queens Hotel on the Common, which was glittering like fairyland as scores of incendiaries spluttered magnesium. From time to time one of them exploded because, by now, each basket of incendiary bombs would include the odd explosive anti-personnel one as a discouragement to firefighters.

We joined a group of night-attired guests around a fire in the hotel lounge. They included some old ladies shivering either from cold or fright. Soon smoke started to filter into the room, it was impossible to tell from where, and then it was rumoured there was a fire in the cellars.

We went to investigate and then decided that the smoke must come from a roof ventilation system. So it proved, when we climbed the stair to the top floor where two waiters at the end of the corridor were fighting a bedroom fire with stirrup pumps and buckets of water. As we went to join them, smoke started to seep out from a door on the corridor; when opened, it revealed bedding and rafters alight round an incendiary bomb.

With handy water bucket, I worked a stirrup pump while my colleague directed the pathetically thin, wavering jet of water to little effect. We were just emptying our third bucketful when there was a whoosh and we were washed flat on our backs in a cascade of water. The fire brigade outside were directing power hoses on the fire through a hole in the roof. Picking ourselves up, cursing and wringing wet, we withdrew downstairs bruised and shivering.

There was no more coal for the fire in the lounge, so we tried to find a taxi to take us and our girlfriends home before we caught our deaths of cold. By luck we found one but, after a few hundred yards, a tyre punctured beside a bomb crater. We abandoned it, and our girlfriends, to walk the two miles back to *Dryad,* still shivering in the freezing air.

By the time we arrived the raid was over. There being no hot water for a bath, I peeled off clammy clothes, towelled myself hard and with teeth chattering climbed under the blankets trying to get warm. During the night I dreamed a vivid dream that I was looking down on my dead body. Awakening with a splitting headache when my servant gave me a call, it all seemed very real. After staggering up, dressed in uniform and descending to breakfast, I found I was not hungry, so wended my way to the sick bay. A young sick-berth attendant made me sit down, heard my story and popped a thermometer into my mouth. When he had removed it and examined it he told me it seemed broken so he went to fetch another. After the second thermometer reading was taken, he went white, told me to stay where I was and marched out. Within ten minutes I had been whisked off in an ambulance to Haslar Hospital. Put to bed deep in blankets, I sank into a disturbed sleep. When I asked the doctor who woke me up what was wrong he told me not to excite myself but my temperature had been a remarkable 105.8.

When I explained I had always run high temperatures in childhood and it would be back to normal in a couple of days, he laughed and willingly gave a promise that, if it were back to normal in two days, he'd let me return to my course in four. This was the maximum missable amount of a course without having to repeat it. In that night's air raid I was lowered down, on a stretcher, to an air raid shelter where I slept soundly; it was the first time I'd visited one.

The next morning I began to feel better and with my temperature back to normal next day, the doctor kept his word while offering me sick leave. I chose to return, completed my course and took the exam with the rest. By luck and possibly friendly marking I was able to add a First in Navigation to my other four Firsts and collect my Admiralty prize of books or instruments. I chose a pair of Barr and Stroud binoculars.

When the siren sounded on the last night before going on leave, having no duties, I decided for once to go down voluntarily to a shelter. It was not a very large raid. A new and unpleasant bombing development at the time had been the dropping of parachute-supported land mines. As they slowly descended they were often spotted by those below. One about to land in a dry dock containing a cruiser under repair had been left swinging precariously from a dockyard crane, a new problem for the bomb disposal squad. Imagine my horror when, having safely survived the blitz up to now, from the mouth of the shelter I observed, silhouetted against the sky, a great flopping mass coming rapidly down. Piling head first down below, I awaited my end. There was silence.

A braver shelterer than I climbed up to investigate and returned in great mirth. "Just come and look."

There outside, like a stranded sea monster, lay a slowly deflating barrage balloon.

Bidding goodbye to Pompey, much battered in the last four months, I went home on leave to await the submarine training class for which I had earlier volunteered in *Vernon* during my Torpedo course.

CHAPTER 6

Standing by a New Ship

A MONTH'S LEAVE AT HOME with still no appointment to my submarine training class began to pall. A trip to the Second Sea Lord's office in the Admiralty revealed they had no record of my having volunteered for submarines and, while those who had volunteered and one or two who had not, were already being trained at *Dolphin*, I was to join a flotilla leader, *Laforey*, building in Yarrow's yard on the Clyde. It appeared that the office containing my letter volunteering to become a submariner had been demolished by a bomb in one of the raids at *Vernon*.

Travelling to Glasgow, I discovered Dockyard Job J1415 still fitting out alongside a jetty in Yarrow's yard and unlikely to commission for ten weeks. It was late at night and drizzling when I arrived in Scotstoun to find just a night watchman on the gate into the yard and no accommodation available. Somewhat disconsolate, after a night in a squalid local hotel, I returned to St. Enoch's Station, the headquarters of Flag Officer Glasgow, to try to discover more about standing by a destroyer under construction. Someone took pity on a naive and unhappy sub-lieutenant and recommended digs off Great Western Road. Taking a tram I eventually reached 22 Hamilton Park Avenue and rang the doorbell.

A maid answered the door and showed me into the lounge where an attractive blonde-haired Wren was writing. She told me Mrs. Paxton was a dear and everyone living in HPA found it most congenial. When the good lady arrived, grey-haired and friendly, she agreed to my sharing a large double room on the first floor with an RNVR sub-lieutenant standing by the battleship, *Duke of York*, building in John Brown's yard further down the Clyde. The rent for supper, bed and breakfast would be £2 per week. Our large, airy room, looking west through a large bay window, contained two beds, a piano and several easy chairs.

At supper, round a long dining room table, I met my fellow lodgers: three naval officers building ships on the Clyde, three signal and cipher Wrens working in naval headquarters and a FANY who drove for the Navy. Supper at seven was presided over by Mrs. Paxton who clearly regarded this use of her house as a contribution to the war effort; it was very unlikely she could have made any profit from it.

Our bedroom, the largest room in the house, was often used by everyone to sit around, listen to the gramophone, dance, sing and drink beer and it was eventually named the Bacon Rind. Many happy evenings were spent there till the sun set and blackout curtains were drawn.

Various decorations were begged, borrowed or stolen, one being a large tram destination board AUCHENSHUGGLE. The capture of this trophy involved leaning out of the front window on the upper deck of the tram late at night to remove the surprisingly long and heavy wooden board. The descent of the tram stair with the board projecting above and below the raincoat worn by its capturer was observed by the conductor who gave chase on the road. A double ring of the bell by the last man off sent the tram on its way, leaving the conductor with tram off in one direction and its board off in another, losing both in an moment of indecision.

Meanwhile, I discovered I was to be the Gunnery Control Officer of *Laforey,* flotilla leader of the L Class destroyers. The leader of a flotilla of eight destroyers accommodates Captain (D) and his staff so that, instead of ten officers, seventeen were to live aboard. I shared a small office in the yard with the flotilla gunnery officer. As the L Class mounted six new design, high velocity 4.7-inch guns to fire heavier shells from twin turrets with power training, elevation, hoists and loading, completely new Flotilla Gunnery Orders had to be written. I helped with these and spent time aboard the ship in the fitting-out basin becoming familiar with the guns and the transmitting station to control them. Two other L Class destroyers were completing at the same time so gunnery officers from *Lightning* and *Lookout* were frequent visitors.

I was sent back to Whale Island for specialised instruction and practice in our spotting rules and to meet and find the right jobs for our gunnery ratings. Then we all exercised together in gun drill, following pointers and control procedures. We watched films and those in telephone communications became familiar with each other's voices. Whale Island, when no longer being ordered about, was far more enjoyable and I was in little hurry to return north to join the Flotilla Gunnery Officer in working out the action and cruising stations of all the gun's crews and control parties and integrating these with other departments into a co-ordinated plan.

The crew of the transmitting station who worked the control tables to control low and high angle firing were a typical cross section. Only Leading Seaman Clark, in charge, had been to sea before. The previous jobs of the other seven were as capstan operator, bricklayer, painter, factory hand, bank clerk, office boy and labourer respectively.

My fellow officers were a mixed lot. Percy, the Gunnery Officer, my direct superior, was a wild enthusiastic extrovert with a zest for life, pronounced by the RNVR doctor, who joined from supervising a mental home just before we were commissioned, to be almost certainly certifiable. Flags, with whom I had served earlier in *Norfolk*, was apt to be dreamy but was a talented artist and musician and a pleasant shipmate. Later on he would practise his flute sitting crosslegged on a rush mat accompanying an imaginary symphony orchestra. As this entailed lengthy pauses following the score as the imaginary orchestra played silently on while he awaited his cue, there was a rumour amongst the crew that he, also, was slightly mad.

Ping, a tough, sardonic, competent man had a caustic wit and I did not enjoy his contempt of my immature enthusiasms. The Pilot was small, serious, strictly on his dignity and unsympathetic. I kept out of his way. Torps, the senior staff officer and the only lieutenant-commander, was a solid, pleasant, wise shipmate with the considerable ability of pouring oil on troubled waters, a virtue often in demand.

Finally, apart from the Commander (E), engineer officer, gunner (T), Secretary and two other sub-lieutenants, both RNVR, there was "D" himself, nicknamed Tubby, an autocrat to be treated with awe and respect, a strict disciplinarian whose first priority was the welfare of the crews of the flotilla, and whose dictum was that a man would serve abroard contentedly if his food was good and his mail as regular as possible: and it was as a result of his endeavours that our flotilla were sometimes the only ships in harbour to receive mail.

There were times, however, when a buzz would go round that the Old Man was in a foul temper and we all watched out. The officer of the watch would be on his toes to answer the Captain's bell, either to account for some oversight or to send to him an unfortunate member of the staff who had failed to live up to expectations. D's Secretary was Richard, goggle-eyed, of great charm, harum scarum and possessing an unquenchable love of beer. Like the rest of us, he carried his gas-mask case around when ashore, but his contained no gas-mask merely a battered pewter tankard of generous capacity. His custom of filing important letters and signals in his bottom drawer, or even the waste paper basket, proved eventually to be his undoing and he left under a cloud. He was cut out for a far more active form of life.

Apart from my action station as gunnery control officer in the director, my duties aboard were to keep watch at sea and, in port, to be divisional officer of the quarterdeck, a division of about forty men, and in charge of wires aft when entering and leaving harbour.

A few days before we commissioned, a nucleus of the crew joined and I was able to discuss the organisation of my division with Chief Petty Officer Windsor, my divisional Chief. He was a great towering figure of a man, a sterling character who held my inexperienced hand till I had learned the ropes. Only one leading seaman and two ABs in the division had any previous seagoing experience. As a result, in the early days it was usually the five of us who secured the ship aft and coiled up wires as needed. Windsor was also my rate officer, sitting beside me with binoculars in the director, while CPO Sharpe, his opposite number in the forecastle division, was the director layer who actually aimed and fired the guns. He was small, thick set, wizened and tough and another exceptional leader. How lucky we were, for on such men is much of a ship's morale dependent.

The evening before commissioning, the crew were met at Central Station and carried in naval buses to Yarrow's Yard. A hot meal awaited their arrival aboard where slinging billets for hammocks were allocated. Next forenoon, we exercised action and fire stations, each cruising watch closed up in turn and guns' crews and control parties started to exercise till, at noon on 12th August 1941 in the presence of Vice-Admiral Troup, the ensign was hoisted for the first time and Dockyard Job J1415 became HMS *Laforey*.

CHAPTER 7

To Sea In Laforey

As WE SHOOK OFF HANGOVERS from the night before's commissioning cocktail party, *Laforey,* with representatives of Yarrow's and the trial Engineer Captain on board, sailed down the Clyde under her own steam at eight in the morning. The sky was blue and cloudless as we steamed past John Brown's yard, where lay *Duke of York* about to commission and two carriers fitting out. As we cleared the lee of the Cumbraes, *Laforey* began to heave placidly to the gentle swell. Descending from the director to the bridge after gun drill practice, I discovered the engines were working up to their full 48,000 HP, 8,000 HP more than that which propelled the mighty battleships, *Nelson* and *Rodney*, over twenty times our size. The hull vibrated to the rapid thumping of the screws. Following two timed runs over the Arran measured mile at well over 30 knots but still with some extra power in hand, by far the most impressive engine trial began.

Steering across the Clyde towards Ardrossan's distant cranes at full speed, leaving a tall white V of wake behind, the telegraphs were moved together from "full ahead" to "full astern". The high pitched whine of the turbines changed to a lower note then ceased and within a few seconds rose once more to a screaming crescendo. The ship shuddered, quivered and shook at the enormous backwards pull and two of us on the bridge, unprepared, fell forward at the rapid deceleration; *Laforey* shaking, thumping and making clouds of black smoke started to gather way astern. The stern sank till it was two feet under white foaming water. Still visible and overtaking were the earlier bow waves gradually merging into the swell. Here was mighty exhilarating power. Many of us felt a surge of sexual excitement at serving in such a remarkable vessel.

Well satisfied after two days' trials of all the ship's equipment, *Laforey* returned to a buoy in Greenock, the civilians left and we sailed for Scapa to work up. On arrival at Lyness it was discovered that the sea had washed the dark grey paint from the bow leaving a dashing permanent bow wave of light grey undercoat.

Our gunnery working up was less than successful. After a sub-calibre shoot had gone seriously wrong due to wrong gun settings, we slid out into the Pentland Firth at dusk for a full calibre night shoot, using starshell to illuminate

Laforey, newly commissioned in Scapa Flow, August 1941.

the target. The bridge gave the order, "Enemy in sight bearing green 45". We trained to 45 degrees on the starboard bow and eventually found the target in our binoculars and telescopes. All was dark in the director except the dim red lights on pointers and rangefinder. I ordered, "All guns follow director" as the 4-inch gun fired its starshell which burst behind our target and just right. We opened fire and soon straddled the target. At last things were going well.

Those on the open bridge were surprised by the very strong echoes reverberating from the cliffs of Caithness to the south and assumed it to be an unusual atmospheric effect. Well satisfied, *Laforey* returned to the destroyer anchorage. Alas, an immediate signal from the C in C Home Fleet awaited us.

The Dunnet Head Lighthouse keeper had protested that shells were hitting the cliffs below him and fragments of rock and boulders were falling close to the light. As we were the only ship firing that night, an explanation was requested. After a long enquiry, it was discovered that the trainer in X turret aft had failed to follow director and thus they fired all their shells straight at the cliffs astern. The officer in charge did not notice and, after other failings, eventually left us.

Having incurred the C in C's displeasure for this incident, things at last began to go better. After a reasonable shoot at a sleeve towed by an aircraft, successful torpedo firings and recovery, and exercise of the Asdic on a submarine, we were considered sufficiently worked up to join the fleet, but continued exercising as well as escorting ships, acting as rescue destroyer to a training aircraft carrier and joining in an unsuccessful U-boat hunt. But our real work lay ahead. Less than five weeks after commissioning, a ridiculously inadequate period for a new class of warship, but every destroyer was vitally needed, we joined a naval force to try to fight a convoy of essential supplies to Malta.

Calling briefly to fuel in Gibraltar Bay, we were part of the eighteen destroyer escort round the new battleship *Prince of Wales, Nelson, Rodney,* the carriers *Ark Royal* and *Argus*, several cruisers, and nine merchant ships in Operation Halberd. We found ourselves to the south of two battleships, *Nelson* and *Rodney*, on the right wing of the destroyer escort which surrounded the convoy and capital ships. *Ark Royal*, maintaining fighter patrols, shot down two shadowing aircraft as the vast fleet sailed south of Sardinia.

Next day, 27th September, the convoy was discovered and air attacks began in earnest. To divert our attention, a small Fiat biplane arrived to the south aerobatically carrying out stunt rolls and spins four miles off. A number of ships wasted ammunition in an unsuccessful attempt to shoot it down as the main torpedo bombing attack moved in from the north. They faced a heavy barrage of bursting shells, dropped their torpedoes at long range and turned away, hitting nothing though several ships were closely shaved. While most attention was being paid to this attack, a further group, the first eleven, far braver, came in low on our side. In company with the rest of the destroyer screen within range we opened fire. Fire control was however, well nigh impossible as there was no way of telling which of the numerous shell bursts were ours.

The torpedo bombers pressed on, two of them passing between us and the next destroyer astern, to intense pom-pom and machine-gun fire from us both. One escaped unscathed but the other nosedived out of control into the sea with a huge splash close to port. The plane sank but a swimming figure and a white box bobbed to the surface. When I told the TS crew down below of this, the suggestion immediately returned that they had heard Italian pilots always travelled with their ice-cream tricycles.

Inside the destroyer screen, a dozen torpedo bombers levelled out under an intense barrage from the carriers and capital ships. One, about to drop its torpedo, disintegrated into fragments when hit by a shell from *Ark Royal*. Others, more fortunate, managed to drop their torpedoes. Their sole success this time was a hit in the cable locker well forward on Admiral Somerville's flagship, *Nelson*.

Despite taking a slight bow-down angle which reduced her speed capability, she was still able to remain with the convoy till, at dusk, the capital ships turned back to Gibraltar with a destroyer screen, leaving the cruisers, merchant ships and the rest of the destroyers to slip through the narrows after suffering the sole loss of one merchantman, torpedoed as darkness fell.

At dawn, with Gozo abeam, *Laforey* and *Lightning* left the convoy and raced down the east coast of Malta to enter Grand Harbour. The shores were lined by a cheering, waving mob as we manoeuvred, one each side of a tanker, to fuel. There were deep gashes of bomb damage in the familiar skyline. My attempt to contact my cousin David, first Lieutenant of the submarine *Urge* based in Sliema Creek, failed as she was at sea on patrol covering our convoy from any Italian surface attack.

Later that afternoon we sailed south to join a long line of cruisers and destroyers creeping westwards, coast-crawling the Tunisian coast. The flashes of Cap Bon Lighthouse lit each ship in turn as we passed less than a mile offshore. Without disturbance, action stations fell out at dawn as, clear of the narrows, we sped to rejoin the big ships returning to Gibraltar. We were credited with a half a plane out of the seven planes shot down by the fleet in this trip, before joining the escort of *Prince of Wales, Rodney* and *Nelson* returning to the Clyde, only to be sent on after fuelling to escort the new carrier, *Indomitable,* to Scapa. Heading at 18 knots into a savage northerly sea, a number of her aircraft which broke adrift in the hangar were damaged and our wardroom steward, caught unawares by a sudden lurch, was thrown into the bulkhead, breaking a thigh and one arm. We were forced to slow down and steer off Stornoway, from where the lifeboat came out to collect him for transport to the local hospital, before we headed back into the teeth of the gale once more.

Without regret, we soon returned with a convoy to Gibraltar before sailing with *Lightning, Legion* and several other escorts on another of the "milk runs" with carriers to fly aircraft in to Malta. On return, within sight of the Rock, *Ark Royal* altered course to fly off aircraft, thereby moving out of the protection of the destroyer screen. Those on our bridge heard a muffled explosion and, turning to look at *Ark Royal*, saw her emitting dense clouds of black smoke and listing ten degrees to starboard.

It was just 1542 on 13th November. I was in the wardroom drinking a quick cup of tea before my first dog watch duty on the bridge. Someone clattered down the ladder and shouted, "*Ark*'s been torpedoed." We abandoned our tea and climbed up on deck. Already "D" had turned to go to *Ark*'s assistance while the rest of the fleet and screen had carried out an emergency turn away.

Ark Royal torpedoed by *U81* off Gibraltar, 13 November 1941.

Lightning, Legion and *Hermione* were ordered to join us and, in answer to *Ark Royal*'s signal that she intended to abandon ship for fear of capsizing, each of the other destroyers in turn manoeuvred alongside while we circled round and dropped a number of depth charges in an endeavour to keep the U-boat deep. After *Lightning* and *Legion* had each collected 500 men, it was our turn. We slid gently alongside *Ark Royal*'s port side away from which she was listing. A shouted conference between "D" and *Ark Royal*'s Captain discussed rescue. The torpedo had hit between the electrical switchboard and the boiler rooms leaving the carrier bereft of either electrical or steam power. It was decided to try to raise steam in her less damaged boiler room, only to discover that some of those needed for this operation had been evacuated to *Hermione*. There was a long delay before they could be retrieved.

Meanwhile, *Ark Royal*'s strongest wire ropes were led across and, from alongside, we began to try to tow the stricken carrier towards Gibraltar, thirty miles away. By the time a large salvage tug arrived after dark, we were no nearer safety due to the flow of water through the Strait. Sadly, soon after *Ark Royal*'s boiler was flashed up, water blocked the furnace outlet, fire broke out and the boiler room was abandoned. As *Laforey* gently towed *Ark Royal*, a steam pipe was led over to try to start one of her dynamos and we also led across an electric cable. All these endeavours were with a view to pumping out some of the flooded compartments. Had counter-flooding been tried to control her list and restore stability, the chances of saving her would have improved.

The salvage tug's tow eventually allowed some progress towards Gibraltar to be made. Admiral Somerville had returned by destroyer and transferred to *Laforey*. We were getting closer to Gibraltar and there was some optimism when I left the bridge at midnight. Patrolling destroyers were still circling and dropping occasional depth charges. I turned in on my bunk in my cabin close above the slowly revolving propellers and was awakened when they speeded up. Climbing on deck, I found out that *Ark Royal*'s list had gradually increased till, with the loom of Europa Point light clearly visible, abandon ship was again ordered and, soon after, she capsized to sink shortly after sunrise.

As we entered Gibraltar Harbour and secured in our usual berth alongside the signal tower opposite the flagship moored on the Mole, ahead of us lay the bare, empty and desolate berth where, since 1940, *Ark Royal* could always be found if in harbour. The sense of loss throughout Force H was only slightly the less because, remarkably, only one man's life was lost in her sinking. That evening, the loss of *Ark Royal,* so often sunk in German propaganda by Lord Haw-Haw, was announced by the BBC. Despite an anti-submarine sweep next day accompanied by three other destroyers and the large submarine, *Clyde*, nothing was found.

The 19th Destroyer Flotilla was the refuge of many birds of passage at this time and once contained twenty-four ships. Among them were Hunt Class Destroyers, the ex-US Navy destroyer *Campbeltown* later to ram and destroy the lock gates in St Nazaire, and four destroyers despatched to reinforce escorts in Malta who distinguished themselves when, on 13th December in passage off Cape Bon at night, Commander Stokes in *Sikh*, with *Maori*, *Legion* and *Isaac Sweers*, managed to sink two Italian 6-inch gun cruisers. On arrival in Malta they joined *Lance* and *Lively*, a month ahead of them, and the whole force gave a most dashing account of themselves till almost all were sunk in turn.

In the weeks before and after *Ark Royal*'s sinking we had been occupied as part of anti-U-boat patrols in the Strait where the Ls and three old V & W Class destroyers had the difficult task of trying to stop them entering the Mediterranean. U-boats usually tried to pass from the Atlantic to the Mediterranean diving by day using the current, then surfacing at night close to the Moroccan coast and heading for safety at speed. By International law we were excluded from attacking within the three mile limit.

Usually, the duty destroyer patrolled just east of a line between Europa and Ceuta Points, the narrowest section of the Strait of Gibraltar. A radar station on top of the Rock swept continuously, to signal to the duty destroyer on patrol any unexpected echo detected. Unfortunately, things were not so straightforward in practice. Numerous small fishing boats burning bright flaring lights dotted the Strait, doubtless some of them co-operating with the enemy. A U-boat surfacing close to a fisherman and then creeping away was a difficult radar target, while the bright flares made sighting a low, dark shape difficult. Many were the unrequited wild goose chases. However, life was by no means unpleasant. Most nights were calm and clear when the lights of Ceuta, Gibraltar and Algeciras twinkled on the horizon. From below the dark mountain shadow flashed Ceuta Lighthouse and on moonlit nights the white water catchments on the Rock's east face stood out bright and clear. Visibility could be so extreme that even the distant snow-clad peaks of the Sierra Nevada to the north east could be seen, ethereal in the moonlit sky.

One night we obtained a confirmed contact with a U-boat which shore radar had detected four miles east of us. The alarm bells rang and we turned towards the position. Radar made contact ahead, as we in the director swept to and fro searching. The enemy was travelling at speed and so we were gaining on him only slowly. At last a lookout reported a dark shape, someone else spotted it and then both lost it. A shout up the voice pipe, "Echo lost, 3,500 yards, Confirmation from the Rock: Lost contact: suggest he's dived."

Laforey slowed down to good Asdic operating speed as we closed the point where contact was lost. The plotting officer continued to report distance from the last contact, "2,500 yards . . .2,000 yards . . . 1,500 yards." The Asdic officer listened intently to the set operated by the HSD till at last, "Echo bearing green 10 range 1,500 yards".

Course was altered "Suggested enemy speed 5 knots course 085."

The Asdic lost contact, then regained it, range 1,100 yards.

"Stand by depth charges: medium setting," from the Captain.

"Marked opening doppler," from the Asdic operator.

"Suggest enemy altering to port and increasing speed," from plot.

"Lost contact: 300 yards red 10," from Asdic.

"Port 15," from Captain.

"Stand by", from Asdics.

We dropped our pattern of five depth charges. The stern lifted as the first exploded, then three, followed by the final explosion.

After speeding on half a mile, we turned to try to regain Asdic contact but as we closed the depth charge disturbance in the water, nothing could be found. The radar searched for signs of a surfacing submarine without success. There was no plan presentation and the primitive sets of the time often collected back echoes, side echoes and, even more perturbing, false echoes.

Dawn broke and we were relieved, returning to harbour to report our attack and the lack of any evidence of success. Such frustrations were typical. The enemy could have altered course after contact was lost. It could have been at a greater or lesser depth that the exploding charges, which required to explode very close to the very strong U-boat hull to achieve a kill.

Early in December, while with a convoy, the first "Woolworth" carrier, HMS *Audacity,* was torpedoed and sunk by a U-boat west of Gibraltar, but then the escorting destroyers succeeded in sinking no less that five of the U-boats against which her aircraft were offering protection. Such converted merchant ships flying anti-submarine patrols were later to become important weapons in the battle to protect Atlantic convoys and Captain Walker, whose escort group had such success on this occasion, became the most successful of all escort group commanders.

Laforey, accompanied by other flotilla destroyers, was also deployed at this time on long patrols into the Atlantic. Aware that convoys were routed some distance west of Cape St Vincent, a pack of U-boats would often patrol in a line at right angles to the convoy's expected route in the hope that one of them would sight the convoy and alert the rest of the pack. One dark, stormy night on one of these patrols in the company of *Hesperus,* a newly joined member of the flotilla, Ping and I, after a wet and cold four hours' watch, were grateful to be relieved to return below, peel off oilskins, wring out the towels round our necks and turn in to a warm bunk.

Insistent alarm bells sounding off a surface alarm later shattered deep and peaceful sleep. It was the work of few seconds to pull on damp clothes before joining dim figures dashing along wet slippery decks to their action station, cursing the inevitable collisions between those making for the bridge and X gun, depth charge and tube crews heading aft. After springing to grab a hold as a particularly large wave splattered the waist, I continued, collided with a stoker making for the engine room and tripped over a ring bolt before struggling up the ladder to the bridge. The director door was always left open, so with a step up, half turn, and wriggle, still half asleep, I pulled on the control officer's phone ready for action.

"Alarm, starboard, all guns load with SAP," was ordered. Then a searchlight pierced the gloom to reveal a U-boat rolling heavily beam on to the swell. The range finder operator obtained a range and we were ready to open fire. Men were climbing over the submarine's conning tower onto the deck where they clung on unhappily. She clearly would not dive and *Hesperus*, whose pattern of depth charges had blown *U93*, a large Type IX U-boat, to the surface, closed in to try to board her. Alas, before she could reach her prize, its bow sank and it slid below the waves tipping a struggling mass of humanity into the water. Both destroyers closed in to rescue survivors who were unlikely to live long in such a sea. With heaving lines and rescue nets *Laforey* saved four men and *Hesperus*, who was closer, about a dozen. Of the remaining thirty of her crew there was no more to be seen.

One of those we rescued was the U-boat's engineer officer, whose first words on being heaved over the guard rails from the scrambling net were, "Thank you, gentlemen". He was sent to the sick-bay to strip off soaked clothes and to be fitted up with dry kit. His belongings revealed nothing and, it seemed to his surprise, were returned when dry. Interrogation was fruitless so he was left alone in the sick-bay.

The Captain decided he would feed with us in the wardroom while each of the other three prisoners would feed in a different mess forward. At meals, as time went on, Hans began to talk in broken English. The excellence of our food amazed him and, even more, the distribution of chocolate rations when he received a bar of Cadbury's Milk. None of this fitted in with expectations from German wireless information. He had been well treated; we did not appear despondent; there was plenty of food; and in no way did the crew of *Laforey* behave like members of a broken race.

As time passed, Hans allowed his command of English language, and accent, to improve. A professor of engineering, he had been called up for U-boat service in 1940 and had friends in Britain. He would discuss anything except the war, but did let drop what a blow to us at Gibraltar must be the losses of *Ark Royal* and *Malaya*. Our denial of *Malaya*'s loss, confirmed when we let him see her alongside on our return to port, really did seem to shake his belief in Dr. Goebbels' propaganda. While he was aboard, a circling Focke Wolf Kondor aircraft was sighted and the Captain decided it was a good opportunity to exercise the main armament in anti-aircraft control. The aircraft alarm was sounded and Hans in his sick-bay prison right under X turret suffered the firing of ten salvoes at extreme range. He must have feared that, after his rescue, his own countrymen were going to finish him off.

On our next anti-submarine patrol in the Atlantic after convoy escort work, three large explosions in our wake seemed to indicate we had been the target of a patrolling U-boat. Despite a careful Asdic search no contact could be obtained of our supposed attacker.

Then, in February, we were despatched on an unusual mission. At Gibraltar, the only flat land in British possession to use as an airstrip lay east and west between the Rock and the Spanish frontier at La Linea, the site of an earlier race course. Its stony ground was used for rugger, both sides wearing knee and elbow pads as protection from injury, but its main use was as an aerodrome. We once found a Hudson parked on the touchline. As thousands of Spanish dockyard maties travelled daily from La Linea, there was ample scope to sabotage bombers parked beside the airstrip. Indeed, General Sikorski was lost early in 1943 when taking off there.

It appeared that a lone Wellington bomber flying to Sierra Leone failed to arrive and, later, faint signals suggested it had forced landed in the Rio de Oro opposite the Canary Islands. We were despatched to rescue the crew before the Spanish authorities arrived to intern them. We steamed down the West African coast five miles offshore, passing the glow of light from Casablanca. When the pilot took his morning sight he was surprised to discover we were three miles inland. Study of the West African pilot revealed the coast had not been properly charted and was believed to be five miles east of its charted position. Only local Arab fishing boats and traders plied those waters, well clear of any shipping routes. After that echo sounder and, when fog descended, radar as well were in constant use.

Later, as *Laforey* approached the reported position of the stranded plane, the fog deepened and the Captain decided, fog siren blaring, to steam twenty miles southward a mile off the coast before turning back north again, hoping then to hear some sound from shore. Shortly before reversing course, in a brief lifting of the fog, there up on the sand dunes above the beach lay the Wellington. As we watched, two airmen ran from the shelter of the fuselage to fire a distress rocket. By the time we dropped an anchor and stopped, the thick fog had descended once more. A motor boat, lowered to meet the aircrew, berthed in a rocky inlet. Arthur Jones, the replacement Captain's Secretary, and the airmen climbed back up the dunes to set the plane alight. On landing, its confidential books had been burned and radar smashed. Next day out of the Saharan dunes had appeared a goat herd who, for the pesetas which they carried, sold them a goat which was cooked over a fire of books and charts and the more inflammable bits of a Wellington bomber. They pronounced it excellent eating and thus, with emergency rations, no one went hungry in the four days they waited hopefully for rescue.

Towards the end of March, invitations were signalled to my friends in the flotilla and Force H to attend my twenty-first birthday party on 2nd April 1942. It was not to take place till six weeks later for, on 31st March, *Laforey, Lightning* and the newly joined *Lookout* escorting *Malaya, Hermione* and other cruisers sailed west into the Atlantic and then south.

I spent my birthday at action stations in the director as the fleet passed Cape Verde and Dakar, still a hostile Vichy French port, even more so since the attack eighteen months earlier. Nothing stirred and the fleet sailed on to Freetown in Sierra Leone. The destroyers berthed close to *Edinburgh Castle* which, with *Vindictive*, acted as base ship. We were surrounded by dugout canoes with outriggers offering fruit and souvenirs for sale and collecting any stale bread or other food which would otherwise have been ditched over the side. Soon a convoy of fast merchant ships with the battleship *Ramillies,* carrier *Illustrious,* cruiser *Devonshire* and a number of destroyers entered port.

With ships refuelled and provisioned, the convoy, including several liners I had last seen during the Narvik evacuation two years earlier, sailed south. As it passed St Helena, destroyers were detached in pairs to refuel from an oil tanker in Jamestown Bay, from which over 300 white painted steps led up the cliffs to the plateau above. Once more we were surrounded by bum boats selling carvings, embroidery and fruit which included huge, fine flavoured St Helena mangoes the size of melons. A trip ashore in the motor boat allowed a quick visit to Napoleon's house, where a tortoise which was claimed to have been his and thus at least 120 years old, was on view. Explosive charges were dropped and hands were piped to bathe in the clear blue-green water. Then our two destroyers rejoined the passing convoy to release other escorts to fuel.

As the convoy, out of sight of land, rounded the Cape of Good Hope, destroyers were again despatched this time to Capetown to refuel during the night before rejoining once more to sail on to Durban, which offered flesh pots at night but five days of work by day with constant staff meetings and preparation for a planned capture of Diego Suarez on the northern tip of Madagascar.

While the First Lieutenant and quarterdeck hands were exercising the handling of dan buoys and their attendant wires and moorings, Guns and I were working at designing celluloid grid conversion units to allow translation of observations from the shore into range and bearing settings for the director and guns. Extra high explosive shells were embarked and a Royal Artillery bombardment liaison officer and a combined operations RNVR sub joined. A slow convoy of transports loaded with troops and escorted by corvettes, minesweepers and destroyers had already been two days at sea before we set forth with the fast convoy.

CHAPTER 8

The Capture of Diego Suarez

ONCE AT SEA, THE WARDROOM was gathered to be told that our task was to buoy a channel between rocks and islands into Courier Bay, twelve miles to the east of the main harbour of Antsirana and separated from it by a steep peninsula. The bay was believed to be mined and defended by two batteries, each of four 6-inch guns, which it would be our task to bombard once action was joined.

As the convoy steamed north through the Mozambique Channel between Madagascar and the mainland, the aircraft carrier *Indomitable* and two destroyers from the Eastern Fleet based at Mombasa joined. *Laforey* and *Lightning* spent much of the day steaming close to each warship in turn and transferring, by Coston gun line, sheaves of amended operation orders collected from *Ramillies,* the flagship. By D-1 the slow and fast convoys had been combined and re-arranged, destroyers had fuelled and our assault force of *Devonshire,* the liners *Winchester Castle* and *Royal Ulsterman* loaded with landing craft and troops, four destroyers, seven minesweepers and five corvettes detached. Hands were piped to supper early before the three destroyers at action stations steamed eastwards in line abreast at 14 knots soon after sunset.

Through the windows of the director the dark shapes of people on the bridge and the glow of dim illumination over the chart table could be discerned. The water curling phosphorescently rippled gently past, its sound mingling with the low hum of the boiler room fans. After an hour a dim light winked from *Anthony* on the right of the line. She had sighted a darkened vessel to starboard. Turning away, the three destroyers joined in a single line ahead and prepared to attack with torpedoes. All guns were loaded. Hushed voices on the bridge passed orders to the torpedo tubes amidships. The enemy appeared to be stopped. As we closed in, there was no hostile sign from her. Then, after long suspense, over my phone from the bridge burst Gun's cheerful voice, "Train fore and aft, Sub, it's an island."

Captain "D" resumed his usual perch in the wooden chair beside the compass pedestal and our course shorewards was resumed. Soon afterwards we stopped again. The sounding machine was recording four fathoms: the bottom was shelving rapidly. As we crept forward it deepened again and it seemed we had

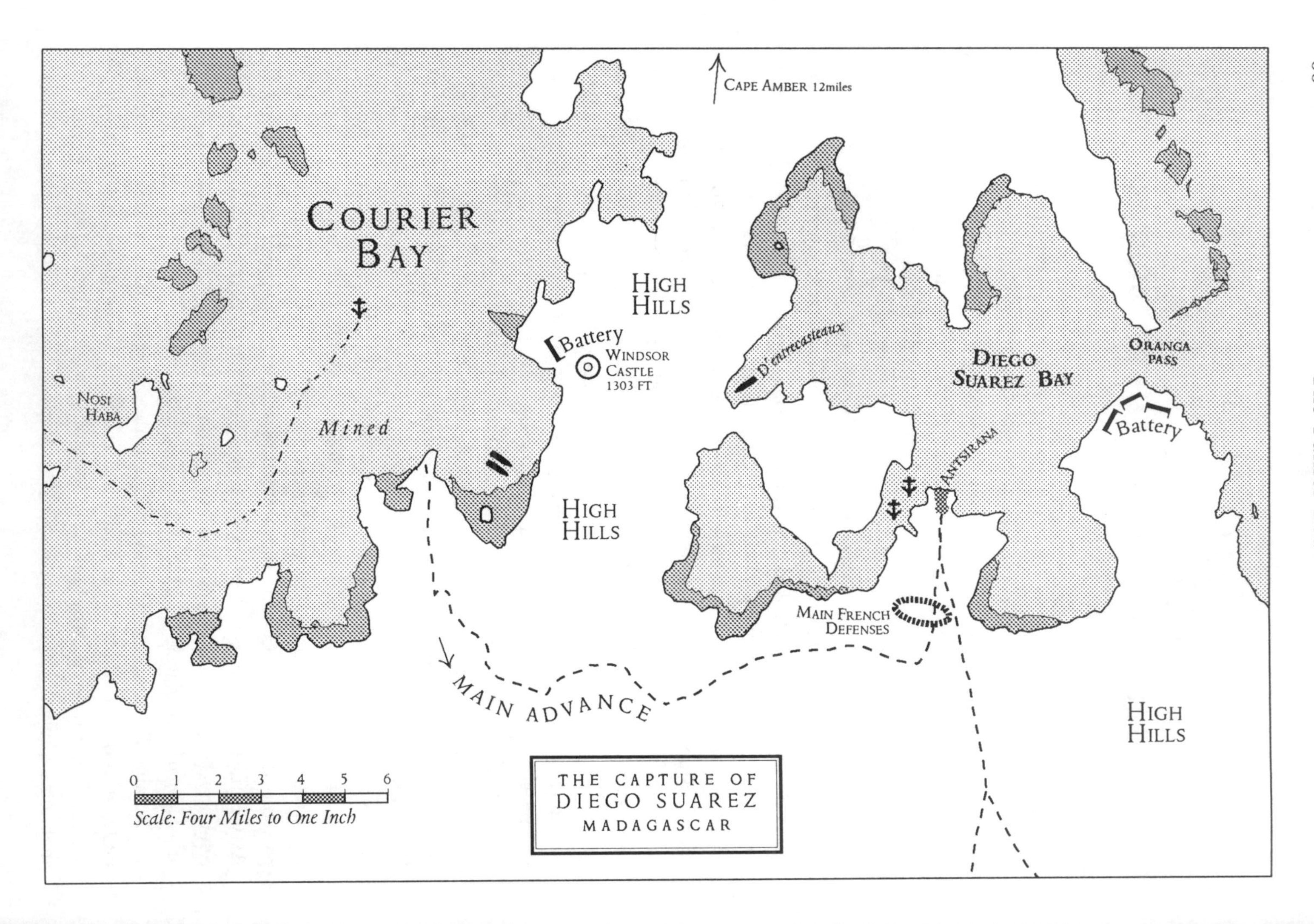
CAPE AMBER 12miles
COURIER BAY
HIGH HILLS
Battery
WINDSOR CASTLE 1303 FT
D'entrecasteaux
DIEGO SUAREZ BAY
ORANGA PASS
Battery
NOSI HABA
Mined
ANTSIRANA
HIGH HILLS
MAIN FRENCH DEFENSES
MAIN ADVANCE
HIGH HILLS
0 1 2 3 4 5 6
Scale: Four Miles to One Inch
THE CAPTURE OF
DIEGO SUAREZ
MADAGASCAR

crossed an uncharted shallow bank. Then a dim white light shone from an island. While high land could be discerned on the western horizon, this light from an agent ashore gave an accurate bearing of the channel to be buoyed into harbour.

During the next three hours, while the dan buoys to mark the channel were being laid, the moon rose, lighting Windsor Castle, the old fort at the top of 1,300 foot mountain above one of the French shore batteries. The islands through which we had been passing were revealed and *Lightning* moved to show three white lights close to a dangerous shoal showing a line of white foam in the moonlight. All the islands on the chart were named Nosi this or Nosi that and it was not long before a wag reported that the supposed destroyer we'd been prepared to torpedo must have been Nosi Parker.

Buoys laid, *Laforey* turned back to report to *Devonshire* that all was ready. In the bright moonlight the whole convoy of approaching ships was clearly visible without binoculars. Surely the French must see us as we advanced? While the minesweepers began to sweep a channel to the assault beaches, *Devonshire* and *Winchester Castle*, with only the barest clanking sound, lowered anchors on well greased cables close to Nosi Hara at the entrance. With the island behind them, they would be more difficult targets for the enemy batteries. Soldiers were manning the assault craft, winches could be heard working and soon all the boats were lowered and ready for the run through the minefield to Red Beach.

At 0230 on 5th May the advance into the bay began. Leaving clear white wake astern, the three leading minesweepers went quietly ahead, followed closely by the ten tightly packed landing craft. Surely we'd be seen as we advanced? My director remained trained on Windsor Castle. Several mines, their cables cut by the sweepers, drifted past, then one exploded with a shattering bang. Surely now the action must begin? But no sign of life from the shore was observed, even after a second mine blew up.

We stopped and the landing craft made for the shore. We were followed by *Royal Ulsterman* steaming along the swept channel to disembark her troops. Our spotter, FOO 2, announced on the radio from the shore that the commandos had landed unopposed. An hour later a white Very light rose from below Windsor Castle, the signal that No.7 battery had been captured. Just as it started to get light enough to reveal the horizon more clearly, machine-gun fire rattled briefly from Blue Beach. The main convoy was revealed at anchor six miles off the islands, all those dark, dangerous Nosis were shown to be soft luxuriantly verdant lumps, with sandy beaches in between surrounding rocks. Apparently the French gunners had been so convinced that it was not possible to enter a heavily mined bay at night through unmarked channels that they were all sound asleep when the commandos, having captured their four modern 6-inch guns, reached their quarters and woke them up with orders to surrender. The sole resistance to the landing was at Blue Beach where a Senegalese machine-gun post had briefly fired at approaching landing craft before withdrawing.

Once the successful capture of No. 7 battery had been signalled, *Laforey* weighed anchor for mine sinking. At least six were sunk by multiple .5 machine-guns on the passage back to the harbour entrance where *Bachaquero*, a merchant ship modified with a front loading bow, was awaiting a lead through the minefield. Meanwhile, the sweepers, in widening the swept channel, had cut loose a score more mines for further rifle and machine gun practice. Most sank and none exploded till *Auricula* struck a mine, was holed forward, and her Captain wounded. *Lightning* went to her aid, but it was impossible to tow her because her sweep wires had snagged the bottom and she eventually sank.

No.8 battery was found not to exist. Gathered in the bright sunshine beside the director at the back of the bridge as we ate a lunch of hot, juicy Cornish pasties, three French twin-engined planes flew over the landing beaches and, despite our leaping back into the director ready for action, they offered no feasible target and climbed over the hills and away. Touch had been lost from our FOO who was on the move but a flashed message from the shore requested a bombardment of the old fort at the pinnacle of Windsor Castle. Standing like a pimple at the very top of the hill, this was not an easy target to hit as only shell bursts below or on the fort could be observed, any "overs" disappeared out of sight and beyond. Starting with single and two gun salvoes we gradually worked up the hill till, after the twenty-ninth shell burst at the base of the fort, the occupants hoisted a white flag. A signal, *Descendez ou nous continuerons,* was flashed at them. Two hours later the shore requested a further bombardment and this time, after a direct hit, the tower crew were observed to come out and disappear over the top, to be replaced by our soldiers to use it as an observation post.

After a night at anchor, with crew fully rested, a signal from shore reported that the French sloop, *D'Entrecasteaux*, was firing on advancing troops in the Diego Suarez peninsula. She had already been hit by bombs from *Indomitable* but fires started then were out and a further attack was requested on her. Only the L Class destroyers had sufficient range to reach. A message was sent to request a FOO to move to a position to report fall of shot and, once he was in position, we were able to fire over the intervening hills at a range of 18,000 yards, where our salvoes were soon reported to be straddling and hitting her. With fires burning and ammunition exploding aboard *D'Entrecasteaux*, after eighty-six rounds fire was ceased to conserve ammunition.

By D+2 troops had advanced a dozen miles, *Bachaquero*'s tanks, guns and armoured cars had landed and an assault on the main defences of Antsirana began. Soon after *Laforey*'s attack on the sloop was completed, a bombardment was requested and the bombarding area and position of our troops reported. It was suggested that, because smoke from bush fires blanketed the battlefield, air spotting could be of assistance. Joined by *Lightning*, single gun salvoes were fired but our FOO was quite unable to see where they were falling, though it seemed clear that our troops were not being endangered. Off and on, both destroyers fired a series of two, four and six gun salvoes, as requested from the shore. Quite unknown to us or the main military force, a company of the South Lancashire Regiment had succeeded in infiltrating behind enemy lines and were practically surrounded under attack when our bursting shells unexpectedly proved most helpful. Luck was with us.

It was only in the afternoon, when the spotting aircraft requested from *Illustrious* arrived, that we received any information on where our shells were landing and a clear target could be identified. At 19,500 yards the first shells fell within 100 yards of the target and thereafter the gun battery was under constant bombardment for an hour, broken off briefly while Fleet Air Arm

Watching *Laforey's* Courier Bay bombardment, Madagascar, May 1942.

planes dive bombed enemy .75 howitzers in the battery. By then the Army Commander had received reports of the South Lancashire's success but still found his main force unable to advance because of murderous Vichy artillery fire.

Desperate measures were called for and a night attack on the besieged town itself between dark and moonrise was planned, though with limited expectations of success. While the Vichy submarine *Le Heros*, was torpedoed on the surface as she steamed to attack ships in the Courier Bay anchorage, the destroyer *Anthony*, carrying fifty marines from *Ramilles*, had rounded Amber Point to the north and steamed at speed and under fire from enemy gun batteries into the port of Antsirana itself. Backing under small arms fire on to the jetty to allow the marines to swarm ashore, she had escaped undamaged back to Courier Bay by dawn, where she was heartily cheered by the assembled ships.

Meanwhile, the marines had stormed the main Vichy barracks and received the Commandant's surrender. As a night assault was mounted on the outer defences by the Army, the Vichy French abandoned any further action, fire was ceased and the gallant artillery battery men who had held up our advance for two days were afforded a marine guard of honour as they marched back to the town under arms. So ended the battle for Diego Suarez. *Laforey* had buoyed the channel and over two days had fired two hundred and ninety-seven 4.7–inch shells, most at ranges of over nine miles from the target, suffering only one gun misfire.

The assault on Diego Suarez served as a prototype operation for subsequent, much larger assaults to follow in North Africa, Italy and eventually Normandy and many lessons had been learned. *Bachaquero* was a prototype for the LSTs (landing ship tank) designed for the purpose. She had shown the importance of advance beach surveys to avoid the frustrations suffered when an undetected reef prevented beaching as planned. The advantage of air spotting of the fall of shot in a bombardment had been proved, while, above all the vital importance of surprise in the timing and location of an attack to allow unimpeded landing had been emphasised. Despite meeting spirited resistance, casualties of 100 killed and 300 wounded out of 14,000 troops had been lighter than feared. One minesweeper had been sunk while five Swordfish, two Fulmar, one Martlet and one Albacore aircraft were lost in the course of 350 sorties.

Next morning, three days after the first landing, the fleet entered Diego Suarez harbour, passing the silent gun batteries at the entrance and avoiding the wrecks of several sunk and scuttled ships, before coming peaceably to anchor in a sharp breeze.

Because the attitude of the local population remained less than friendly, no shore leave was granted, but the Admiral gave permission for the gunnery officers, director layers and bombardment liaison officers of *Lightning* and *Laforey* to land with their COs to investigate the effects of their gun fire. Climbing a hill topped by wireless masts, we looked out over the scrub covered rolling plateau between the town and its main defences. It was dotted with thatched native beehive huts, each with a patch of dead looking corn-cobs, among which half naked children played. A thin hump-backed ox was dragging a primitive wooden plough across one plot of dry dusty soil. Lizards sunned themselves on bare rocks. When we had crossed to the line of earthworks and fortifications with .75 howitzer emplacements, machine-gun posts, barbed wire and deep anti-tank ditches, it became obvious why the main frontal attack had failed and most of our tanks had been destroyed.

After some searching, we found several shallow craters a few feet in diameter. There was no sign of direct hits on guns, but one had landed on a magazine which appeared to have exploded or burned out. These were the remains of the bombardment spotted from the air, but what we really wanted to discover was where our earlier unobserved shells had exploded. Eventually, in a wooded area, we discovered trees embedded with shell splinters and more shallow craters. It had indeed been fortunate that these had landed on Vichy troops rather than the South Lancashires who, unbeknown to the force commander, had outflanked them. Clearly it had been impossible for our FOO to see where the salvoes were landing.

On our return past the scuttled German ship, *Wartenfels,* we noticed a small tug moored to the jetty bearing the name *Count Benyowski*. When back aboard, with a chameleon collected ashore for wardroom anti-cockroach duty, I was sent for and told to see if she could be put to use towing lighters to speed the unloading of stores from the merchant ships anchored in the bay.

Count Benyowski, about thirty feet long and broad of beam, had a high snub-nosed bow which fell away to the tall wooden bridge. There was a small platform either side of it for handling the ship and, above it, a 6-inch brass flashing lamp, looking like a minor searchlight. Abaft of that came a true masterpiece of a funnel, grey-painted, slim, smoky and reaching nearly to the sky. This sat on a coaming which supplied the only ventilation to the combined engine and boiler room below. Finally, there was the broad round-sterned towing platform with a primitive winch and a tow rope of large dimension.

While an ERA and two stokers delved into the mysteries below, PO Wolfe and I explored the cable locker and small crew space forward. We found a coil of brand new 3-inch hemp rope, some fenders, a collection of old paint pots and four wicker-work covered glass flasks of about 2-gallon capacity, one of them full and containing a rank and acrid red wine. Then there was an old and grease-covered primus-type cooking stove and some very dead fish. Two seamen were left to clear the mess below while we went up to the bridge. The glass windows in front could be opened and there was a telegraph with orders written on it in French and Greek, why the latter we never discovered. We tested it and found it worked and that there was a dull clanging gong to enable the engine room to reply to the telegraph orders. The next item was the compass. We opened the magnet boxes and connectors and found them rusted in and performing little useful functions. It seemed best to leave well alone till we could swing and find out our compass errors. The large steering wheel took some strength to turn and was more the type to be worked from the side than from in front, as it was nearly as high as the helmsman. Luckily, I had been given a really first class three badged petty officer as my coxswain, and he was well able to cope with the intricacies of the wheel and telegraph.

Once the seamen emerged from below to report the fore cabin clear, we all got together and hosed down the decks and paint work which were filthy and deeply coated in coal. A smart teak deck was revealed and there seemed possibilities of becoming a "tiddly" ship. We opened the bunkerplates and discovered a plentiful supply of coal, with plenty more when required in a pile on the jetty. The ERA came up to report progress. While we had been clearing up, the engine room people had raised steam in the old Scotch-type fire tube boiler and had even started the dynamo to charge the small battery which supplied lights and searchlight. The engines proudly bore a brass plate announcing their German origin and the date showing that they were installed during Queen Victoria's reign. Of a two stage reciprocating type, they had a form of Stevenson Link Gear for reversing.

After a reasonable head of steam had been raised, and the smuts and smoke from the funnel had drifted in black clouds across the harbour for about an hour, we decided to try the engines. We tied the great vessel even more firmly to the dockyard wall and then slowly went ahead. All was well and a swirl of water appeared astern. Next the same was tried astern. Again, all seemed well. The lights were tested and then the searchlight. They worked. I flashed a signal to *Laforey* asking permission to go for a trial trip and approval was granted.

Having carefully arranged what each position on the telegraph facepiece was to mean, we let go from the shore and I rang, "slow astern"; the engines started in response to the bell down below, and then "dong" went our gong on the bridge in reply. We slowly drew astern and PO Wolfe and I exchanged cheerful glances. I rang down "stop engines" and soon after, "slow ahead"; then "half ahead", and finally, that being satisfactory, "full ahead".

We steamed at about 8 knots close to *Laforey* where we were the object of great interest and some derisive cheers from a number of the ship's company who were sunning themselves before supper. Stopping off *Laforey's* starboard side, I shouted to the officer of the day, who was on deck, to see if we could have permission to come alongside. After a considerable pause, the starboard ladder was hauled in and we were told to try very slowly. We arrived with the gentlest bump and tied up, proclaiming indignantly that it was unnecessary to have raised the ladder.

Captured tug *Count Benyowski* at Diego Suarez, Madagascar, May 1942.

That night D19 signalled our success to the Admiral and received a reply that the tug was to be available at eight-thirty next morning to assist ships berthing, and that orders for us would in future be issued by the signal station set up on the main jetty. A number of lighters were in use and ships at anchor were loading cargo into these. We would be needed to tow them away when full, to be unloaded ashore. I turned in happily, though feeling somewhat apprehensive as to what would happen next day. A stoker was left on watch in *Count Benyowski* to maintain steam.

We set forth at eight o'clock. The cool morning breeze had died down, and it was starting to get hot. The leading stoker had found a spare canvas wind chute and this was led down through the engine room skylight but, nevertheless, the heat below was terrific and whenever it was unlikely that we would need engines for a few minutes, the stoker would sit at the top of the engine room ladder with his coal-grimed head and naked shoulders in the fresh air. Little rivulets of sweat glistened as they washed clean tracks in the coal dust on his chest giving him a streaky, zebra effect till, on wiping a particularly itchy drop with his filthy sweat rag, he would turn his torso grey once more, though one tone lighter, like a blackboard after the instructor has wiped it. Then the process would start all over again, till a shout from the bridge sent him clattering into the inferno below.

On reaching the jetty, I was told that the ship movement had been postponed till the afternoon and that I was to collect three empty lighters from a buoy off the dockyard and tow them to *Duchess of Atholl*. It took about half an hour to tie the three cumbersome, rusty barges together satisfactorily and start to tow on the centre one. Slowly we brought the tow rope taut and started off. It seemed to be going fairly well but the considerable problem loomed ahead of how we were to secure them on arrival. I flashed up, *"Duchess of Atholl"*, but got no reply: so, slowing down, we crept within hailing distance and demanded through a megaphone to know where they wanted their barges.

Two fully laden lighters lay on the port side aft and I was told to remove them and then put the three empty ones in their place. Such a problem would surely have been simple to the original tugmaster, but to me it seemed almost insuperable. However, nothing daunted, I slid *Count Benyowski* very slowly alongside the two loaded lighters. In spite of our slow speed, the tow behind was sufficiently heavy and had sufficient momentum to continue when we stopped. They met their loaded sisters with an almighty clang, thereby parting the forward breast rope to the liner. Luckily the after breast held. The outer member of my tow now turned well out from the ship till it was just clear of our stern.

I decided the problem was too great for me and that with such a tide running I'd better get away as soon as possible with my two full barges. Sending a couple of sailors over, we led the remaining after breast rope to the empty trio and I shouted for a second rope to replace the parted one. Before we could get it, however, the tide had started to take charge of the two full lighters and the only way of avoiding a worse mess was to go ahead with them. This I did. The sailors above returned with the new rope to find us under way and their empty barges lying further aft on one very taut hawser. They shouted to me to come and do something about it. Only too glad to be clear, with my charges safe astern, I had no intention of taking the risk of trying anything more before they were safely parked. A very voluble merchant service officer's oaths rang in our ears as we drew out of earshot.

Another problem now faced us, which was how we were to dispose of our two without damaging them or us. As the tow rope was tied to only one barge, they were towing crabwise, well out on one quarter. We slowed down, only to find the tow overtaking us. I was beginning to appreciate that towing inert objects was not anything like as easy as it looked. Letting the two barges get alongside, I put a sailor over on one of them and then went ahead to avoid the tow rope fouling our propeller.

My idea on coming alongside was to steer in towards the jetty at slow speed, then to turn sharply and pull back on the tow rope, thereby starting to swing the bows of the barges out and, at the same time, taking the way off them. After the recent débâcle, hope of success as we approached the jetty was not great but there was an audience of Frenchmen and soldiers. It would never do to let the Service down in front of them. By drawing on the experienced guidance of the coxswain our object was achieved, the lighters arriving alongside with the faintest shudder, and the sailor aboard them secured the ropes with commendable speed before they could drift off once more. After he had slipped the tow rope we turned in a circle and slid past close to the outer lighter when he leapt cat-like aboard. The landlubbers were visibly impressed, quite unaware how large an element of luck was responsible for our success. *Count Benyowski* returned to the dry dock to moor up for dinner.

In the early afternoon we were waiting off the jetty while a lumbering 10,000-ton cargo boat weighed anchor and steamed slowly whale-like for the jetty. A wind had risen offshore and her Captain had difficulty in securing. "Tugmaster," shouted the Captain from his bridge high above, "give me a shove forward."

The sub-lieutenant's stripe on my shoulder strap seemed to swell to the broad gold ring of a commodore as I put the telegraph ahead. Tugmaster Durham, Master of His Britannic Majesty's tug, *Count Benyowski*, was going into action. Black smoke poured from the funnel; the engines ground thumpingly up and down; a faint wisp of steam escaped from the whistle as we rapidly approached the merchantman's bow. Stop engines; hello, we are getting rather close; half astern together; full astern together; fender forward; crump, clang, crash.

Count Benyowski was on the job all right but, the round fender having rolled to one side, we were pushing from inside instead of outside our charge. The bow had punctured one of the cargo boat's plates and made a small hole, luckily well above the water line. Her Captain, spotting my tender age and the single forlorn stripe on my shoulder quite mildly shouted, "Never mind, we can repair that dent quite easily. I'd take it a little more gently next time, Tugmaster."

"Aye, aye, Sir."

My golden moment had not totally disintegrated, remaining still a tugmaster, though admittedly a rather deflated one.

After the ship had secured, we chugged to the jetty to refill the coal bunker, and I went off with the coxswain, determined to steal a sausage fender for our bow. After searching the dockyard store and huts, we eventually found one. In the course of our search we also discovered the dockyard wine store. Instead of the tot of rum issued daily to our sailors, the French ration was half a litre of red wine. Despite smelling raw, some was taken back to *Laforey,* which, being too fiery for drinking neat, was mixed into vicious red cocktails that evening in the wardroom. We all survived.

Next morning a mail arrived containing an official letter promoting me to lieutenant. Having missed a twenty-first birthday party, to combine this with a second stripe party was an obvious solution. Unaware that it was the custom to ask the Captain's permission before putting up a second stripe, and wearing a borrowed pair of lieutenant's shoulder straps, I asked him to be allowed to exceed my wine bill and have a party that night and permission was granted. *Count Benyowski*'s work was over early that day so I was able to enter into my party to the full. *Lightning*'s and *Lookout*'s wardrooms had both been asked and we downed large quantities of black velvet till eight-thirty, when the mess sat down to a cheerful dinner followed by port and liqueurs. At ten-thirty all were comfortably settled round the ante-room club fender playing "liar dice" when a messenger knocked and handed me a signal "*Count Benyowski* is required to collect an empty lighter from the jetty and tow it alongside *Oronsay* in the main anchorage."

Unsteadily, I weaved to my cabin, changed into a polo necked sweater, dunked my head into a basin of cold water, and safely climbed aboard the fully manned *Count Benyowski* ready with steam up. Unnecessarily explaining to the coxswain that I had been celebrating my second stripe, and telling him he was to take over should we appear to be heading for disaster, we let go and steamed forth into the night in a shower of sparks and billowing smoke. Shore and loading lights of ships in the anchorage left tracks of brilliance across the water. Somehow we carried out our orders and safely returned to *Laforey*. Next morning, PO Wolfe reported that my ship handling had been masterly using only two speeds, full ahead and full astern. The devil cares for his own.

After happy days butterfly chasing and riding French cavalry horses ashore, orders arrived that the three Ls were to escort *Indomitable* to Mombassa and join Admiral Somerville's Eastern Fleet of four R Class battleships, two carriers, some cruisers and two flotillas of destroyers. Colombo had been abandoned as a base since the Japanese attack six months earlier. *Count Benowski* was handed over to another destroyer and we set sail north.

CHAPTER 9

Eastern Fleet

A CLOVE-SCENTED STIFF OFFSHORE BREEZE wafted from Zanzibar as we sailed past to enter Kilindini Harbour, the port of Mombassa. The azure sea was topped by hissing, sparkling white horses under a sky of scudding white clouds as we passed the line of R-class Battleships, the carrier *Formidable* and several cruisers riding at long stay and pitching slightly. Passing a destroyer depot ship, the three Ls anchored and we lowered a boat to allow D19 to call on Admiral Somerville flying his flat in *Renown*. He returned with the news that *Laforey* and *Lightning* were to sail next day as rescue destroyers to the carriers *Formidable* and *Indomitable* and arrangements were made for us to weigh and proceed alongside our respective carriers to discuss procedure. Safely secured alongside *Formidable* we were invited to dinner in their ample wardroom and thereafter competed in a hard "liar dice" contest against skilled opponents before descending unsteadily back across a narrow gangway well after midnight, content that honours were about even.

Next day, following our carrier, we were impressed by a squadron of nine Swordfish aircraft landing-on, in quick succession, in just over a minute. She also carried newly acquired American Grumman Martlet bombers. Sadly, in a simulated dive bombing attack, the Swordfish squadron leader and his observer were killed in a steep dive, when his starboard wing broke off at the root leaving the plane to spin like a leaf in an autumn breeze and hit the sea with an almighty splash. Despite our reaching the point of impact very quickly, no sign of plane or crew remained, merely an oil patch, rainbow coloured in the overhead sun. We safely rescued a fighter pilot who had overshot the landing deck and returned sadly to harbour. After I had fallen prey to Indian dealers in the market during our week in Kilindini, returning aboard with a shark vertebrae cane and various sandalwood boxes, the fleet sailed east for Ceylon.

The L-class destroyers of the 19th Flotilla were detached to refuel from a tanker moored off Fort Victoria in Mahé Island, the principal island of the Seychelles, at the time with no airport and undiscovered by tourism. As soon as we secured alongside the tanker, a fleet of pirogues, unsafe-looking outrigged dugout canoes manned by the Creole inhabitants of the islands, put out from the beaches to trade tortoiseshell, bread-fruit, copra carvings and *bêche-de-mer* double shells polished like ebony, which would hold nearly a gallon of water like a double calabash but make rather bulky souvenirs. The waist amidship below the searchlight and alongside the torpedo tubes seethed with life. Because of the very high incidence of VD in the islands no shore leave was granted to the crew, but officers were allowed to land for a couple of hours.

The motorboat made for the jetty with an escort of tiger sharks, known locally as Demoiselles. A limp flag drooped from the flagstaff beside the Governor's house at the end of the jetty. Walter Gath, the RNVR sub-lieutenant, who, in a later commission, took over my job in the director and sadly was killed when *Laforey* was torpedoed and sunk off the Italian coast on 30th March 1944, and I climbed the hill above the town under the grilling midday sun. We passed huts of split bamboo roofed by fronds of coconut palm and surrounded by coconut, bread-fruit and banana trees till we reached the 1,000-foot summit and sat to enjoy the panoramic view.

The lush green slopes we had climbed fell to golden sandy beaches washed by the greeny-blue Indian Ocean. To the right and high above rose Mont Seychelles, the highest point in the islands, wooded by vegetation to the top of its 3,250-foot summit. Below lay the straggling town and a sprawl of small islands dwarfing *Lightning* and *Laforey* like toy ships in the bay beyond. A Creole arrived and shinned agilely up a palm to collect and cut a green coconut with a machete for us to drink, only to depart delightedly with a sixpence. Exotic birds fluttered in the trees.

We descended by a different route and discovered a beautiful botanical garden dotted with multi-coloured flowers and flowering shrubs around dark green lawns of a shamrock like plant. Under the trees sheltered dark grey tortoises two feet tall and three feet long which lumbered off with an ungainly rolling gait when approached.

All too soon our ship had to sail from these enchanting islands, passing several sturdy old schooners which traded copra and guano from outlying islands and fished the teeming waters. Our last sight was of shapes low on the horizon lit by a deep red setting sun as we hastened to rejoin the fleet for our next call at Addu Atoll in the Maldive Islands. This coral atoll, considered the Scapa of the Indian Ocean, offered a safe, submarine-free haven for the whole fleet. The surrounding coral islands were inhabited by voracious land crabs in place of rats as indigenous scavengers.

Landfall at Colombo two days later revealed a thin line of vegetation in the morning haze, with a large hoarding DRINK CEYLON TEA dominating the horizon. Accompanied by a Dutch destroyer, *Van Galan,* who had joined the flotilla, we patrolled offshore while the big ships entered the harbour abandoned since *Hermes, Dorsetshire* and *Cornwall* based at Trincomalee on the east coast had been sunk by a Japanese fleet seven months earlier. Then the flotilla followed into port to fuel from a tanker moored off the Yacht Club.

Next day, leave was given but as duty officer I remained aboard and the following day the officers of the 19th Flotilla were bidden to a party in the cruiser, *Gambia*, who had worked with us on passage. The highlight of the evening was a crab race with Addu Atoll land crabs. *Gambia's* carpenters had built a line of starting traps with a long hinged gate to be opened by the starter. Each ship's jockey complete with cap was to encourage his own crab.

A bookie presided over a blackboard listing the runners: amongst them Lightning, by Vulcan out of Thunder; Lookout, by Horizon out of Sight and Gambia, by Gad out of Station.

With a shout, "They're off," the starter opened the gates. Pandemonium ensued. Two crabs attacked the onlookers who were urging on their own ships' jockeys with shouts of encouragement. Two crabs fought each other, and Lightning's jockey was bitten. The Laforey crab was facing the wrong way in its trap and so made a slow start but with a few well aimed kicks by Ping, our jockey, it crossed the line second to the loser of the fight, who made for the line to escape his heavier opponent, a clear winner without any jockeying assistance.

Next day accompanied by half a dozen sub-lieutenants from various ships in harbour, I landed to dine and wine in the Galle Face Hotel. The evening ended with a rickshaw race back to the jetty, a bonus ride for the rickshaw boys. Passenger Jetty, Colombo is covered by a roof supported by solid cast iron pillars. As we made our way along the pier we watched an extremely drunken commander weaving along till he met a pillar to which he would solemnly apologise.

Captain D's boat was alongside and when I asked the coxswain whether his boat was doing the midnight trip he replied he was. It being after midnight, we climbed aboard and I told the coxswain to return the others to their ships before returning to *Laforey*. When we came alongside the officer of the watch asked where D was. Replying that I had no idea I made for my cabin. Some time later, I was woken by an unhappy OOW. "You're for it. Report at once to the First Lieutenant."

"What for?"

"Pinching the Captain's boat."

When I reported, I was informed I was under close arrest for a gross error of judgement. Ruefully, I returned to my bunk and next morning, under arrest in my cabin while eating breakfast in bed, Wally came down to tell me the

Captain would see me on the quarterdeck at 0930. He then gave me a graphic description of D's return to Passenger Jetty after wining and dining with the American Naval Attaché who had driven him back to see him to his boat. As D reached the destroyer steps he saw his boat full of sub-lieutenants singing loudly shove off, preventing the crew from hearing his shouts. By now the drunken commander had weaved up to ask what the "blurry" row was about, then, seeing the American captain's uniform and remarking "another blurry Yank," he aimed a blow at him. Ducking, that officer withdrew, to D's profound apologies. What then happened before the boat returned for the furious Tubby Hutton half an hour later Wally did not know, but D's return aboard was explosive and he indicated retribution would follow.

When I reported, I was made to "Off caps" like any rating defaulter and was charged that at 0010 I did take my Captain's boat from Passenger Jetty, Colombo. Asked what I had to say I could only apologise. Courts martial were mentioned till eventually I was told I would be "logged". When the entry in the log was made I was instructed to sign it and then dismissed. Arthur Jones, Captain's Secretary, cheered me up by informing me that, as long as I avoided a second "logging" there would be no permanent record of my misdemeanour.

Laforey refuelling at sea from *Indomitable* before Pedestal Malta convoy, August 1942.

On return to Mombassa, the three Ls were detached to fuel in Durban and again in Cape Town, where the lower decks were cleared to the waists of the three destroyers moored alongside for D to inform us we were to escort the carrier *Indomitable* back to protect a convoy to relieve Malta, which was running out of food, fuel and ammunition. Next port of call for the destroyers was Pointe Noire, 100 miles north of the mouth of the Congo River. Forty miles to seaward, a lookout reported an island in sight. Pilot was summoned to the bridge but the island seemed to be uncharted. As we approached, the echo sounder recorded thirty-five fathoms. Our island, renamed Laforey Island, was afloat, a two acre mass of vegetation on which palm trees and shrubs grew and birds nested. Such islands, rafts of fallen timber, break away from the river banks when the Congo is in flood and occasionally end up in mid Atlantic till broken up by rough weather.

The tanker from whom we fuelled gave us their pet monkey. By nightfall a hammock had been made in the seamen's mess deck for Minnie, which she immediately accepted and used. Rejoining *Indomitable*, we sailed round the bulge of Africa at 20 knots and, instead of calling at Freetown, the destroyers were fuelled in turn at sea, steaming up alongside the big ship about fifteen yards clear, when her crane lowered a steel hose which jumped up and down as fuel was pumped along it. Careful helmsmanship was called for to avoid getting either too close or too distant. And so we approached the Strait of Gibraltar.

CHAPTER 10

Operation Pedestal

BACK ONCE MORE IN FAMILIAR WATERS off the east Moroccan coast, *Indomitable* was escorted to join a large convoy approaching from the west while, after dark, the three Ls fuelled in turn from a tanker anchored out in Gibraltar Bay. When dawn broke on 10th August 1942, the convoy and its escort steaming east were well within the Mediterranean. Fourteen fast merchant ships, one of them a tanker, accompanied by two battleships, four carriers, seven cruisers, two fleet tankers and an ocean going tug, sailing in four columns, were escorted by a circle of twenty-four destroyers, with a further eight destroyers as carrier escorts.

In brilliant sunshine, the vast assemblage of ships maintained station as they followed a complicated zigzag pattern as a deterrent to U-boat attack. Not a breath of wind ruffled the surface of the azure sea. During the forenoon watch, "D" put a file of operation orders on the chart table for the information of officers of the watch. It seemed that Malta, under siege, had only a fortnight's food remaining, while petrol supplies for her fighters were exhausted. Unless a convoy, despite inevitable heavy losses, could be fought through the Sicilian Strait to relieve the island, it would soon fall. If the tanker, *Ohio*, and several cargo ships could reach Malta, Malta would be relieved.

It was not till after daybreak on 11th August that enemy reconnaissance aircraft found our Armada. During the forenoon *Furious* detached, with an escort of two destroyers, to fly off Spitfires for Malta after which she would return to Gibraltar. The other three carriers practised co-operation between their squadrons. This entailed steaming head on to the freshening breeze which had risen and thus having to steam clear of the Asdic-swept water covered by the destroyer screen. Hands at action stations had barely finished their meal when two dull thumps broke the peace. Everyone on the bridge was looking aft. Contorting myself in my director seat, I was just able to see the heavily listing carrier *Eagle* emitting dense clouds of smoke three miles astern of the convoy. Within minutes she had sunk.

Ordering *Lightning* and *Lookout* to close the gap, D took *Laforey* back through the convoy to rescue survivors. Joined by a rescue tug and two other destroyers, over 900 men, some of them injured, were hauled to safety up the survival nets over the side. Our doctor, sick-berth attendants and others were kept busy giving artificial respiration and dressing the wounds and other injuries of the dripping survivors who were then transferred to the V & W destroyers returning to Gibraltar with *Furious*. *Eagle*'s airborne planes landed on the two remaining carriers, *Victorious* and *Indomitable*.

Laforey seemed fated to rescue survivors of torpedoed carriers: first *Ark Royal* now *Eagle*. We could only hope all would be well with *Indomitable* and *Victorious* over the next two days. We steamed to regain our station at the head of the escorts with one *Eagle* survivor aboard to act as a most useful aircraft air warning liaison and fighter direction officer ahead of the main fleet. Enemy air attack could be expected before sunset.

During the first dog watch the first of many air attacks began. After a report from a carrier's radar of approaching aircraft, the director was ordered to sweep the likely sector. Then a bridge lookout shouted, "Enemy aircraft bearing green 10". A short sweep revealed a V formation of five Junkers 88 bombers. No echo showed on our primitive radar to reveal their range so everything depended on Able Seaman Daft, manning the director range finder, producing the answer.

"Range, Daft," I shouted.

"Director, what is the delay in opening fire?" in my earphone from Captain D.

"Daft, Range."

"Can't make it out, Sir."

"Name and nature," muttered CPO Windsor beside me.

There was nothing for it but to pass on estimated range down to the TS deep below.

"Range 100, Commence, Commence, Commence."

Fuse settings were passed to the turrets and, in turn, "Ready" lights from each gun glowed beside CPO Sharpe, the director layer, whose trigger would fire the salvo. Dong Dong. The whole ship shuddered as the three twin turrets fired together. Now to see where the shells would burst in that blue, cloudless sky. Would they be anywhere near the target?

Dong Dong. Another salvo off before six flashes and puffs of black smoke appeared close behind the bomber formation. I reduced the enemy speed set and turned the graticule in my spotting binoculars to adjust the settings in the TS. Another salvo exploded close behind the target. Then, the corrected salvo pockmarked the sky, bursting right amongst the Junkers 88s. One fell away, trailing smoke and flames and plummeted into the sea a couple of miles to port. A second plane showed a streak of smoke behind one engine but flew on, maintaining formation. Almost at once, the whole sky round the aircraft blackened with myriad shell bursts. I ordered "cease fire" because there was no possible way to distinguish which bursts were ours.

Ping on the bridge semaphored, "Fluke". Then D's quiet voice in my earphone, "Well done, Durham." Possibly, I was the only one to realise the sheer good fortune of making my guess of 10,000 yards at the one and only moment when it would be almost exactly the true range. Skill? Judgement? No, luck! Oh such fates are reputations made or lost. To me it seemed a most unsatisfactory revenge for the loss, a year earlier, of my cousin and best friend Walter Beatson, shot down in his Blenheim bomber attacking a German convoy off Texel.

Laforey had at least fired the first shots in what was to become an epic convoy battle. The bombs eventually dropped by the remaining planes exploded harmlessly within the lines of merchant ships. Later, in the dusk, a half hearted attack on the convoy, with torpedoes dropped at long range by over thirty Heinkel and Junkers bombers proved unsuccessful, while four of them were shot down by fleet gun fire. As they attacked from out of the setting sun on the far side of the convoy, we were not involved.

What would tomorrow bring? Soon after dark, action stations fell out and everyone settled down to snatch as much sleep as watchkeeping duties would allow.

Dawn on 12th August broke and, as a reddish rising sun rose to golden brilliance, not a cloud marked the blue hemisphere of the sky. The tannoy blared out for action stations to close up. During the long day when wave on wave of high level, torpedo and dive bombers, escorted by numerous fighters, unleashed successive attacks on us, my clearest memory was of the convoy and its escort slowly steaming eastwards, its wake ruffling the polished, sparkling mirror of the sea.

Violent attacks were hurled at the convoy from above and below, ships were sunk or damaged, but those lumbering grey-painted merchantmen steamed ever onwards with purposeful determination, giving the impression that nothing could stop those remaining afloat from reaching their destination 400 miles distant. They appeared withdrawn and detached from the flame, smoke and noise of battle. Let the warships and naval fighters defend them, but as long as they were able and remained afloat they would continue to move forward at a steady 14 knots. Retaining excellent station, even when emergency turns were ordered to reduce the risk of torpedo damage, they would soon resume their course for the Sicilian narrows. They seemed to put their naval escort in place as the mere means to ensure the end of their safe arrival.

An early, rather half-hearted, torpedo attack from a score of planes proved abortive when the assemblage of ships turned safely away and fleet fighters gave chase. Later in the forenoon, following this hors d'oeuvre, the first prolonged and determined air attack was launched.

A large squadron of bombers escorted by fighters arrived from Sardinian airfields to circle the convoy at long range. Sweeping round in the director, I counted over eighty planes. Out of effective range, they circled for about half an hour before breaking up into two separate torpedo attacks. From our screen position on the port bow of the convoy, attention was concentrated on around twenty planes flying low over the sea. They spread over about five degrees of the horizon and turned towards us. As they advanced to within gun range, the peace was shattered by a crescendo of gun fire from around and behind us as the guns from our side belted hot metal into the sky.

The planes were not deterred, as had been those of the earlier attack: they pressed on through the barrage of bursting shells almost to within range of the multiple pom-pom and Oerlikon guns which clattered into action before they released their torpedoes and turned away. Some destroyers turned towards them to comb torpedo tracks and, remarkably, no casualties were suffered in this attack. That from the far side of the convoy four miles away had more success when a torpedo hit a cargo ship though, despite her damage, she was still able to continue to maintain station in her line of ships. During these torpedo attacks high level bombers bombed the convoy but scored only one direct hit, a large bomb which broke up without exploding on *Victorious'* armoured deck.

As the enemy withdrew the racket died down, till only one ship was firing, then she stopped, leaving only the sound of the gentle lapping of water along the hull and the hum of boiler fans to break the peaceful silence and relieve aching eardrums. Soon, however, two loud blasts of the flagship's siren ordered an emergency turn to port. Depth charges had been dropped on a possible U-boat contact on the starboard quarter. Several other emergency turns followed in the next few hours, one depth charge attack having surfaced an Italian submarine which was rammed and sunk to severe damage of the destroyer concerned. Our Asdics made no contact and the director's crew were able to leave the baking heat inside their steel cage and enjoy the afternoon sunshine till, after tea, reports of further approaching planes were received. We climbed back into the director to haul on anti-flash gear and earphones. Soon, wave on wave of what seemed every sort, shape and size of plane appeared on the horizon.

Twin and single engined bombers mingled with little single seater Italian fighter gnats. Attacks were launched from high and low level. The main gunnery problem lay, not in finding a target, but which one to choose. The cacophony of guns firing, shells bursting in the air and bombs exploding in the water, rose and fell. One clear memory is of swarms of torpedo bombers circling out of range low over the horizon. In one small sweep with binoculars over fifty in one sector could be seen. For about twenty minutes we slowly trained the director round following them before they broke up into several groups of a dozen or more and turned towards us.

Rather than individual gun fire a concerted HE barrage was ordered about two miles outside the destroyer screen, the likely dropping area for torpedoes. It seemed to take an age for them to arrive that close, but then heavy anti-aircraft guns, Bofors, Oerlikon, pom-poms and multiple machine-guns all belched forth ammunition. The sky ahead blackened with bursting shells while strings of tracers followed, with their typical slow and leisurely trajectory. Most attackers were deterred and dropped their torpedoes early to turn tail, leaving only a few braver pilots to zoom over the screen to attack close to the convoy. In these concerted and co-ordinated attacks from all round the horizon, casualties on both sides were inevitable. On the far side a destroyer was torpedoed and sunk as was one of the precious fourteen cargo ships.

There as a short lull while the torpedo attackers withdrew, then an umbrella of fire over the convoy was ordered. As this entailed firing at a pre-arranged range and sector, I was able to look around and so watched as, without warning, out of the slowly setting sun, a procession of Junkers 87 bombers dived on *Indomitable*. Surprise was complete as bombs burst in the water alongside the carrier and four gouts of flame rose from her deck. As visibility cleared, smoke almost hid the fire on her flight deck.

Only *Victorious* was left able to fly and land planes, her own squadrons, those airborne when *Eagle* sank, and now those which had taken off from *Indomitable*. There were too many for her to accommodate, so she had to fuel them and fly them off while others landed till, after dark, emergency repairs restored *Indomitable*'s flight deck for use. She had suffered severe casualties in her hangars and gun turrets, one of which received a direct hit, while one of the bombs exploding deep inside the hull had blown out a jagged plate on the ship's side three feet above the waterline. A double decker bus sized hole gaped from a fuel tank.

When, at sunset, we turned back west with the heavy ships, just four cruisers, twelve destroyers and a tug remained to tackle the desperate passage of the convoy through the Sicilian narrows to Malta. While still within sight astern, they suffered their first casualties when *Nigeria,* flying the Admiral's flag, was torpedoed by an Italian submarine, as was *Cairo*, which sank; also torpedoed, but not terminally, was the vital tanker *Ohio*. *Nigeria* was too badly damaged to continue east and rejoined the fleet to return to Gibraltar, her flag transferred.

The convoy's struggle to Malta is now history: *Manchester* sunk; *Kenya* also torpedoed but able to continue; in the end four of the cargo ships, two severely damaged, and the torpedoed, bombed and finally towed tanker *Ohio*, whose Captain received the George Cross, were at last able to reach Valetta out of the fourteen who set forth from the Clyde.

On our return to Gibraltar, with less than a quarter of our HE ammunition remaining unfired, *Laforey*'s commission had drawn to a close and a refit lay ahead. Our one casualty in Operation Pedestal was the monkey Minnie, who had been discovered cowering in a dark corner, her teeth chattering and on the verge of hysteria. Sadly, the tot of rum given her to aid recovery led to severe alcohol addiction and eventual DTs and a drunken death.

We sailed independently at high speed escorting the ferry *Royal Ulsterman*, an old friend, bound for the Mersey where, after mutual exchanges of regard on siren and fog horn, we turned round and sailed to unload remaining ammunition into a lighter before passing through the lock gates into Southampton old docks. The engines which had propelled us over 100,000 miles in the last year began their well earned rest.

Social life one more, but the prospect of ten weeks' idleness while *Laforey*'s refit continued did not appeal, so I volunteered once more for submarine service and was accepted, but had to await a relief's arrival. Before he arrived, I was told at short notice to replace one of five officers due to receive the Freedom of the town from Northampton, who had adopted us and whose ladies had been valiantly knitting balaclava helmets, sweaters and sea boot stockings for our crew. In the forenoon a party of forty descended from a mainline train at Bletchley from which a short branch line leads to Northampton. The three-coach local train across the platform was already well loaded when the crew climbed aboard. By the time Captain D and the other four of us had crossed, there was not a seat to be had so we climbed into the guard's van, joining a tethered but none too friendly looking goat. The guard blew his whistle and climbed in with us as the train rattled off for the ten minute journey.

As the train drew into Northampton, a band on the platform struck up "Rule Britannia". After a brief shunt the engine driver manoeuvred the first class compartments opposite the red carpet leading to the entrance hall. Alas, no officers emerged and the reception committee were informed we were in the guard's van. There they met the goat blocking the door. In due course we proceeded along the platform to the red carpet to make a proper, if belated, arrival. A car awaited D and two officers. Doc and Scratch pled non-executive officer status, leaving Flags and me to march off at the head of the party who had fallen in, three deep.

The band playing "Here the Conquering Hero Comes" led the march along the street lined by cheering citizenry. Somewhat uncertain of what conquests we could claim, we marched on till we reached a road fork where the band took the right leg and we followed. Ahead lay a blank wall: shades of the signal course with a fleet heading for the rocks for lack of the correct order to anchor. The band countermarched through their own ranks and seemed somewhat surprised to find us following through their advancing ranks. As the Bandmaster passed Flags in command he shouted that we had passed the town hall, where we were supposed to halt, fifty yards before the road junction. With the counter-ranks of the band still intermingled with sailors, Flags wisely ordered first, "Halt", and next, "Dismiss", leaving a party in disarray to make their way back as best they could up the steps and into the town hall where crest and coat of arms were duly exchanged between Mayor and D. Thereafter, all went well and the visit was pronounced a great success.

On our return to Southampton, my relief had arrived and I was able to go on leave to await the metamorphosis from hunter to hunted.

CHAPTER II

On Patrol in a German U-boat

WHILE ON LEAVE, it was a disappointment to discover that, having missed the start of a three-month submarine officers' training class, I would need to await the next one in January. My proposal to spend the intervening weeks attached to a non-operational submarine was accepted: thus I found myself in *L26*, a First World War boat based on HMS *Cyclops*, a cargo steamer converted into a submarine depot ship in Rothesay Bay.

After spending a fortnight of daily seagoing, diving, gunnery practice aboard and carrying out a torpedo firing, I had followed and made drawings of air and electrical systems, and was able to trim and handle *L26* dived. To spend a further six months before being given an operational appointment looked more and more a waste of time. It was thus a delight when Jackie Slaughter, the jovial Rabelaisian Commander S/M, perhaps encouraged by noting the gazetting of my Mention in Despatches for my year in *Laforey* and also by increasing losses of submarines and experienced submariners in the Mediterranean, sent for me. He said he planned to test me on what I had learned in *L26* and, if satisfied, would dispense with the training class and send me straight to Londonderry for three months in a more modern training boat after which I could join an operational submarine: three months saved. A couple of days later, an even more surprising advance followed.

In the Holy Loch, *Graph*, the captured German *U570*, was due to sail on patrol to the north coast of Norway. Because her First Lieutenant had just left to do a perisher (Submarine Commanding Officers Qualifying Course), her third hand had taken over as First Lieutenant, so a replacement officer was needed. As this was not the job for a green, newly trained RNVR sub-lieutenant. Jackie Slaughter offered me to her Captain, warning him of my lack of training but suggesting that, as I had no knowledge of how a modern British submarine was handled, at least I had nothing to unlearn in finding out how a U-boat worked. Bravely taking a considerable risk in accepting unseen such a replacement third hand, Sam agreed to chance it. However, one essential item of the basic training missed was the use of Davis submarine escape apparatus. With no time to travel to the heated escape tank at Gosport, I found myself despatched in a motor boat to the head of Loch Striven, where men were being trained in a top secret establishment to handle X Craft (midget submarines) and Chariots (manned torpedoes). There, on a bleak December afternoon, clad in two thick sweaters, I was forced to face a descent into the icy waters with my nose sealed by an uncomfortable nose clip and breathing neat oxygen from a chest bag through a rubber mouth piece. In the black depths I was grateful for the lifeline attached to my waist band, with which I had eventually to be hauled up a ladder back into the boat, blue, goose-pimpled and shivering uncontrollably.

The supervising doctor took pity and, ashore again, allowed me to warm up in a hot bath and fortified me with a deep dram of neat whisky. I was left seriously doubting the advisability of attempting to escape from a sunken submarine in the winter depths of the Atlantic. I am glad I never had to put it to the test.

Next day aboard *Forth*, the depot ship of the 5th Submarine Flotilla in the Holy Loch, I was introduced to Peter Langly-Smith, newly promoted First Lieutenant of *Graph*, who took me to meet Sam Marriott, my new Commanding Officer, in his depot ship cabin. A small stockily-built Lieutenant RN, with light brown hair, ruddy complexion, bright eyes and rather a serious frowning countenance, stood up to greet me. Fingering his tie, he made it clear that he was under no illusion about the risk he was taking in accepting me. As he explained my responsibilities, I could see he was sizing up this tall, ex-destroyer gunnery officer whom he was to take untrained to sea in five days. I was to become navigator, signal, cipher and Asdic officer. Thank heavens for Peter, who had patiently to hold my hand and help to cover up my technical deficiencies.

Burning midnight and early morning oil, I settled once more to making diagrams of a submarine's air and electrical circuits and its torpedo firing mechanism. Trying to follow captured German layout drawings and understand how various systems worked, inevitably wasted Bert Pinch, the warrant engineer's valuable time in answering questions.

The control room contained a bewildering mass of pipes, gauges, dials, levers, switches, hand wheels, air bottles, electrical control boxes for rudder, fore and aft planes and, centrally, the aluminium ladder leading to the conning tower and the outside world. Housed in a pit in the steel deck was the patrol periscope. At the side was a wooden chart table under which were stored charts, navigational books and sextant below a handsome chronometer. In the kiosk at the side, half-way up the conning tower, the attack periscope was housed. It was worked from a revolving saddle on which the Captain could perch to train on any target. No attempt seemed to have been made to alleviate or soften the stark basic utility of the mass of equipment. Although some of the more essential valves had been given replacement English tally plates, most of them were the original German ones making it difficult to discover what did what.

The day before we were due to leave on patrol, while I was still in a haze of undigested information, Sam sent for me and issued a string of instructions on preparing charts of our likely patrol areas, drawing signal, code and cipher books, checking the North Atlantic Pilot, celestial navigational tables, the Nautical Almanac for 1943 when we would still be at sea and much else. Still fuddle-headed by *Graph*'s complicated electrical system, where the two 120-cell batteries could be used either in parallel or in series, I tried to remember everything. At least the tiny wooden locker left no scope for taking more than the most basic essentials of spare sweaters, long johns, battledress, sea boots, sponge bag, writing pad, cigarettes and a month's ration of nutty. Exhausted and slightly drunk, I enjoyed my last night's comfortable sleep in a civilised bed in my depot ship cabin to await the morrow and my first submarine patrol.

On 27th August 1941 *U570,* commanded by Korvetten Kapitan Hans Rahmlow, had been on her maiden patrol in the North Atlantic when, eighty miles south of Iceland, he had surfaced the boat directly up from ninety feet. Unfortunately, at that very moment, an A/S sweeping Hudson aircraft passing overhead was able immediately to drop four depth charges directly round its unexpected target. Rahmlow panicked, ordering his men up the conning tower from below, only to face machine-gun fire from the circling aircraft. A white flag was waved and eventually the surrendered U-boat was taken in tow by a trawler and temporarily beached. After a local inspection revealed only minor damage, a British crew manned and sailed the boat back to Britain where it was renamed HMS *Graph* after the code name of the retrieval operation.

There followed twelve months of investigation and trials of all the U-boat's equipment. Some minor modifications to the tubes, in order to fire British torpedoes, were made before it was decided to carry out normal British submarine patrols and learn more of the strengths and weaknesses of the design in patrol conditions. Before I joined her, *Graph* had spent one fortnight and one three-week patrol off the French coast in the Channel, during the second of which she had carried out a torpedo attack on a surfaced sister ship returning to harbour. Torpedoes had exploded at expected intervals and a U-boat sinking was claimed. Now she was to spend four weeks at sea within the Arctic Circle off the Norwegian coast.

Within the limitations of materials and technology available, designers of a certain size of submarine have to decide between demands for killing power, speed, endurance, diving depth and toughness under water, buoyancy on the surface, ease of operation, robustness of life of machinery and comfort of the crew who man her. U-boats forced to operate far out in the Atlantic required longer range, greater speed to home on convoys, and tougher hulls to resist explosions of our amatol depth charges, more formidable than their TNT. The British "S" Class of similar size to the standard Type 7C U-boat operated closer to their home ports and could be slower, less deep-diving, more stable on the surface and less uncomfortable.

U-boats accepting a maximum salvo of four torpedoes forward were able to use a more streamlined hull than our boats with six torpedo tubes to be accommodated. Both nations carried in all twelve torpedoes forward, and each had a stern tube, the Germans with a reload torpedo aft. The U-boat 88-millimetre streamlined gun, specially designed with watertight binocular sights, was far superior to the clumsy surface ship 3-inch, and later, 4-inch gun fitted to British submarines.

Under water, both nations had a maximum speed of about 8 knots but on the surface the German highly supercharged MAN diesels delivered 19 knots, 4 knots faster than our Perkins designed to last the life of the submarine as were our heavy duty batteries. The Germans managed to achieve similar battery capacity with cells half the size or weight, filled with over twice the number of thinner battery plates. The resulting high capacity batteries and aluminium alloy engines had a short life requiring annual replacement. This weight saving allowed a 7/8-inch thick steel hull with twice the diving depth of our 5/8-inch hulls. U-boats, however, were able to maintain a far greater range only by carrying nearly twice the amount of diesel fuel, even risking some carried outside the pressure hull, and the only way this could be achieved was by a considerable sacrifice of surface buoyancy and crew comfort.

U-boat electrical circuits were complicated, with switching making extensive use of relays leaving faults far more difficult to trace and repair than our simpler more robust manual copper switching. They accepted the risks of air bottles and fuel outside the hull; we kept ours inside. They had separate diesel and electrical air compressors, a better system than our two, both electrical. Our gyro compass was more reliable: their echo sounder better. We opened the vents allowing us to dive by hydraulic power; theirs were hand operated and used clumsy long shafts fore and aft from the control room to open forward and aft vents ninety feet away. With ample hydraulic power available *Graph* had modified these to power working. They had twin rudders for extra manoeuvrability and were able to use steel for propellers and periscopes, far lighter and stronger than ours; yet U-boat designers never produced a tight stern gland and, as a result, required deep bilges needing constant pumping out.

The resultant discomfort from the U-boat's design was notable. Their crews were forced to live in conditions which, if imposed on farm animals, would likely have involved prosecution for cruelty. In cramped quarters with inefficient sanitary arrangements, meagre fresh water supplies and even officers', petty officers' and ERAs' messes bisected by an open corridor, there was no privacy and seamen and stokers ate and slept in any corner of the deck they could find. On the surface, with its limited buoyancy, the boat bucketed about so violently in rough weather that it was not possible to stand or move without holding on.

In an "S" Class submarine the crew had mess tables and benches, there were separated boxed-in messes for leading seamen, chief and petty officers and ERAs while the wardroom mess had bunks and lockers round a table and offered comfortable privacy. We enjoyed three times the fresh water capacity.

Graph sailed in the afternoon of 21st December, roughly a month after I had first set foot in any submarine. In accordance with wartime custom, a few minutes before submarines sail on patrol, people congregate on the depot ship's upper deck and line her rails. Most of the flotilla seems to be there. Last to board the departing submarine is her Captain, escorted to the top of the ladder by Captain S/M. They shake hands and salute before he is piped over the side, down the ladder, across the plank, and once more is piped aboard his command. Wires have already been singled, the plank is hauled aboard and stowed in the casing as he climbs the conning tower to the bridge, receives brief reports before shouting an order down the voice pipe.

The boat shudders as her screws boil the water, wires are slipped and she gathers stern way. The telegraphs clang and she stops before moving ahead and, as she draws level with the depot ship once more, a shrill whistle brings the white sweater-clad crew lining the fore casing to attention, the depot ship pipes in reply, then both sound off the "carry on". As the departing submarine turns away to head to sea Captain S/M gives a farewell wave and in the depot ship men disperse, leaving small parties chattering for a few minutes before returning to their work. There is an unspoken feeling of "When shall we two meet again?" in the air.

A stiff breeze was blowing from ahead slicing the tops off the short sharp waves into flying spume as *Graph* turned round the shore at Hunter's Quay. An order was passed down the voice pipe to open up for diving and, once in the open water south of Bute, we dived to check the trim and either pump or flood tanks to achieve rough neutral buoyancy under water. To surface on completion, compressed air was blown into the ballast tanks while the Captain waited up in the conning tower to open the hatch as soon as the bridge could be heard to break surface.

The sleeping warrior of Arran was silhouetted by the setting sun when I climbed once more on to the bridge. A T-class submarine, to come on patrol with us sharing our escort, was approaching. She also had carried out a trim dive and, once she had surfaced, we took station astern of her following the submarine escort *Cutty Sark*, a pensioned-off First World War destroyer converted into a yacht by the Duke of Westminster and now returned for wartime service. Allied submarines on passage in home waters were always escorted by a surface ship as protection from the trigger happy.

In a wartime submarine, two hours were considered the longest it was possible to remain sufficiently alert, so watches were arranged two hours on and four hours off. Because lookouts' watches changed on the hour those of the officers began at the half, thus ensuring always having at least one lookout on watch with eyes fully accommodated to the dark. As a further precaution, the control room, from which men climbed the conning tower to the bridge, was lit by red lights at night. When I next emerged on the bridge at 2030, it was dark and blustery with a cascade of spray from every third wave. Ahead glowed the dim stern lights of the two ships we followed.

To maintain station, the engines' revolutions had to be adjusted neither to lag behind nor to come too close. During my watch, the T-boat ahead drew out to the port quarter of the escort vessel as if to overtake. I thought I should inform our captain so ordered "Captain on the bridge". In a few seconds half dressed and shoeless he arrived.

"What's up?" he demanded. I explained, "Nothing, sir, only *Trespasser* has drawn out on *Cutty Sark*'s quarter."

"Well, next time just inform me and not use an emergency order." He crossly explained that "Captain on the bridge" was for emergencies.

I lamely replied that in *Laforey* a bell was used for emergency while "Captain on the bridge" was less urgent.

I had a lot to learn, and Sam Marriott was bearing the brunt of my education. As he withdrew once more, soaked through by an unfortunate wave, I had no doubt he was regretting taking such an untrained officer to sea on patrol.

Quarter of an hour before the end of my watch, a shout up the voice pipe enquired if the messenger should call Peter Langly-Smith, my relief. Agreeing, I happily imagined the pleasure of a warm dry bunk. By 2235, with no sign of relief I shouted down the voice pipe to find out if Number One had been called. It was not till ten minutes later that a rather sour Peter climbed out of the conning tower, apologising but claiming no one had called him. I soon discovered he slept so deeply that it was almost impossible to wake him up and we arranged he would be shaken as much earlier for the next watch as he had been late for the watch before, thus compensating for my earlier overtime on watch. I was told later that my predecessor had tried telling the messenger to give him a cigarette and light it for him but, after a fire alert when his blanket began to smoulder and emit clouds of smoke, this system was prohibited by order of the Captain.

Two days later we reached Lerwick and secured to a fuel barge anchored offshore to top up diesel and food and enjoy a last night's rest before sailing north. It was not to be; in the middle of the night a boat bobbed alongside and we were ordered to sail immediately. Once at sea, the boat was opened up for diving and by dawn we were out of sight of land as a watery sun rose to primrose-tint clouds strung above the horizon like streaky bacon.

As navigator, it was my duty to take a midday sun sight, the first time I had handled a sextant since the pre-war training cruiser. It was a very different proposition trying to see in the sextant telescope the image of a watery sun on top of a wave-broken horizon which rose and fell as *Graph* rolled fifteen degrees either way. My doubtful fix was far out of accord with our dead reckoning position on the chart, which, understandably, the Captain preferred to accept. Full disclosure of the abysmal inadequacy of my celestial navigational endeavours was fortunately delayed by forty-eight hours of overcast skies where no sun, moon or star could be seen as we made our way north-easterly to a point off the Norwegian coast within the Arctic Circle.

Alas, the skies cleared and I found myself once more armed with a sextant on a lurching platform twelve feet above sea level. Taking sights of three stars, I descended to the chart table below to produce a position. The three lines met in a wide triangle, sadly not over the sea but inland over a 2,000-foot mountain. Sam, with a scowl of irritated disbelief, despatched Peter, from whom I had taken over as navigator, to take sights and fix the ship. From his chart position we turned east and soon the mountains of the island of Soroy, guarding the entrance to Alten Fjord, base of the German battle fleet, were sighted. Our patrol area was north of the entrance while another submarine had a billet to its south. *Graph* settled down to patrol up and down a few miles offshore.

Arctic winter nights can be memorable for, whenever the sky was unclouded, the Lord provided His own illumination to lighten our darkness. Aurora Borealis was revealed in all its magical glory. Rays of red, green, orange and purple light would flash on and off suddenly, like heavenly searchlights. Up above, curtains of light would dance to and fro, up and down; a shimmering effect was produced by brighter patches which rippled in waves all along the curtain; they themselves would open and close, advance and retire, pass through each other at will and, as suddenly as they had appeared, be gone. Soon another would appear, perhaps of a different colour. It really lived up to its Scottish Highland description: the fairy dancers. A considerable effort of will was called for to continue sweeping to and fro with binoculars searching for that break in the continuity of the horizon which betrays a ship.

It was only later that I discovered how much wetter and more uncomfortable was watchkeeping on the bridge of a Type 7C U-boat than on a similar sized British S-class submarine. Because it had only a quarter of the buoyancy, the narrow platform, in stormy weather, dipped, plunged and rolled under repeated deluges of stinging salt water. It was well nigh impossible to keep binocular object lenses from filming over and, in the worst weather, watchkeepers needed to wear a safety girth with a spring clip to attach to an anchor rail which surrounded the bridge casing. In these conditions, the conning tower hatch was kept shut, the engine intakes being able to collect air through ducts down each side of the bridge astern of the hatch. Whenever the hatch was opened to allow relief of watchkeepers, water would gush down on to the steel deck of the control room below, where it sloshed about before draining away to a sump needing frequent pumping out. Despite every effort to remain alert on a dark stormy night, it could be difficult to spot an approaching ship before it was unsafely close.

Watchkeepers wore liberally Vaseline-coated watertight Ursula suits of hooded jacket and separate trousers tightly tied outside sea boots, but there were three vital entries for water. We tried, usually in vain, to tighten the collar of the Ursula jacket between a thickly towelled neck and hood under the chin. The glands at the wrists were more difficult to pack: there were two schools of thought; glove over sleeve or sleeve over glove, neither successful. Even if a big wave washing over the bridge burying the officer of the watch and lookouts up to the waist in salt water, failed to penetrate between trousers and jacket, the necessary holding of binoculars to the eyes entailed bent elbows. Once a trickle of water had infiltrated under or over the bottom of the gloves, raising the arms allowed it to run coldly down to the elbow where a small pool would accumulate only to flow back and fill the glove when arms were lowered once more.

During the Arctic winter, submarines on patrol would dive only for the few light hours in the middle of each day and then often had to descend to sixty feet to keep control, just coming up to periscope depth for an occasional periscope sweep or, at fixed times, to point towards Rugby and receive any ciphers of information or instruction. Only ultra long waves could penetrate under water. It was often difficult to navigate off this rugged coast, where there were so many similar shaped peaks, so great reliance was placed on the sounding machine.

Only during the dog watches was there much recreational activity aboard. Then those off watch would stir, maybe two serious stokers would concentrate on a draughts contest, a gramophone would blare forth Vera Lynn in the fore ends, while from the ERAs' mess would come the rattle of dice on the Uckers board. This violent form of ludo was often played in other messes and the wardroom. Sam like to win and it was often politic to see that he and his usual partner Bert, the Chief, on whom an unholy gloom would descend as soon as we left harbour, finished up victors.

Their opponents round the small square wardroom table, surrounded by wooden lockers and opposite two bunks, one above the other, and a small wash basin across the passage, were the two remaining officers off watch. Neil, the long haired RNVR fourth hand and torpedo officer, was irresistibly cheerful unless roused, when a wild Irish temper could explode. If there seemed any chance of avoiding detection, all of us would cheat in our moves of the counters so as to uck back to the start any counter nearing its final safe haven. Sometimes fierce arguments ensued.

Neil and I were reputed to be a pair of gannets, from our capacity always to finish our food, even in the roughest queasy stomach-turning motion of *Graph* in a gale. One of the most important submarine crew members is the cook. In a space where there is hardly room to turn round he has, on one small electric cooker, to produce three meals a day and each night to bake forty pounds of bread. Should the beef be underdone or the jam tarts be burned or tasting of soap he will hear all about it. He must not suffer sea sickness. Cooking on a stove that heaves thirty-five degrees either side of vertical in addition to sundry other corkscrew swings calls for a cast iron constitution. Remarkably, even in *Graph* so much less stable than a British counterpart, it was seldom that opening tins of soup and bully beef was all our chef could achieve from the exceptional quality of food available.

Especially tinned for submarines were whole tongues and hams, vegetables and varieties of soup, asparagus, lentil, tomato, chicken and Scotch broth, all so nearly solid as to make a meal on their own. No deep freezers then, so these were for use once fresh meat and vegetable supplies were exhausted. In addition to making stomach-clinging figgy duffs and jam pastries, ample tins of fruit were available. Thus the coxswain in charge of stores could, in co-operation with the chef, stock up supplies for a month's varied and appetizing menus for over forty men. In addition, we had supplies of honey kindly contributed by a group of English apiarists and large rectangular tins of boiled sweets always available to compensate smokers for dived abstinence.

In the days of severe rationing ashore we were privileged, but still many suffered bleeding gums, a form of scurvy, from lack of sunlight and Vitamin C. The depot ship dentist was later able to contribute a paper to a learned medical journal on scurvy and its treatment in modern times.

Life off Soroy Island on patrol followed its regular pattern as gale succeeded gale, but of the enemy there was neither sight nor sound until, on New Year's Eve, distant sounds of intermittent underwater explosions were heard. The previous night's gale had moderated and, when we surfaced, the night was bright with snow-clad peaks to the east clearly visible. Motors were stopped, engine clutches engaged and after a hiss and one or two thumps, the diesels clattered into life and the battery charge began. Descending to supper at eight-thirty I had left Peter to enjoy the dance of the Northern Lights. All too soon, at a quarter past midnight, in the bunk across the passage from the wardroom table I was being shaken and handed a cup of thick steaming cocoa known as kai. The messenger reported that it was dry but cold on the bridge. After piling on sweaters, sea boots and Ursula suit, checking the chart and deck log in the corner of the control room and having a word with the helmsman, it was time to clank up the ladder to relieve Neil on the bridge.

The air was sharp and crisp and the looming mountains rising sheer from the sea seemed ready to jump out at us. Dark shapes of snow-clear precipices stood out black to the naked eye and it was difficult to believe that we were seven miles from the shore. At one o'clock lookouts changed over and sharp eyed signalman Freddie Cheale took over the port side. Soon after, as *Graph* steered north, he reported an island on the port beam. Sweeping round I was just able to make out a break in the horizon. The enemy was in sight. I bellowed down the voice pipe, "Sound the night alarm; break the charge; Port 30." As *Graph* swung towards it Sam bobbed breathlessly out of the conning tower hatch. Unable to distinguish the target, he ordered me to point the ship towards it and rang down full speed ahead.

The rattle of the engines rose to a high pitched scream as the superchargers came into play and the whole U-boat began to vibrate with her wake creaming astern. Soon it became obvious that the target was moving left. By now, with eyes accommodated, Sam had seen it and altered course to intercept. There seemed little doubt that this was a large vessel travelling at high speed. Alas, the bearing continued to draw ahead and it soon became clear that, unless she altered course towards us, there would be no chance of a successful torpedo attack. Using an estimated range of ten miles, the plot calculated from the change of bearing a speed roughly 30 knots and that her course was straight for the entrance to the fjord. If only we'd been at the other end of our patrol line. Sadly we could only watch her disappear from sight. Diving stations were ordered to fall out, the signalman was commended for his sighting and patrol resumed. My watch complete, Peter came up to take over. Climbing into the comfortable warm bunk he had just left, I was soon asleep.

My awakening was rude. A messenger was shaking me violently. "Sir, we are at diving stations and starting an attack." I had slept though the night alarm gong. Heaving out and ducking through the hatch into the control room, I clattered up the ladder to my action station in the kiosk on the fruit machine. This box worked out a sine curve to produce from the enemy's course, range and speed a director angle, the number of degrees off the bow to aim when firing torpedoes. Each torpedo would follow the same track at intervals so that, should the enemy speed be underestimated, the first would hit and, if over, the last of the salvo might do so.

When I arrived I discovered Neil had taken my place, so I climbed down to take over the plot.

Every so often a bearing and estimated range of the enemy would be shouted down the voice pipe to be marked on the plotting table. It soon became clear that this time, with a reported beam-on target and no change in bearing, the enemy must be stopped. I shouted this up to the Captain on the bridge in confirmation of what he had already decided. We were running in silently on the motors. In sight were two stopped ships beam-on and close together. It seemed most likely that the heavy ship had detected us and sent two destroyers out to listen for us. At that time it was believed that enemy anti-submarine measures were more based on listening than transmitting, so Sam decided to advance towards them warily, fire torpedoes at long range and then silently withdraw.

A torpedo depth setting of six feet was passed to the tube space and each tube in turn reported ready. At 45 knots, each torpedo would run roughly for ten minutes till its fuel was exhausted when it would sink to the bottom. When the Captain estimated the range as about 6,000 yards, he shouted he would fire on a slow swing, necessary with a stopped target.

"Fire One, starboard 5," was ordered; then "Fire Two," followed at short intervals by Three and Four. The boat shuddered as each was fired and the hydrophone operator reported them running. It was time to turn and flee.

The second hand of the stop-watch, started with the first torpedo, ticked round deliberately as we turned away and, after eight minutes, there were two loud explosions a few seconds apart followed two minutes later by a couple more. Those on the bridge had seen nothing. It seemed possible two hits had been scored with the other two torpedoes exploding on the sea bottom at the end of their run.

When ten miles clear, *Graph* dived and the fore end men were ordered to reload torpedoes from the racks each side of their accommodation space. This can be a tricky operation in rough weather with every reasonable precaution to be taken to avoid three tons of torpedo running amuck in the restricted space or sliding back out of the already half loaded tube. Propeller clamps must be removed and firing mechanisms engaged. Apart from the CO, everyone believed we had scored two hits and spirits were high, not least with the fore end men. With the reload torpedo space now empty and available for their narrow mattresses, their accommodation space had doubled.

That evening, New Year's Day 1943, after surfacing for the long night we heard the BBC News announcement that, two days earlier, north of North Cape, Captain Sherbrooke had valiantly led his destroyer flotilla to drive off an enemy assault on a Murmansk convoy, inflicting some damage on enemy ships who had withdrawn from the action leaving the convoy intact. Clearly what we had mistaken for a depth charge attack on a consort must have been the sound of that action to the north of us. We had seen either the pocket battleship *Lutzow* or the cruiser *Hipper* to seaward and it seemed likely that, instead of having come out to hunt us, one of the stopped destroyers may have been trying to tow a damaged consort and had stopped to adjust the tow. With hindsight, it might have been safe to risk our attack closer before firing torpedoes, particularly in view of the difficulty of range estimation in conditions of such extreme visibility.

Without any sign of movement from the entrance to Alten Fjord, ten days of uneventful patrolling up and down followed. With relief we would dive for a few hours of light, when only the hum of motors and the occasional sound of a pump starting or a hydroplane moving would break the welcome calm of life at sixty feet. All too soon would arrive time to close up at diving stations, to open the lower hatch for the Captain and signalmen to clump up the ladder below the dripping conning tower hatch, to blow main ballast tanks in a hiss of air and, as the bow began to rise, once more to heave and bucket to and fro in time with the waves above. Ears would click as the hatch opened, releasing pressure in the boat and, after a pause, the thump of starting diesels would mark the end of those few blissful hours of peace.

Graph, replaced by a T-boat on completion of her three week patrol, was ready to return to base. By then the sheer discomfort of patrolling in a U-boat was beginning to affect everyone's efficiency and alertness. With only a daily litre of fresh water in a slopping tin basin available for each man to clean his teeth, shave and then wash, all in the same water, the aura of underwashed bodies mingled with the smells of damp wool, diesel fuel, battery gas, greasy overalls and the last meal cooked on the galley stove. In this atmosphere, with condensation dripping from above, men in the cramped fore ends squatted to eat and lay to sleep on the heaving deck above the two remaining reload torpedoes in a well below. Officers, petty officers and ERAs could at least eat at a narrow folding table and did have the use of a curtained bunk with an aluminum rail to stop them falling out, each side of the central passage.

On watch, nursing the thundering diesels in the engine room, men were unable to hear the loudest shout and had to communicate by signs or by scribbled chalk messages on a slate. To detect trouble, stokers would listen to individual cylinders and valves through an inverted trumpet held to the ear as, oil can in hand, they lubricated each reciprocating rocker arm in turn. With the superchargers engaged it was even more of a screaming inferno.

As we set off south, a south-easterly gale began to blow, the wind rose and also the sea; skies were overcast, heavy and menacing and, with the bridge dipping deep into grey-green seas, speed had to be reduced. The wind was blowing off the tops of breaking waves into long streaks of spray. The Captain, ever prone to seasickness, had taken to his bunk.

An attempt to obtain a wireless direction finding fix failed and, uncertain of our position, the sounding machine was our only navigational aid. Even regular half-hourly soundings revealed no shallow patches which might have given some idea of where we were. The weather was too rough for cooking but hot soup and bully beef were on hand for those with stronger stomachs. Water from down the hatch slopped about on the steel control room deck. It had been hoped to make a Shetland landfall in daylight but, as one sleet shower followed another, our speed reduction made this unlikely.

Uncertain of our position to within fifty miles after three days' dead reckoning, a further speed reduction was ordered. Sam, green-faced after half an hour poring over the chart and fiddling with dividers and parallel rulers, decided the soundings indicated we were probably about thirty miles north of Muckle Flugga in the north of the Shetland Isles and should make a landfall in daylight next morning. Leaving an underlined reminder of the importance of good lookout in the Captain's Day Book, he returned to his bunk.

"Quarter of an hour to your watch, Sir, and Mr Strouts says it's very wet and cold on the bridge".

Oh, the blessing of a steaming thick cloggy sweet cup of kai before heaving on a damp Ursula suit, sea boots, oilskin and thick gloves, girthing tight the leather safety belt, making a careful study of the chart, then climbing up the dripping ladder till, steadying yourself braced against the roll as a wave washes over the bridge, it is off spring clip, up through the open hatch just in time to kick it shut again, clinging to the periscope standard as the next icy wave cascades over; then crawling to the front of the bridge, clipping on harness to a ring bolt when, safe from being washed overboard, there is time to have a careful sweep of the horizon before taking over the watch.

Neil, with a curt, "All yours, Phil," unclips himself and, hanging on, moves aft to time the hatch opening, jump below and clang it shut before the next wave washing over could pour down to the control room below.

On the bridge, spray stung our cheeks and our eyes smarted with salt. Streaks of foaming wave crests were the sole light patches breaking the blackness of the night. They would sizzle past, bridge high as the bow plunged deep into the heart of the following wave. There is a fierce exhilaration, on a bucketing platform only a few feet above the surface of the sea, in facing the fury of a gale, buffeted by the waves but defiantly battling on till sea, ship and seaman seemed to form one heaving entity. The cold rush of wind makes a high pitched shriek in the jumping wires. Every time her nose buries deep in a wave the hull shudders before once more the sharp pointed bow rises, with water streaming off the flat deck in torrents till it seems to point high in the sky before descending once more to thump into the next hissing roller.

In one of my binocular sweeps of the horizon half an hour into the watch and soon after lookouts had been relieved, I thought I saw the flash of a faint yellowish light. Was it real or had I perhaps spotted the foam or yet another breaking wave crest and imagined a phantom light? I shouted to the port lookout to sweep the sector close on our port bow where I continued anxiously searching. Worrying minutes passed and then just when I decided it was all imagination, we both saw it, a rather watery yellow glow which showed for a second and then was gone.

"Port 30. Inform the Captain there is a flashing light in sight and I have altered away," I shouted down the voice pipe to the helmsman. As *Graph* swung beam on to the sea she rolled heavily, lurching to leeward, and then, turning further, the wind and sea fell on the quarter, the ship became steadier with waves no longer breaking on the bridge and the scream of the wind faded, with the sounds of the gale so diminished that all seemed suddenly quiet and peaceful once more. Sam opened the hatch and clambered up. Nothing was to be seen, so he ordered a further reduction in speed to await the dawn.

Four hours after being relieved, I was back on watch once more. As the sky lightened, the dim shape of a hill and later a white painted lighthouse perched on top of sheer cliffs above jagged pinnacles of rock, were revealed. The waves sweeping in hurled themselves into spouting geysers and cascades of spray only a few miles astern. We had been lucky. Instead of making our landfall to the north of Shetland we were off Out Skerries half way down and only twenty miles north of Lerwick.

The Captain decided to steer south down the coast to see if we could risk trying to make harbour. The wind having by now veered south, it meant we were once more heading straight head to sea to continue the buffeting of the last few days. However, the chef had taken advantage of the earlier calmer conditions to cook bacon and eggs. How welcome, on relief, to eat a cooked breakfast with coffee and a freshly baked roll before joining Sam at the chart table.

"Well, Pilot, are we going to have a shot at making harbour?"

I could see no reason why not until it was pointed out that we'd first have to cross two miles of lee shore off Bressay and then run a similar distance with wind and sea right astern over a shallow bottom. It might be wiser to heave-to till the gale moderated. Eventually he decided to chance either being laid over on beam ends or being pooped, and to have a go.

The plan was for the Captain and me to stay on the bridge, securely lashed in position with the hatch below screwed up tightly. At the chart table, Number One in the control room would mark our compass bearings on the chart but, unable to see the chart, we would memorise various compass courses and when to alter to them. Meanwhile the Coxswain, in preparation, had checked that all portable equipment was lashed down even more securely than usual.

When all was ready, we climbed up top, relieved Neil and both lookouts, and clipped ourselves securely by our harnesses to the front of the bridge. Then, when the headland was abaft the beam, Sam cautiously altered course to starboard. This was it; no turning back now. The boat's pitch changed to a violent lurching roll. Despite being two miles up wind of the sheer cliffs we could hear the roar as each wave smashed ashore and bounced back to meet the next in chaotic foam, almost doubling the size of each wave's crest and trough. Then an exceptional wave smashed into the port side, lifting 750 tons of U-boat bodily, like a cork skidding it listed over thirty degrees sideways till water streamed over the starboard side of the bridge to swirl around waist high around that, pouring over to windward. There was just time to snap shut the voice pipe cock and save the helmsman from a drenching. Ice cold water trickled slowly down the inside of sea boots to form pools at the heels. After *Graph* had righted itself, a shout up the voice pipe confirmed that little damage had been suffered below.

As we slowly altered course round each headland, the seas began coming more over the port quarter turning the violent rolls to a gentler corkscrew motion. From time to time the stern would rise and the diesels would race as a screw lifted out of the water but, adapting to the rhythm of the waves, it became drier on the bridge. The town of Lerwick came in sight as the last headland was rounded.

"Only two miles to go, Pilot. Alter course to 338."

The rolling had ceased as *Graph* steadied on her new course. Instead, she began to skim along like a surf rider on the crest of each overtaking wave which lapped over the flat after casing till the stern lifted once more.

An extra large hissing breaker hove in sight.

"Look out, Pilot, this is it."

I turned to watch, fascinated and hypnotised into inactivity as the stern sank. The surge of hissing water raced towards the anti-aircraft gun platform at the rear of the bridge as the stern continued to sink. Ducking and late in shutting the voice pipe, the sea gurgled over and swirled us up till we were swinging face down, moored by our harness lifelines high above the deck of the bridge. As we swung to and fro I looked up at the surface of the water, green and sparkling several feet above. Strangely, there seemed no trouble in breathing as if the coaming of the sides of the bridge had imprisoned an air bubble. Eventually the green mirror descended and we landed back on our feet again with a thud. Re-opening the voice pipe allowed more cold sea water to drench the wretched helmsman who shouted up that at our deepest, the depth gauge had shown the boat down to thirty feet.

Twice more we were pooped by the following sea till we reached some shelter in the lee of Bressay Island. "Harbour stations" was passed over the intercom and the casing party climbed up to the bridge and clambered over to the casing below to bring out wires so as to secure alongside the submarine escort which was to lead us back to the Holy Loch. A friend on the casing of the S-class submarine berthed on the far side of the escort claimed he'd never seen wetter or more cheerfully exhilarated submariners than Sam and me. As a fuel lighter came alongside to replenish our diesel supply, a signal from the Senior Officer ashore enquired whether Sam would prefer to go straight south after fuelling or to spend the night. It seemed so calm inside the harbour that there might never have been a gale blowing outside. We stayed and a boat collected all our officers except the duty officer to bathe, dine ashore and enjoy a blissful night's sleep in a long, wide comfortable bed.

By next morning, we were able to stand straight without feeling the imagined rolling of the land, the gale had moderated and Sam, bearing on his chest the newly awarded red, blue and red ribbon of the DSO gazetted during our patrol and sewn on while he slept, was piped back aboard for the passage south. On the way, he prepared, and Neil Strouts typed, the patrol report, an abbreviated

'Sam' Marriott who commanded *Graph, Stoic* and *U776*

account of the submarine's movements and activities over the past twenty-eight days. In that time I had learned how to move inside a heaving steel tube, keeping balance while swaying along the central corridors, ducking through the circular hatches in and out of the control room and, by taking the ring out of an old naval cap and stuffing the top with cottonwool like a soft crash helmet, to avoid cranial damage. So ended my first submarine patrol, memorable for the discomfort, lack of buoyancy and seakeeping qualities of a captured Type 7C U-boat.

Above *U570*'s engine room control panel was a board stating in bold letters "FUHRER BEFIEL, WIR FOLGEN" (The Führer leads, we follow). While the main trials were being conducted in Vickers Barrow yard after *Graph*'s capture, an oak carving of a giraffe above the motto "THE FUHRER LED, BUT WE OVERTOOK HIM" had been attached to a wardroom locker.

Sadly, defects were beginning to overtake us as, soon after our return alongside *Forth* in the Holy Loch, continuing serious mechanical problems began to dog our future utility. Since *U570*'s launch in the Blohm & Voss yard in Hamburg in March 1941 and completion and commissioning two months later in Keil, none of the normal German metric spare parts had been available, though for the short-life battery plates, Exide Ironclad had been able to provide replacements so that full electrical capacity had been maintained.

It was a different picture where replacement parts were needed for ballast, trim and fuel pumps, for blower, compressor, evaporator, or for electrical control and relay equipment; to maintain them each item required individual fabrication. Worse were problems with the Krupp designed diesel engines. Cracked engine cylinder heads had allowed salt water to cause severe piston and liner wear. Despite the best endeavours of leading welding specialists up from Birmingham, welds in the high grade steel alloys used were only temporarily successful before cracks again began spreading, with resulting loss of power in the engines from serious and continuing liner wear. In addition, the main ballast pump failed, as did blower clutches and, of vital importance for safe surfacing, the Krupps air compressor was allowing air to blow back into its crank case, limiting the air pressure available to blow tanks.

While all this time-consuming repair and maintenance work was being done, the continuing demands for our services could not be met. We were not mechanically fit for patrol. Western Approaches training base at Londonderry wanted us to carry out special dived trials as a target for surface ships and aircraft; further tests were required at the Loch Goil noise range; "huf duf" (high frequency direction finding) equipment in selected escort vessels needed transmissions on different wireless frequencies and courses for testing and improving equipment; and there were several other requests for tests and trials. Until repairs could be successfully completed none of these demands could be met.

Meantime, Sam Marriott had closeted himself in his depot ship cabin with strict orders that no one except the First Lieutenant was to disturb him. When he re-emerged into circulation after several days, he outlined what he had been doing. He had rightly considered that the use so far made of *Graph* in carrying out patrol work like any British submarine was a waste. Could she not be used as an anti-U-boat weapon, using her silhouette to join a U-boat pack gathering on the surface for a convoy attack?

It was known that U-boats sailing from Norway, Brest and St Nazaire combined to form packs which should give a reasonable chance that an extra boat would pass undetected for long enough to be able successfully to torpedo a sister ship. One such attack might cause sufficient confusion to disrupt U-boat operations on the surface, uncertain whether there might not be a nigger in any particular woodpile. Special arrangements to protect *Graph* from friendly air or surface attack would be required and success might depend on Naval Intelligence Division's knowledge of German signal procedure, call signs, wavelengths, codes, pyrotechnics and recognition signals. The whole proposal was forwarded to Admiralty for urgent consideration and decision.

During much of February 1941 *Graph* remained alongside *Forth* under repair. Life aboard the depot ship settled into peaceful routine. Several afternoons a week I would land with a friend at Strome Pier on the east side of the Holy Loch and we would walk round the head of the Loch and visit Loch Eck before reaching Sandbank Pier for the boat back for dinner. Fierce poker games would follow into the small hours.

One Sunday afternoon, as duty officer, I was settled comfortably in *Graph*'s wardroom when my thoughts wandered to the primitive arrangements for submarine gun control which, to an ex-destroyer gunnery control officer, seemed remarkably hit or miss. To work out degrees to aim off in allowance for the target's course and speed, a cumbersome metal-framed box with an extending arm had to be hauled out of a cupboard below the chart table in the control room. All this Dumaresq calculator did was to solve a sine curve. For torpedo firing the "fruit machine" mounted in the control room worked out a similar calculation. By fiddling, I discovered that a torpedo speedsetting of 30 knots would provide the same answer as the Dumaresq, so saving having to carry and store it. A memorandum to this effect was passed to Sam, who forwarded it through the proper channels to Admiral Submarines whence it was distributed as a Submarine General Memorandum.

It was not until two years later that I received a letter from the Admiralty that "While their Lordships appreciate the zeal and ingenuity displayed by Lieutenant Durham in this matter, they are unable to approve any award under the Lott Naval Trust Fund." A pity!

Then, at the end of February, Peter Langly-Smith was suddenly appointed, at short notice, to replace the First Lieutenant of a T-class submarine about to leave for the Mediterranean. Despite my serious lack of experience, I was accepted as First Lieutenant in his place and an RNR sub-lieutenant joined as navigator. Perhaps it was a matter of any excuse to remove such a proven navigational incompetent by kicking him upstairs.

One of the responsibilities of a first lieutenant in harbour is the carrying out of "trot fobs", manoeuvres to alter the positions of the trots of submarines alongside the depot ship. Only in the inner berths can the depot ship crane hoist in and out torpedoes, periscopes or other heavy equipment, and the supply hoses for diesel fuel, lubricating oil and distilled water be connected.

A typical day's movement might be that, alongside to port, *Forth* has berthed in order *Graph, Tantalus, Surf* and *Utmost* with the starboard side occupied by a store ship. *Tantalus*, newly in from patrol, has a leaky torpedo air vessel for repair; *Utmost* must embark torpedoes, stores and 8,000 gallons of fuel. When *Tantalus, Surf* and *Utmost* all tied together kick out their sterns, remaining attached to the depot ship forward, *Graph* is allowed to slip out astern and move to a buoy out of the way. The crane can then hoist out *Tantalus*' torpedo. At 0845 *Utmost* lets go to lie off astern allowing *Surf* to sail. As soon as *Tantalus* alongside has removed torpedo rails and shut her fore hatch, she will let go to lie off astern while *Utmost*, ready to store ship, replaces her. It will depend on future movements planned whether *Tantalus* or *Graph* next berths alongside *Utmost*. It will have taken two hours before *Graph*, who merely wished to continue routine work and cleaning, is settled alongside once more.

My first trot fob was similar to this. I had never manoeuvred in anything larger than *Beryl* or *Count Benyowski* and was now required to move a submarine, with the added disadvantage that *Graph*, with fixed drowned foreplanes six feet below water level, could act as a very effective tin opener unless way had been safely taken off when securing alongside. Beside me on the bridge at the electrical steering box and rudder control was her coxswain, Brigham Young, DSM, and Bar, whose eighteen stone frame was deemed too tight a fit through the conning tower hatch and thus for safety he was prohibited the bridge on patrol.

He and I had the day before suffered a difference of opinion over stores and I had a feeling he might not be too unhappy to see me make a mess of things. Feeling insecure and pocketing my pride, I admitted this was my first trot fob and I would welcome any advice he cared to offer. As a result, big man as he was in every sense, he virtually did my ship handling for me, suggesting when to go astern so as to make a perfect come alongside. Thereafter we became firm friends, and I soon learned how to handle the boat on the surface myself.

Fortunately, during the month's Arctic patrol I had learned the art of trimming and controlling the boat when dived. This was particularly important because, in a U-boat during a dived attack, the Captain moved to the kiosk above the control room, and was in no position to correct any error by the First Lieutenant in charge of the trim. The Captain in a British submarine carrying out a dived attack at the periscope was surrounded by the attack and control team and in touch with everything going on around him.

German practice was for the engineer officer to trim the boat while the Captain above concentrated on the attack, seated in the saddle of the massive

A trot of S-class submarines alongside their depot ship. (From a painting by Tom Dowling.)

attack periscope which he controlled up, down and round by foot pedals undistracted by the hubbub of activity below. This periscope could be used when ten feet deeper than the control room one which suffered more limited visibility in rough weather.

In our submarines, both patrol and attack periscopes operated at a similar depth in the control room, the former with improved magnification and clarity but with a fatter and more easily seen head above the surface. Thus, the Captain could shift from one to the other as he closed a target. He could move to look at the plot, talk to the Asdic operator, and watch depth gauge, trimming team, fruit machine operator, torpedo firing controls and the whole team round him feeding him with information.

The duties of a submarine First Lieutenant were varied, with many of them new to an officer pitched in at the deep end with neither training nor experience. Relying on the coxswain to look after stores, food, rum and the medicine chest, responsibility for the discipline, welfare, health of the crew and general cleanliness aboard was not arduous, particularly with *Graph's* highly experienced complement; it was care of batteries and electrical motors and equipment and calculation of the trim to adjust the contents of tanks so that, when the boat dived, it would be in rough neutral equilibrium that had to be learned.

After the Stoker PO has sounded and dipped the contents of each fresh water, lubricating oil and distilled water tank and noted the amount of diesel in the compensated fuel tanks, allowance must be made for the weight of the torpedoes, ammunition, stores and food aboard to calculate the amount of sea water to be either flooded in or pumped out of each tank. After this comes the reckoning during the trim dive soon after sailing. How skilful was the First Lieutenant's calculation? Will the boat be bow or stern heavy? Will it be so light as to need high speed and dived planes to force it under water, or so heavy as to take all their effort to avoid plummeting to the bottom? Only the trim dive, watched with interest and amusement by all the other forty-three men aboard, will tell. Then, the care of batteries has to be learned. They must be charged, but not overcharged, to maintain full capacity. The specific gravity of the acid in battery cells must be read with a hydrometer and, as it rises, the charging rate reduced so as to avoid overproduction of battery gas or loss of acid.

At last, after two months out of operation, *Graph* was ready to visit Londonderry for a fortnight's exercises with the Western Approaches Anti-Submarine Training Base. Arriving off Moville in Eire at the mouth of the River Foyle after a night passage, a boat from *Philante,* Sopwith's yacht, now headquarters ship, came alongside to collect Sam, who later returned with a sheaf of exercise orders; we returned to sea, followed later by an escort group of a destroyer and six corvettes, and spent ten days acting as their target dived by day and surfaced at night. Using deep diving and silent running tactics, we endeavoured to make life for our hunters as difficult as possible. The opportunity of having a U-boat rather than a British submarine added zest to their endeavours.

On completion, we sailed seventeen miles up the narrow and winding River Foyle to Londonderry. We passed Boom Hall, site of the chain boom sealing the channel during the siege of Londonderry and now a Wrennery. Being tidal right up to the city and beyond, care was needed to turn in good time before coming alongside on a flood tide. To be pinioned against the bridge by the tide, and spat upon by a cheerful horde of ragged children, had been the fate of several careless newly qualified COs in their first command. The submarine base there, Transatlantic Shed, lay close downstream of the bridge, well beyond the Guildhall, the centre of the city, and the riverside berths of frigates and corvettes in escort groups training for convoy protection against U-boat attack. On its other side was the Derry terminus of the Emmett single track railway to Enniskillen.

Wartime Derry was sheer joy, offering dances, Wrens and other activities at the Allied Officers' Club, railway trips to Buncrana in Donegal where rationing was unknown, Guinness flowed and one could order one or two-egg steaks, the size measured by the area covered by one or two fried eggs without overlapping, while smuggling trips of unrationed chocolates, sugar, nylon stockings and other scarce commodities on the train back were usually successful. From the city wall beside the cathedral and high above the town one could look down at the Bogside, unaware of the civic strife to follow: poor beautiful Derry.

Returning once more to the Clyde, a new cobweb of cracks appeared in a main engine casting. Two civilians from Naval Intelligence Division awaited our return alongside *Forth*, confirmation that Sam's proposals to join a U-boat pack were receiving serious consideration.

While further efforts to be made to weld the engines were awaited, *Graph* spent a couple of days at the Loch Goil sound range. Sam went ashore to listen, leaving me to dive the boat without him. By a phone connection to the shore we were told to run different motors and pumps, open and shut vents and valves, sound klaxons and alarm bells, talk loudly, stop and start the gyro, put up and down periscopes so allowing a study of detectable sounds under varying conditions of range and water noise to be made. Most U-boat machinery was mounted on buna, ersatz rubber, to deaden sound.

On one of these trips to the range, a press artist specialising in sectional diagrams was embarked, a very demanding gentleman who emphasised the importance of meeting deadlines and of his catching a train from Gourock back to London. As he became more and more insistent how calamitous it would be if he missed it and how important was his part in getting his magazine to press, we decided to test this out by concluding our exercise and returning to Tail of the Bank just in time to allow him to watch his train steam out opposite. His magazine appeared as usual without apparent difficulty.

Two cheerful staff officers arrived while Sam was on leave to announce that, with our help, they proposed to sabotage us. We worked out the most accessible inlets on which to attach demolition charges and these were then photographed; we gathered that a commando raid on submarine pens on the Continent was under consideration. John P. Monk, *Daily Mirror*'s Buck Ryan series artist, arrived to draw people in and based on *Forth*, among them Brigham Young the coxswain, and Lieutenant "Puck" Durham of "Giraffe", later to appear in a copy of "Good Morning", a daily paper for submariners produced free by the *Daily Mirror*. Boats would leave for patrol with a few sets of daily "Good Mornings" and one copy would be issued to each mess daily, welcome compensation for the lack of daily papers, and an imaginative gesture.

One day, in deep water off Arran, *Graph* was taken gently down to 500 feet, a far greater depth than was deemed safe in comparable British submarines of the time. Apart from the less watertight stern glands which leaked far faster, the probable reason for the extremely large capacity bilge in a U-boat's stern compartment, she behaved perfectly. Then, a Russian submarine of the L-class was due alongside *Forth*. Unfortunately, *Sokol*, a British U-class submarine handed over to the Poles, was in harbour. Her CO made clear that he feared trouble should his men meet Russians, so unhappily she was banished to a distant buoy during their stay. *L11* was a minelaying submarine of considerable size and was open to visitors while alongside.

The mines were laid from two parallel large diameter pipes in her stern. Off her long dingy grey painted control room lay nine individual cabins. The largest belonged to the political Commissar, with a smaller cabin for the Captain, who, it seemed, was required to defer to the latter in all operational decisions; this and the unwieldiness of the boat might explain why, despite their Murmansk base being so close to the German anchorage off Alten Fjord, patrols there were left entirely to British controlled submarines. Apart from Baltic operations by small coastal submarines, our Russian allies were noticeable for their absence from Atlantic waters.

Sadly, it proved impossible to repair the engine castings and *Graph* was removed from the operational list until she could undergo a full dockyard refit. Sam Marriott was replaced as CO and left to join an S-class submarine building at Cammel Laird's yard in Birkenhead. His replacement, Shaver Swanson, who

The crew of *Graph* (ex *U570*) alongside their depot ship, February 1943.

had earlier served as Number One in *Graph* and left for a perisher, now returned as Captain. His attitude was a great deal more relaxed and, as a married man, he spent most nights ashore, leaving me to cope with the extra responsibility, which by now I had sufficient experience to handle.

Because of a shortage of wireless equipment, we were sailed to Barrow where Vickers removed our British equipment fitted for operational patrols and replaced our original German sets. Returning to the Clyde, we lay at a buoy while a tug towed us slowly round and round transmitting on their normal frequencies to exercise and allow calibration of various shore D/F stations which operated in the detection of U-boat positions in the Atlantic.

By early June it was decided that *Graph* should proceed for an extensive refit in Chatham dockyard, with anti-U-boat plan abandoned. Behind a trawler escort, we sailed through the Pentland Firth down to the Firth of Tay where a further setback was to be suffered.

Dundee was the shore base of the Allied Submarine Flotilla, made up of French, Dutch, Danish, Norwegian and Polish submarines, whose unfortunate British Captain S/M had the unenviable task of maintaining international discipline. How does he punish a French stoker, who in a private fight with a Norwegian cook, has inadvertently knocked out the Dutch ERA who attempted to separate them, particularly when the French stoker does not speak English?

Because U-boat diesel engines were remarkable in being reversible, Shaver decided to enter the dock through its narrow entrance on to the tideway using engines rather than motors. The delay from changing from going ahead to going astern with diesel power was greater than that with electric motors. In the strong ebb tide he turned towards the entrance too soon and when it was clear *Graph* would not be able to negotiate the gap, it took too long for the reversed engines to stop us before, with an almighty thump, the drowned starboard hydroplane hit the stone jetty to starboard bringing us up all standing. Backing away, engine clutches were released and a safe entry made on the motors. When a diver later examined the hydroplane its 6-inch diameter steel shaft was so severely bent that the after edge of the plane had ground against the hull, fortunately without causing the gland to leak. Yet another major repair was added to the length of the refit list.

Shipping steaming up and down the east coast was subject to air, E-boat and occasionally U-boat attack and it was thought too risky to sail *Graph* on her own with an escort independently. Instead we were added to the tail of a regular convoy with our own trawler escort. As a deterrent to low flying aircraft, several of the coasters in the convoy that we joined flew barrage balloons. These failed to deter a covey of Heinkel 111s who flew in low off Scarborough, dropped their bombs on the convoy without hitting anything and were away before anyone could open fire. Everyone was alert to E-boat attack. These fast torpedo boats were apt to tie up to a navigational buoy to avoid detection till, with a roar of engines, they would attack a passing convoy, fire torpedoes and turn away. Our convoy escaped. Then at dusk, wave on wave of heavy bombers rumbled overhead bound from their East Anglian bases for the Continent. Sadly, later in the night a single plane approaching the convoy from the east was shot down by an escorting corvette, only to prove to be a damaged bomber trying to limp home.

Entering the Thames estuary next morning, we all felt grateful not to have to face the uncertain ordeal of the coasters regularly sailing in convoy up and down the east coast.

Berthed out of the way at an isolated jetty in Chatham dockyard, a month of indecision about *Graph*'s future followed, with dockyard staff insisting that the time and labour involved in repairing *Graph* equalled that needed to refit ten British submarines, where spare parts were available. While refit conferences sat, adjourned and sat again, those of the crew not on leave continued the commissionaire work of showing visitors round a real live (well nearly) U-boat. A visit by a very senior Wren officer (three rings, no less) provided me and the sub with the chance to plead successfully the granting of an all-night leave pass for two of her Wrens normally required back in barracks by midnight: dancing in a sleazy Soho night club and contented sleepy return to Chatham next morning in the milk train was the happy result. When at last the dockyard took over and the refit started, only a skeleton care and maintenance crew remained and the rest of us were despatched on leave to await new appointments.

Subsequently, *Graph*'s refit started, stopped and started again, only to be abandoned till in 1944 on tow to a scrapyard, she broke adrift from her tug to be wrecked on rocks off Islay, a far better end for her than the knacker's yard.

My next U-boat encounter was taking over with a Polish boarding party the first one to surrender after VE Day. Filmed by a whirr of news cameras we sailed her into Portland Harbour. Soon after, Sam, I and several other *Graph* veterans were to sail one up the Thames to Westminster Pier.

CHAPTER 12

Working up in Stoic

AFTER ONLY A WEEK ON LEAVE, on 2nd July 1943 I was phoned at home by a Wren officer on Flag Officer Submarines' staff. She informed me that the First Lieutenant of a newly commissioned S-class submarine had fallen sick and I was to join the night train to Glasgow that evening to take over from him. Security regulations did not allow her to name the submarine on the phone but, in reply to my enquiry of her Captain's name, I was told it was Lieutenant P.B. Marriott. So, Sam and I were to be reunited after four months.

Next morning, a picket boat from the depot ship *Forth* in the Holy Loch collected me from Greenock pier. Alongside her lay *Stoic* in pristine grey paint. Once my gear was safely stowed in a depot ship cabin, I descended the port ladder and crossed the plank for a quick look. On deck, greasing the 3-inch gun was a scruffy overalled AB, cap flat aback with a cigarette drooping from his lips. Without even stopping work, he gave a surly reply to my query whether the First Lieutenant was aboard: not a promising start. Down the hatch in the fore-ends I joined hands working on torpedoes and, moving aft to the wardroom, met Number One, a cheerful Canadian, very fed up at having to leave. He had been diagnosed as suffering from TB after several months' standing by the boat while it completed fitting out in Cammel Laird's yard.

After arranging an afternoon takeover of stores, electrics, trimming, rum and numerous other details, we climbed back up to the depot ship wardroom to meet Sam and, after a quick gin with him, to find the rest of *Stoic*'s officers.

The navigating officer needed no introduction. Subby Pratt (despite promotion to lieutenant RNR, he remained Subby) was the navigator who had taken over from me in *Graph* when I became First Lieutenant. Small, rotund, reliable, hard working and harder drinking, Subby was good news. The fourth hand, Prosper Dowden, a real RNR sub-lieutenant this time, with a morose and lugubrious visage, had been a *Daily Mirror* reporter before the war, hated the popular press vehemently, wrote poetry and regarded Subby and me as frivolous and somewhat irresponsible. Last, but by no means least, there was George Herbert, the warrant engineer. Chiefy, in his first operational appointment after promotion from Chief ERA, was a cheerful and competent engineer, with a rather slow sheepish smile and a little too great a liking for whisky, which had given him a thick speech even when perfectly sober. He and Subby could usually be found with glasses in their hands before lunch or in the evenings. They contained either "something to warm one up" in cold weather or "something to cool the blood" when it was hot. Sweltering in equatorial heat or freezing in the Arctic, the contents of their glasses did not vary.

Finding myself once more in a situation without training or experience on how to carry out my job, I was grateful for the support those officers gave me. Here I was in a modern British submarine, with totally different handling systems from either the First World War *L26* in which I had served only three weeks or the German U-boat *Graph*. Once more I had to get down to follow out different trimming, air and electrical layouts, with insufficient time to understand them before I would have to try to make use of them. I was to be allowed only one day's exercise at sea as a passenger before taking over.

Next morning, harbour stations closed up and *Stoic* sailed to exercise in Kilbrannan sound between Bute and Arran in the Firth of Clyde. There the crew practised diving and surfacing, closing up for gun action, torpedo attack drill and various breakdowns. When the boat first dived I was able to watch how my predecessor, whom I was to relieve that evening, trimmed the boat. In *Graph*, there were two separate and unconnected trimming systems. To adjust the weight of the U-boat to equal that of the water it displaced, there was a central tank into or out of which water could be flooded or pumped. Then, to ensure that neither bow nor stern was heavier, a trim pump could move water fore or aft along a separate trim line to achieve equilibrium. The British method, however, was to make a combined adjustment of both displacement and fore and aft movement using one main line either to flood in or pump out water to fore, midship or aft tanks.

In control of trimming, the First Lieutenant stood facing a box above the depth gauge, which could order the pumping or flooding of the chosen tank. Seated in front of him were the coxswain and second coxswain controlling fore and aft hydroplanes facing bubbles and indicators showing their planes' position. When the klaxon sounded to dive the boat, engine clutches would be taken out and the main electric motors would each be run at half ahead, thus giving sufficient speed to allow the planes to be effective. The fore planes would be moved to a dived position to force down the boat. As the bubble moved aft, the after planes would be moved parallel to the fore planes till the boat could be steadied and levelled off at periscope depth. It was then possible to judge whether the boat was heavy or light and to pump or flood the necessary tanks. Gradually, the planes would be less and less needed to maintain depth, the speed could be progressively reduced until the boat was in satisfactory trim, neither light nor heavy even at slow speed. On completion, after returning alongside an inner berth ready to load torpedoes from *Forth* next day, my predecessor sadly said goodbye with a curt "all yours".

I found myself alone in the wardroom contemplating my inadequate training to tackle what lay ahead and studying the trim book, in which had to be worked out, before sailing, the contents of each tank, allowing for any alterations in weight aboard. A considerable adjustment would be needed for the twelve torpedoes forward and one aft which were to be loaded next day.

While torpedoes were being lowered by crane from the depot ship to slide down rails through the fore hatch to the tubes and reload storage below, I had a chance to size up our crew. On the whole, what I saw cheered me. CPO Wales, the Scots coxswain, was quiet but sufficiently forceful to stand no nonsense. In charge of torpedoes was a wise old three badge petty officer, respected by the fore-end men under him and as familiar with a torpedo's byways as a cockney cabby with London streets. Ryder, the outside ERA, tall, slim and well spoken was a gem and utterly reliable. His job under two masters, Chief and First Lieutenant, was of vital importance to the safe handling of the boat under water. Hydroplanes and main vents were controlled by telemotor pressure, while surfacing depended on sufficient high pressure air groups being available and connected to the panel. These and all machinery outside the engine room were his responsibility. Jock Smith, with a broad Scottish accent, despite coming from Newcastle, who was HSD responsible for Asdics, and the PO Telegraphist were both reliable and competent, while Chiefy Herbert seemed happy enough with his engine room staff. That left the PO LTO with charge of motor room watches and the maintenance of the 240 half-ton cells in the two batteries. This petty officer had a tendency to be surly, offhand and unwilling to be corrected or told anything, and it was clear that he would need to be firmly handled. Finally, the gunnery department was under the sloppy individual who had given me such an unhappy impression when first coming aboard. He might have to learn the hard way.

By evening we had loaded our torpedoes, each fitted with a blowing head to bring it to the surface on completion of its firing run. These were to be our first outfit and, on satisfactory conclusion of our practice firing, would be returned to the depot ship, routined, fitted with warheads and then returned to us ready for our working up patrol off the Norwegian coast. First, however, they had to be fired for practice and thus we found ourselves next day at the torpedo trial range at the head of Loch Long.

A trials team came aboard to check that the tube firing gear was in working order before we carried out a trim dive. Main vents were opened and, if all my calculations of the water to be put in each tank were correct, we would settle happily at thirty-two feet. Not this time however: at twenty-six feet we seemed stuck and, despite speeding up to full speed with both planes hard-a-dive, failed to get any further down. I was flooding through the main line as hard as I could, having been forbidden during our working up period to open kingston valves to allow emergency flooding. It took nearly twenty minutes to achieve a rough trim. I had applied my calculations to allow for torpedoes being embarked the wrong way and thus finishing up with the amidship's trimming tanks full. We had to surface while the Stoker PO pumped 1,000 gallons out amidships and added 500 gallons each end. Not an auspicious start. Sam, showing remarkable restraint, remarked that such things did happen in working up boats but it was not to be repeated. Did I detect sniggers amongst some of the control room crew?

Belatedly, we dived for the first firing run. No.1 tube was flooded and brought to the ready. Time and pressure recorders were fitted and the firing reservoir charged with compressed air. The report "No. 1 tube ready" was passed by phone to the control room. On reaching the firing position marked by a buoy, the Captain ordered, "Fire One". After a moment's pause there was a thud, the boat gave a shudder, then a hiss of escaping air sounded from forward and the increase of pressure could be felt on the eardrums. The Asdic operator, once he heard the rattle of the torpedo engine, reported, "Torpedo running". Blowing main ballast, we surfaced to watch for the torpedo surfacing at the end of its run to be retrieved by the torpedo recovery vessel waiting at the end of the range. This was then all repeated five more times until each torpedo had been fired.

All next day was spent working at, round and about torpedoes. The reload fish had to be heaved into the drained down tubes before the previous day's torpedoes were re-embarked and lowered down rails to replace in the racks those we had just loaded.

The following morning broke fine when a full salvo of six torpedoes was to be fired, an anxiety for several of us. The torpedo officer with the TI had to be sure each fish was properly prepared with the right valves opened, the igniters properly cocked, the gyro correct and various other details checked. Neglect of any of these precautions could lead to faulty running. I had, without practice, to hold the boat down, if necessary speeding up to avoid breaking surface at this most critical time. It was a rule that any working up submarine which broke surface while firing her salvo must repeat the firing later, a most unpopular extra task delaying the working up patrol and the chance to become fully operational.

As we set off down the loch to our diving position Sam ordered down the voice pipe from the bridge "Open up for diving".

Pressure must be raised on the telemotor system before steel cotterpins are removed from the main vents, air bottle groups have to be connected to the blowing panel, kingston valves at the bottom of some tanks opened and all valves on the main line checked shut. Sea water density is taken, battery ventilation valves shut and foreplanes, which are folded flat in harbour, turned out and tested. Finally, Q tank, the quick diving tank of five-ton capacity to speed the boat on its descent, is flooded. Once all these details have been checked, Number One reports the boat ready for diving.

Soon "Diving Stations" are ordered, the signalman bearing ensign staff and ensign comes below, and the Captain, pressing the klaxon twice, shuts the hatch and clatters down the ladder to the control room. Engines are stopped, clutches removed and the main motors put at half ahead both. Their hum seems quiet after the noisy rattle of the diesel engines. The outside ERA, after pulling the levers to open main vents, starts a second telemotor pump. Outside the low roaring of air from the external tanks slowly ceases and the boat, encouraged by the planes which both coxswain and second coxswain have put to dive, takes a bow down angle as the depth gauge needle is moving: ten . . . twelve . . . fifteen feet.

An experienced first lieutenant will by now have an idea what corrections to trim are needed and will start pumping or flooding, forward amidships or aft as required. At twenty feet the Captain will order, "Open Q kingston. Blow Q." There is a clomp as the telemotor controlled kingston valve opens and air hisses into the tank. A few seconds later an indicator lamp flashes, blowing ceases and the kingston valve is shut. On the order, "Vent Q inboard," air escapes with a roar into the control room. The vented air has a musty salt smell and ears pop. Finer adjustments to the trim allow the boat to slow down, conserving valuable battery capacity.

As we approached the firing buoy, the Captain ordered, "Stand by, all tubes." Being already flooded all that was needed was to open bow caps and charge up the firing reservoirs to the correct air pressure. One after another the tube ready indicator lights glowed on the firing order panel. There was tension in the control room. Forward, the helmsman with the telephone operator perched beside him kept course with the slightest wheel movements. Jock sat listening in his earphones as he trained round the Asdic. Leaning intently over the plotting table, the navigator, dividers in hand, called out the distance to go to the firing point from the check periscope bearings which the Captain gave him from time to time. On the panel behind the two periscopes the outside ERA stood alert and ready, watching air and telemotor pressure, while his mate, wheel spanner in hand, worked the periscope hoist for the Captain, ready to hoist or lower it to avoid more than the minimum breaking surface.

The port side of the control room was occupied by the trimming team: coxswain seated in front of the after plane control wheel, facing a large depth gauge and bubble to show the angle of the boat; beside him on his right, the second coxswain faced similar controls for the fore planes under the indicator light FORE PLANES TURNED OUT; and above them myself, as First Lieutenant, leaning back on the conning tower ladder and anxiously tapping the depth gauge to detect the least flicker of the needle up or down, whispering orders to planesmen if necessary. Above it the pump order instrument gave alternatives of PUMP, FLOOD and STOP as well as FORWARD and AFT.

Should the boat show signs of being light, a little water could be flooded in; meanwhile the periscope must be watched to see that only a little was showing above the surface. More alarming was a tendency to be heavy as, below thirty-five feet, the periscope would be dipped even when fully hoisted. This was as great a crime as breaking surface, because it prevented the Captain from seeing the target and knowing when to fire torpedoes. How well I was to get to know Sam's anguished and ferocious cry of, "Don't dip me, Number One." as the tops of waves started to lap over the periscope glass. Controlling depth in rough weather left little margin between the Scylla of breaking surface and the Charybdis of dipping the Captain.

However, in the calm water of Loch Long there was no enemy to miss, merely much extra work to face should the firing be unsuccessful.

"Stand by," ordered Sam. Then "Fire One," - wham h'sssss.

"Half ahead together. Full dive fore planes," I ordered.

"Torpedo running," from Asdics. The bow started to rise.

"Fire Two" - another shudder and pressure on the eardrums.

Thirty-one feet; bubble moving forward. The bow was coming up. I signalled to the periscope workers to lower it slowly. It hissed down gently till a flick of the Captain's hand stopped it.

"Fire Three." Thirty feet, bubble still forward.

"Full ahead together." The telegraphs clanged round together, each with a different toned gong.

"More dive after planes." Twenty-nine feet, bubble moving aft.

"Fire Four," from Sam. "Group up if necessary, Number One." Twenty–eight feet, bubble one degree aft. We'd got the bow down at last.

"Fire Five." Twenty-nine feet, bubble two degrees aft.

"Level her off, coxswain. Less dive, fore planes."

"Holding her, Sir," I reported to Sam.

"Fire Six." Thirty-two feet, bow still down. "Rise fore planes, hold her up."

I put the pump indicator to pump forward, as we appeared to be bow heavy, and just avoided dipping the periscope. The Asdics had reported each torpedo running, so all would appear to have been well.

"Whew, well that's that!" said Sam. "Check main vents, Number One." This order is a precaution to be sure that the main vents are shut before surfacing, as otherwise the air blown into the ballast tanks would merely bubble out at the top. I reported all main vents checked shut.

"Surface."

"Blow One. Blow Three." The valve gave a jar as the outside ERA opened the blows to tanks One and Three. There was a throaty hiss as the air flowed into the tanks.

"Blow Four." The bow is coming up.

"Stop blowing One." She lists a shade to port.

"Stop blowing Four starboard."

As she levelled, "Stop blowing." The shriek of compressed air ceased, and gave way to the lapping of water on the hull.

The Captain meanwhile, had gone up the conning tower followed by the signalman. The latter clasped his hands firmly round the Skipper's legs and the ladder as he removed first one and then both clips. As the hatch flew open, there was a whoosh of air up the conning tower as all the extra pressure from Q and the tubes escaped above. Unless the Captain is held, there is a danger of his being blown out, and the Captain of a British submarine was tragically lost in this way off Norway.

As soon as the water from the voice pipe had been drained down into a bucket, Sam passed an order from the bridge to put in engine clutches and then to go half ahead together to follow up our torpedoes. Several could be seen, red noses up, above the lopping little waves looking, except for the stream of bubbles foaming at the side of each, like bobbing buoys. One torpedo had steered about twenty degrees to the left of the rest and was a few hundred yards from them. Eventually all six had been safely spotted, and the torpedo officer and the TI were informed, much, I am sure, to their great relief.

Following a successful dance arranged by the ship's company in Arrochar Hall that evening, *Stoic* returned to the Holy Loch to complete working up. Much practice was possible alongside the depot ship which contained a torpedo attack teacher worked by Wrens on which the attack team could practise on realistic looking targets in a dummy conning tower fitted with periscope, fruit machine, navigating table and Asdic. There was a spotting table as well, to allow gunnery control practice, complete with resulting shell splashes short, over or straddle, right or left resulting from the orders given. Wireless and Asdic operators could practise and cipher officers train on deciphering dummy messages. Aboard the boat, guns crews could practise using solid shells.

The fourth hand usually acted as gunnery officer but, because of my gunnery experience and interest, Sam was happy for me to tackle this job as well as my normal duties. While drilling at the 3-inch gun on the fore casing it was not long before, not unexpectedly, the gun layer proved slapdash and slack in obeying orders. Loudly, in front of the gun's crew, he was threatened with the Captain's Report if he failed to improve. Seemingly dazed in disbelief, he staggered back against the guard rail and made as if to protest, but thought better of it. The resultant marked improvement in his performance thereafter led to drill at the gun soon reaching an acceptable standard.

However, in a submarine, there is a lot more to efficient gun action than firing a gun. First, the gun's crew have to reach it from down below as soon as the boat has broken surface. In the wardroom a ladder to the bottom of the gun tower must replace an upper bunk while shells are brought up from the magazine. Then, once the casing breaks surface, the hatch must be opened, three men climb up, gun layer and trainer each carrying telescopes to ship in gun brackets, sights then set and the gun elevated and trained on to the target. While this is being done, a supply of ammunition has to be hoisted up through the hatch from below, collected, loaded and the breech shut. Speed is essential and much practice needed to cut down the seconds until within less than a minute from breaking surface the first round can be fired. All movement must be carried out "at the rush".

Sometimes the target may prove too formidable, as was to happen later in the Java Sea, or an enemy aircraft may be sighted or, for some other reason, it is necessary to crash dive. Then the gun's crew have to get below before sea water can lap over an open gun tower hatch with disastrous results. Speed here is even more vital. Men have to learn to pile down the ladder, one foot either side sliding down without using the rungs. It was made clear that tramped-on knuckles was proof of failure to drop fast enough. The gun's crew were aware that, during every gun drill, there would be an unexpected order of "Dive" with a stop-watch started. Gradually, accompanied by such sarcastic shouts as, "Do you think this is a nursery school?" seconds were knocked off the time before all were safely below with the hatch shut.

Last down were always gun layer and trainer who had first to train the gun fore and aft and unslip telescopes. In encouragement I would, from time to time, pile down after them, jumping on top of anyone seeming slow. Gradually, we knocked off seconds and the men seemed quite to enjoy the challenge. One day, however, coming down last, I accidentally stamped on the gun layer's knuckles. Later that evening the coxswain informed me that Able Seaman Smith had put in a request to see the Captain with a complaint that the First Lieutenant had intentionally kicked him. I summoned Smith, told him I should forward his request to the Captain but warned him that, should the Captain view the complaint as frivolous, he would be liable to punishment.

After investigation next day, Sam told him that he was welcome to leave the boat and be replaced if he wished. Soon after, a crestfallen gun layer asked to be allowed to withdraw his complaint and stay. The coxswain had already made clear that Smith's shipmates shared my irritation. We had little further trouble with the chastened gun layer.

Following the well established working up routine, we exercised first in the Firth of Clyde practising torpedo attacks, with a smoke candle released to indicate firing, carrying out a gunnery shoot, and a deep dive to 350 feet, and also exercising Asdic in mine detection on the dummy minefield laid for the purpose and undergoing sound trial at the Loch Goil range. Then, based at Scapa, where we were just too late for a fleet visit from the King, who had signed *Stonehenge*'s visitors' book a few days earlier, we acted as a Home Fleet destroyer target; next morning to Larne for further exercises with escort groups training for the continuing Atlantic battle to protect convoys from U-boat attack.

Our ten week working-up period complete, we awaited orders for our first patrol. Before this, however, we sailed to Campbeltown where we embarked three officers, two naval and one army. Earlier, two of our reload torpedoes had been replaced by folboats, light canvas canoes of similar length to a torpedo. Now, at sea, we began to practise in daylight the opening of the fore hatch, a far larger hole than either conning tower or gun tower hatches, the heaving up from below of the folboats and equipment and their preparation for launching. Our early attempts were noisy with much shouting as the folboats jammed on obstructions below, while the timing stop watch showed it took over twenty minutes to complete the operation, with the fore hatch open for more than five before it could be shut again. This time-lapse gradually reduced till we were able to hoist and launch the folboats in four minutes with the hatch open for less than two. After supper, in pitch darkness, we continued the activity, showing no light, finally launching canoes for a short paddle before a timed return alongside, up and back down below with, again, the hatch open for less than two minutes. Exhausted by these endeavours at anchor, everyone turned in, some on camp beds, for a well earned sleep. In compensation, next day, the crew was given a make and mend while Sam and visitors busily studied the chart, noting angles, distances and bearings in preparation for that night's beach reconnaissance.

After a few glasses with our guests in the wardroom and a late supper, anchor was weighed at midnight and we sailed north about two miles offshore till we reached the position off the bay that COPP10 were to survey. These Combined Operations Pilotage Parties were designed to obviate problems like that met by *Bachaquero* when, attempting to land troops in Courier Bay during our attack on Diego Suarez in Madagascar eighteen months earlier, an uncharted obstruction prevented her reaching the planned landing place. They hoped to carry out undetected surveys of the angle and composition of beaches and to discover any likely obstructions to landing.

Stoic turned slowly to close the shore on the motors. The night was dark and moonless and even the stars were hidden in a blanket of cloud. Then we stopped and the whispered order, "Launch folboats" was given. Climbing over the bridge down to the fore casing, I heard the padded thump of the fore hatch opening. Gym shoe wearing fore-end men jumped up followed by the face and hand-blackened landing party. The two canoes were hauled through the hatch and lowered over the sides into the water, the sound of the splash lost in that of waves lapping the saddle tanks. Equipment gathered, their crews successfully dropped catlike in turn over the gun rails into their easily capsizable and bouncing craft. With a whispered farewell they paddled off and were soon lost amongst the wave tops. *Stoic* turned away, then dived to sit peacefully on the sandy bottom till, ninety minutes later, it was time to re-surface and search from half a mile offshore for the flash of a light from the returning canoes.

A short, sharp sea had risen to lop against the seaward saddle tank. With a light drizzle reducing visibility, nothing was spotted till, after half an hour of vain searching, alongside without warning bobbed the two folboats. Catching heaving lines thrown from the casing and attaching them, the paddlers climbed out to help heave up their fragile craft. The fore hatch was opened and, faster than in earlier practices, men and folboats were below and the hatch clanked shut allowing the boat to sink below once more to the sounds of air expressed from ballast tanks and of butterfly clips being hammered tight.

Waves had been breaking heavily and one canoe had capsized when our commandos landed on the beach that they were to survey. After making measurements and taking samples, they found themselves unable to make any headway into the breaking surf, so had to re-beach and move along the shore till a rocky outcrop gave them sufficient shelter to get clear and paddle furiously to seaward. As a result, their course to reach the rendezvous required re-calculation, no easy task in a bumping folboat with only a swinging magnetic compass for navigation and it was great relief to sight *Stoic*'s dark shape above the lopping waves.

Stoic's crest (I stand fast)

Surfacing at dawn revealed an overcast sky as we hastened back to the security of the Holy Loch before the gale broke. With mutual expressions of esteem, COPP 10 departed leaving us to prepare for patrol.

Torpedoes, fitted now with warheads, had to be routined and loaded, the magazine filled with a full complement of both 3-inch and Oerlikon shells, batteries topped up, the distilled water tank filled, charts and navigation aids brought up to date, rum and provisions for two months embarked and stored and, at the last minute, fresh bread, meat, milk, butter and fish collected. Then, following a last whole night's sleep in a comfortable depot ship cabin, we sailed in company behind an escort to Lerwick and, next day, with fuel and fresh provisions topped up, were off north to patrol off the Vaagsfjord, the very entrance to Harstad which had been *Echo*'s base in May 1940 during the attack on Narvik.

I had remembered the tall Andenes Lighthouse at the tip of a low spit of land guarding the entrance and now was to use it for fourteen days to fix our position when on watch. There were a few excitements, once when a small ferry crossed close to us and again when the Asdic reported propeller noises despite no vessel being seen. One night the normally darkened light flashed from the lighthouse for a couple of hours and we had unfulfilled hopes of a target. Meanwhile the cipher officer became more and more unhappy as we received a series of messages on long wave radio from Rugby which he was quite unable to decipher. Only on return to base did we discover these were connected with the midget submarine attack in progress on *Tirpitz* further north which effectively disabled her.

We were among several submarines patrolling possible exits of German warships as a result of that raid. Then a signal ordered us and two other submarines to sail south at best speed to appointed positions to patrol near Kya Lighthouse guarding the entrance to Trondheim. Diving at first light two days later we closed the lighthouse at periscope depth. Nothing was seen before our later recall to berth alongside in Lerwick harbour. A number of our crew visited a dance ashore, of whom one or two celebrated their first submarine patrol a little unwisely and had difficulty negotiating the plank back aboard. It was low tide, making the descent at a steep angle precipitous. In the wardroom we were entertaining the Commander from our escort vessel to a post-prandial drink or two. From time to time the duty officer would be called by the trot sentry to assist in heaving out of the water a returning libertyman who had failed safely to cross the plank and fallen in.

Our guest, a retired officer of World War One vintage recalled to service, was scornful of the sad inability of the modern sailor to hold his drink. A number of gins later our guest, a little unsteadily, rose to return to his ship. Politely, we followed him up the fore hatch to the casing from which the plank climbed precipitously up to the jetty with just a single lifeline. The plank swayed as he started up it, his left hand holding the lifeline tight. Half-way up, missing his footing, he slithered sideways while grabbing the lifeline with both hands. The extra weight on the lifeline was too great; it sagged, and our guest was left suspended ankle deep in oily sea water till he managed to sprawl on all fours and land on the safety of the saddle tank. Heaving him up to the casing with nothing said, with squelching footsteps he made a successful second try to climb up to the jetty and away without further comment. World War Two officers controlled their glee with some difficulty.

In preparation for joining an operational flotilla, a few days' leave was granted in two watches. While Sam was away on his, a spare CO took over to take us up the Clyde on a Sunday to dry dock at Govan. Once safely moored inside with the dock gate shut, pumping out began.

Submarines in dock, with only a narrow keel and a circular hull, require to be well supported by tightly wedged timber supports. Waiting on the jetty to position these large baulks were about eighty dockyard maties. They were not an impressive sight, lolling against bollards, some playing cards, others reeling about drunk and only about a dozen showing any sign of helping to tow the floating supports into position. On the fore casing our crew watched in frustration and requested permission to help, but when the works overseer was approached he warned that if one of our men were to make as much as a move to assist, the whole squad, who were being paid double time, would down tools and walk off on strike. With over twice as many available as were needed to do the job, it took twice as long as it should. So much for working hard for Victory in November 1943, as the posters urged.

In addition to the usual work in dock, removing weed and barnacles from the hull, scraping and repainting it, replacing zinc blocks, checking propellers for dents or chips which could cause them to sing and betray the boat's presence, adjusting the Asdic set, and checking underwater valves, *Stoic* had fitted experimental laminated plastic propeller, hydroplane and rudder bearings in place of the more traditional self-lubricating lignum vitae. Shafts required to be withdrawn so that their bearings could be checked for wear and, if necessary, replaced.

Out of dock, with leave complete and men kitted up with tropical rig, *Stoic* sailed south from the Clyde bound for Portsmouth. When in bright winter sunshine harbour stations were piped, there to starboard lay the shining white finger of the war memorial beside the deserted Southsea funfair, seeming strangely out of place amidst anti-aircraft batteries, barrage balloons and Napoleonic war fortifications. Once through the narrow channel with, on one side, houses on the Portsmouth shore jostling for position, so tightly crammed they seemed to risk leaning out too far and splashing into the harbour, and the modern red barrack building of Fort Blockhouse on the other, and, after giving way to a clanking chain car ferry, we turned west to come alongside and secure to the jetty in Blockhouse Creek.

Dolphin, that establishment of modern buildings, with a tall submarine escape tower amidst the solid fortifications built to resist French invasion a century and a half earlier, was where in peacetime Admiral Submarines flew his flag before moving in wartime with his staff to London, and also the training depot for submarine crews. Opposite lay *Vernon*, the torpedo school, and the burnt out remains of Portsmouth Harbour station, well remembered from our sub-lieutenants' courses during the blitz.

Over the next week, more and more piles of equipment were delivered to the jetty. There were twelve pistons and liners for diesel engine cylinder replacement, armatures and other electrical gear, valves, tool boxes, and engineering spares of all sorts and sizes. The coxswain and I became more and more convinced that stowing all this away within the limited confines of an S-class submarine was well nigh impossible but, by turning the leading seamen out of their mess and building a false deck of boxes, we somehow managed to cram it all in.

In addition, we painted ship. The accepted colour for Mediterranean submarines was a dark blue but, this being unavailable, we were able to sport a vivid bright royal blue, midway twixt Oxford and Cambridge. Gone was the dirty grey of northern climes, here was the exotic colour of Mediterranean blue sea, a feast for the eye amidst the cold winter hues of home waters.

Before we sailed a fifth executive officer joined. This would allow two hours "on" and six hours "off" instead of the normal two "on" and four "off" possible with only three watchkeepers. Joe had recently completed three months in a training submarine and this was his first operational appointment. Married young, with his home in the Isle of Wight, we allowed him two days' leave at once. During his absence we were visited by King Ibn Saud of Saudi Arabia and his brother and foreign minister, noting with amusement a natty pair of pinstriped trousers below his robes as he climbed the conning tower ladder. Our distinguished visitors were accompanied by Admiral Sir Charles Little, C-in-C Portsmouth.

While Sam and I accompanied the royal party, Subby showed Sir Charles around, taking great trouble to explain the equipment simply so that he understood. He was non-plussed when the C-in-C gravely thanked him for explaining everything so clearly adding, with a twinkle, that a lot seemed to have changed since his first submarine command. "And to think I explained to him that the main vents were to allow the air to escape and the boat to dive," ruefully remembered Subby over a large gin when they had left.

Following a farewell cocktail party, *Stoic* sailed southwards.

CHAPTER 13

Eastward Bound in Stoic

AFTER A DIVED DAY IN THE BAY OF BISCAY, in the unfulfilled hope of meeting a U-boat leaving or returning from Brest, *Stoic* proceeded on the surface to Gibraltar. Berthed alongside *Shakespeare*, which was bound for home refit after returning from her final patrol in the Gulf of Lyons, we were allowed to remain and enjoy a traditional Christmas with *The Messiah* sung by service choirs in the cathedral, before sailing on Boxing Day as part of an east bound convoy. For safety, we were stationed between the Commodore's ship and the leading ship of the next column.

Four days later, north of Malta, our convoy split up, some ships sailing to Valetta and others joining other groups, one steering up the west coast of Italy and one up the east coast into the Adriatic: changed days from fifteen months earlier when *Laforey* helped fight the Pedestal convoy to the rescue of besieged Malta. Now, with the demobilised Italian fleet moored in Grand Harbour, Valetta, Allied forces were driving up the Italian mainland north of Naples. After sailing on independently, we found ourselves two hours later out of sight of ship or shore once more.

During my watch before dawn south of the German occupied mountainous Cretan shore, with spray splattering the bridge, the port lookout reported three vertical lights in sight between us and the shore.

Delighted at an opportunity to abandon a miserable wet surface watch, I dived the boat. Perhaps because of the rough sea and water noises Jock, the Asdic Operator, could hear nothing. Half an hour later, with dawn breaking and my watch nearly over, I took the boat up to twenty-eight feet for a really careful periscope search, only to sight a trawler well inshore of us. I called the Captain, who considered it far enough inshore for it to be safe to surface and proceed. As he blew main ballast I was happy to advise my relief to be sure to wrap up well as he'd find the bridge cold and washing down with spray. He was unamused, claiming I had only crash dived as an excuse to escape the unpleasant conditions up top; he may well have been not entirely wrong.

Early in the New Year, 1944, *Stoic* entered Beirut Harbour. Since the torpedoing of *Medway*, depot ship of the First Submarine Flotilla, her replacement *Medway II* was a barracks taken over from the French four miles inshore of the harbour, with only the repair workshops and stores in a warehouse close to the submarine berths. This necessitated considerable transport being available. In addition to regular buses between barracks and jetty, each submarine was allotted its own car with a Lebanese driver. Due to lack of space, submarines were secured bow to the wall, with their sterns secured to buoys, while wooden floating catamarans provided access between them. Also moored inside the harbour were a Greek submarine depot ship and its submarines, a floating dock and numerous caiques and schooners, some of them part of the Levant Schooner Force carrying out raids and reconnaissance amongst the German occupied Dodecanese islands.

It soon became clear what a splendidly happy place and flotilla we had joined. The French were unpopular locally, but the British, who had not discouraged the Syrian controlled Lebanese independence movement, were well liked. The wardroom in a large villa was comfortable, its bar well stocked with, in addition to normal bottles, absurdly cheap local wine, liqueurs and fiery vodka. There was no mistaking those at the breakfast table who had over-indulged in such firewater the night before.

Night life was hectic. The British-controlled Mimosa served bacon and eggs all night and provided exotic over-made-up hostesses with whom to dance. The pleasures they offered in the rooms above the restaurant were never pressed on customers and several unsophisticated souls ate there quite unaware of the establishment's true nature.

Amongst Beirut's numerous night clubs and bars, one of our favourite haunts was Le Bar Russe where we tossed back tiny glasses of neat, good Russian vodka, far purer than the Lebanese variety, between substantial bites of zacouska, of which a fresh plate arrived at the table with each replacement vodka bottle. A Cossack would play his concertina while large, black bearded men sang and danced in wild abandon.

Up in the mountains, Brigham Young, *Graph*'s ex-coxswain, temporarily relieved from sea service, ran the ratings' rest camp. On the slopes of the Lebanon mountains off the main Beirut-Damascus highway there was ski-ing, while officers could arrange trips to Jerusalem or Damascus in their submarine's private car between patrols.

Stoic's future destination was undecided and we should all have been happy to stay and patrol the Greek and Turkish coasts and islands; it was thus with some sadness that the decision was received that we were to continue east. Before sailing there was just sufficient time for Sam, Subby, Joe and me to take a day trip up the coast to Tripoli in our car.

Making an early start, our drive north soon cleared the several miles of primitive wooden and baked mud shacks on the outskirts of Beirut to enter real Phoenicia, little changed by Egyptian, Assyrian, Greek, Roman, Islamic, Crusading and Turkish invasions. The hard-baked, sandy coloured land was dotted by banana, orange and olive groves, small flocks of sheep grazed scruffy vegetation and, in villages, untended goats and donkeys foraged to try to scrape a living, scattering scrappy chickens in their path. The parched landscape seemed to cry out for moisture. Our Jehu of a driver, in stained khaki topee, was wont to remove both hands from the steering wheel to point out places of interest in barely comprehensible English. Every few miles Sam, in the back, would demand he drive more slowly, to little effect as we progressed at a steady 50 mph, tyres screeching round bends and children, chickens and dogs scattering right and left in our path.

Entering one village, the entire population seemed to be gathered on the beach. With relief the driver was ordered to stop and we went down to the foreshore to find out what was afoot. Under the control of a spindly legged, grey-bearded patriach, to the furious barking of dogs, all the fit and able, women and children included, were hauling on the two sides of a seine net which a boat had curved to enclose a fifty yard circle offshore. The bell of the fine meshed net closed as it was hauled up the beach to reveal a few silvery sardine sized fish, a large octopus and a scattering of shellfish and small crabs. The men stood back while the barefooted, dark skinned, drably clothed women gathered the catch in to buckets, discarding the shells but keeping the octopus and crabs. It could well have been the Sea of Galiliee two millennia before.

Soon after leaving this biblical scene, as we drove out of one village our car rounded a bend, where the road narrowed, to meet a ramshackle lorry advancing towards us at an equally furious speed. If both vehicles had braked all would have been well, but our driver, losing his head, accelerated and thus, in scraping past the rapidly approaching lorry, could not avoid hitting, with his near wing, an old Arab woman balancing an earthenware pitcher on her head. The poor lady somersaulted sideways, landing on her head, smashing the pitcher to fragments.

With utter disregard of the victim moaning and bleeding in the dusty gutter, Jehu climbed out to start a furious and vociferous argument with the lorry driver who had climbed down from his cab, leaving us to lift up the woman's head and comfort her. At least she was conscious. With his most compelling and ferocious scowl, Sam sent Jehu off in the car to seek a doctor. Returning after discovering a French doctor in the village, a furious babble of arguing Lebanese was gathered round the village constable who had been summoned. Stopped once more between the old lady and the lorry, again completely blocking the road on a blind bend, Jehu leapt out to join the crowd with everyone screaming at the top of their voices and no one listening.

Contemplatively, Subby remarked it was unlikely to be long before there would be a further crash to occupy the policeman. The doctor was unsure whether the old lady's skull was cracked and recommended a precautionary X-ray in Beirut General Hospital. While this was being discussed, the inevitable second lorry came round the bend running slap into the first. More pandemonium ensued and, while both lorry drivers shouted at the constable, our driver tried, to no avail, to persuade Sam to tell the policeman it was not his fault. He was told in the clearest terms that it would be made clear on our return to Beirut that he shared the blame. Next he refused to allow the old lady into his clean car. I though Sam was about to strike him, so did he because, without further ado, he bundled her into the back seat and with Joe beside him, set off very slowly back to Beirut.

The policeman asked Sam to sign a statement. However, speaking no English and able to write only in Arabic script, he eventually abandoned this demand and allowed the lorries to move. As both lorries were old and battered it was really only our car, with one door jammed shut and the mudguard and wing bent which had suffered real damage.

Facing a long wait, we went exploring and, eventually, in the baking heat, had a swim in the warm sea before drying off on return up the beach.

At last the car returned, the old lady having been kept in hospital, and Jehu, who had taken the chance to get his story in to the naval garage first, seemed to have recovered good spirits while Joe had collected a case of beer and a picnic lunch. Hot and hungry, we decided to turn off the main road as soon as we could find a suitable side road. The surface of the road we found soon deteriorated. Leaving the car, we lugged our lunch basket on up the track, which ran down one side of a steep valley. Just as we were about to stop, a broken down bridge came in sight round a bend in the valley, Sam and I agreed this would be ideal for lunch. Joe and Subby, lugging the heavy lunch basket, were not so enthusiastic. As we rounded the bend further the remains of a Roman aqueduct became clear. Only two of the main arches were complete, with three smaller arches above them, as well as the remains of several more crossing the valley. Nearly 200 feet high, it was a massive construction of huge square blocks of sandstone. Our driver could tell us nothing about it.

After lunch, enlivened by the antics of dozens of lizards on the stones, we made our way back to the car to observe, crossing the dried up water course just short of the modern road bridge, an old high arched stone structure. When we reached it we discovered it to be a perfectly preserved Roman bridge with a cobbled road surface built, like the aqueduct, of interlocking sandstone blocks without any need of cement. Of very similar design and shape as the Telford bridges built in the Scottish Highlands centuries later, it had remained unchanged in the dry Lebanese climate.

As we drove north. Byblos was signposted twenty kilometres ahead. Tripoli being too distant to reach, due to the time lost, and having heard that this town was worth a visit, we decided we would stop there. There was no mistaking it when it came into view as the car topped a rise. Dominated by a solid square stone castle were a few two-storied European houses, a convent and a sprawl of native dwellings, markets and shops. Unlike our deserted valley, Byblos was well aware of its assets and tourist appeal.

Below the castle, through a wicket gate, was a white painted hut with placards advertising postcards, souvenirs and guides in several languages. We eventually found a smartly dressed guide with some English and followed him up a bank to look up at the solid grey castle walls. He pointed out round stones, the remains of earlier Greek pillars, projecting from the foundations. After entering a low portcullis gate, we had to pause in the cool interior to accustom our eyes to the dark before climbing a spiral stair out on to the battlements. The view was breathtaking. Between us and the azure Mediterranean sea lay the remains of an ancient Greek town. Several Doric pillars still stood while others lay around in pieces, some of which had clearly been robbed for the castle foundations. Embedded in the castle wall was a Turkish cannon ball. To the right, between castle and town, spread the geometrically laid out ruins of Roman occupation.

After touring the castle dungeons we visited the Roman remains. Inside knee or sometimes shoulder high walls, were tiled floors; Sam discovered a hypocaust with its channels and runways to let in and out water to and from a solid stone tub. With much of the town unvisited but with dusk gathering, we regretfully paid off our guide and set off towards the glow on the horizon above the bright lights and street signs of modern Beirut.

Sadly, next day we shook the dust of Beirut off our heels and also, quite literally, out of our white uniforms and the following morning passed the imposing de Lesseps statue on the end of the breakwater guarding the entrance to Port Said harbour, where we had to wait two days. After Beirut, Port Said appeared drab and unexciting, most of the crew were too broke for a run ashore and everyone made up a considerable quantity of lost sleep. The Sea Transport Officer in Charge (STOIC) had suffered some muddled signals since our arrival, so we invited him for a gin in his namesake ship.

On the third forenoon a Canal Pilot boarded and we slipped, turned and set off down the canal where our round hull proved an advantage. Cargo ships were often required to stop and tie to the bank when meeting another vessel. As this was regarded as impractical for a submarine oncoming large ships had to give way, allowing us to sail past, nose in the air. With smaller craft it was possible to slide past at low speed. Due to the enclosed water of a canal, collisions are impossible. Each ship pushes a mound of water before it so that even on an apparent collision course a wedge of water cushions them apart till, as their sterns clear, each moves back mid-channel once more, for all the world as if they had passed right through each other.

On reaching Suez, a signal from the honorific SNORSCA, shades of Rip van Winkle, ordered us to secure at the coaling jetty opposite the town to fuel before sailing south in the afternoon out of the control of Senior Naval Officer, Red Sea and Canal Area to steer between the jagged Egyptian mountains and the pinky-brown Sinai Range bound for Aden with, at sunset, the tops of the mountains of Hejaz dimly visible above the haze. A fresh northerly wind chilled the air and the sea sparkled with phosphorescence. Fearing torpedo attack from one of the Italian submarines known to be in the Red Sea, the streaks of the wakes of numerous sharks coming towards us caused constant false alarms till each watchkeeper in turn decided to disregard them and hope for the best. The sea sparkled and twinkled, shimmering with life and activity so that the school of dolphins which joined us left behind a glow like an underwater city. Each leap sounded like a popping champagne cork followed by a hiss of foam as they landed back in the water.

Halfway down the Red Sea off Port Sudan, the wind backed south and strengthened till, by daybreak, spray was coming over the bridge to reveal a cold bleak day of heavy rain showers one after another reducing visibility till after passing Perim we turned into the Gulf of Aden.

So much for the grilling heat of the Red Sea and Port Out, Starboard Home for comfort. With that illusion shattered, we prepared to check the claim that those stationed in Aden became mad.

First impressions of Aden from a distance were of an arid, bleak outpost of Empire below a shimmering haze of heat, from which a winking lamp on Signal Hill flashed berthing instructions. No longer needed as a coaling station, even the oil installations lay across the bay from the town. Berthed alongside, and due to sail east that evening, lay another S-class submarine a few days ahead of us. Over a cool midday beer with her first Lieutenant, an old friend, I heard tell of their goings on. It was a welcome custom for visiting submarine officers to be offered generous hospitality by a retired Colonial Office gentleman who had settled in Aden. On their first night in port, two officers had stayed in his spacious, airy house, looking out from near the top of Signal Hill over the built up plain towards Crater City. At breakfast in the morning they were asked to tell the next evening's visitors to meet Mr Briggs at the Aden Club for dinner before returning to his villa for the night.

When Bill and their recently married third hand reached the Club, their host, a little unsteady on his legs and blurred in his speech, had clearly reached the bar some time ahead of them. A tubby man of expensive complexion and bright twinkling eyes, Mr Briggs sported a cerise polka-dotted bow tie, monocle and a wide purple cummerbund covering the expanse between white silk shirt and immaculately creased trousers. Perspiring a lot, he constantly mopped beads of sweat from his brow with a large silk handkerchief.

After dining they returned to the half empty bar, most club members that evening having attended Guest Night in the Naval Base mess. Somewhat furtively, with one finger up beside his nose, Mr Briggs confided to his guests that it was his wont to receive occasional Arabic lessons so perhaps they would come to join him for one that evening. Surprised, but still unsuspecting, they politely agreed. Returning from making a phone call, he announced that Ali, his boy, had taken the car to collect the teachers so, after one for the road, they would all walk in the cool of the evening along the shore and up to his house. On their arrival Ali, his barefooted, grey moustached Arab servant wearing white shirt and shorts piped in red, opened the door for them. Following the gently weaving Mr Briggs to the lounge, their eyes fell on a waiting middle-aged and pregnant lady accompanied by two slim and shy looking, cotton frocked girls.

Formally, they were introduced: "This is Fatima, my girl friend and these are," (pause) "Lulu and Fifi: hope you like them."

George, the third hand had gone a little pale; here was he, a strictly faithful, newly-wed husband, finding that, quite unbeknownst to him, a nubile Arab bed mate had been laid on for the night. Ali having been despatched to feed the visitors, their host went through to his study to collect something.

"What the hell am I to do?" queried George.

Bill replied that they really must not prejudice future hospitality to submariners so, as far as he could see, they would just have to get on with it.

"I won't; I don't care if I do upset Mr blasted Briggs; let's quickly make back to the boat."

Bill repeated they must stay and play along with the arrangement.

Before George could argue further, their host returned to say he believed the girls were clean and that, on awakening, they should each be given ten chips and sent packing. Then, stating it was getting late, he led the submariners up to their spacious bedroom, bare of furniture except for two beds, a mat on the polished floor between them and a bedside table each side furnished with separate whisky bottles, water carafes and tumblers. Against the inner wall lay a wardrobe and chest of drawers, while overhead in mid ceiling revolved a large fan. Leaving through the veranda door, their host told them Ali would send the girls up as soon as they were fed.

Alone once more, they earnestly discussed a plan of campaign. perhaps they could lock the bedroom door, but this still left the other door out to the veranda. If that were locked also to prevent the ladies entering they would almost certainly complain and Mr Briggs was bound to arrive to investigate what went on. Perhaps a better idea was to arrange for themselves to share one bed leaving the other for the young women.

After each had knocked back a generous fortifying dose of neat whisky and half undressed, but before even having the time to unpack pyjamas from overnight bags, in through the door bounced Lulu and Fifi, twittering together in Arabic, to advance, neatly wriggle out of their cotton frocks and then, stark naked, sidle simpering alongside the half undressed pair. Doing all he could in support of his reluctant shipmate, Bill in his loudest and most compelling voice ordered, "Now look here, you two, we are going to sleep in this bed, and you are to share the other."

The sole reply to this announcement was, "Have some whisky"; it later becoming clear that this was the full extent of the English vocabulary of the dusky maidens who, perplexed but unperturbed by this reception of their freely offered charms, snuggled even closer.

All thoughts of unpacking pyjamas abandoned, the two decided they would in unison cross the mat to the empty bed opposite. On Bill's "Ready, steady, GO", elbowing their unwelcome companions aside, they bounded over the mat together on to the unoccupied bed. Mystified by the nature of this new game, their visitors followed in an endeavour to try to climb in as well. "The veranda" shouted Bill. Rushing out of the veranda door, they had just time to slam it in the faces of Lulu and Fifi in pursuit. Thwarted, but by now enjoying these surprising romps and determined to join in and not miss the fun, the naked pair ran out through the main door, along the passage, and out of another exit on to the veranda. Sighting them advancing once more, George and Bill with a cry of "Hell" (or was it "Help") returned within, bolting the veranda door. Frustrated, the girls noisily hammered on its glass panes to be allowed back in.

It was at this point that Mr Briggs, clad only in a pyjama jacket, stumped out on to the other end of the veranda, hand in hand with the naked and very pregnant Fatima. "What the hell are you two playing at?" he demanded of his guests. "Surely you can be a little quieter about it. Now, let's have no more nonsense. For heaven's sake, go to be bed like normal civilised human beings."

Admitting defeat at long last, Bill and George, urged on by repeated invitations to have some whisky, accepted their destiny. Bill, having done all he could to protect the third hand's virtue, did admit that for him the night's endeavours were not entirely bereft of enjoyment. So ended his tale of Aden life.

That afternoon a message inviting two of *Stoic*'s officers to dine that evening and spend the night with Mr Briggs arrived. Prepared for anything, Chief and I agreed to go.

On arrival up the hill at the villa, we were greeted by a tough looking Army Intelligence Officer, Major Roberts, newly returned from leave in East Africa, who shared the house with Mr Briggs. While awaiting Mr Briggs' emergence from his bath, Rob regaled us with a lively account of doings in the Aden Protectorate, where intertribal wars still broke out whenever the British appeared off guard. Aden was one of the few Crown Colonies traditionally governed by an RAF officer and we were in the middle of hearing Rob's views on the failings of the present incumbent when our host, wearing Red Sea Rig of black trousers, shoes and cummerbund topped by an open necked white shirt, ideal for keeping cool in the tropics, descended.

After a few sherries Ali arrived to announce dinner. "Just one more sherry," pressed Mr Briggs. Several drinks later Ali returned to repeat that dinner was served. "Perhaps you'd like a sherry before we feed?" asked our host, refilling our glasses without waiting for any reply. Afloat with sherry, Chief and I were becoming more and more hungry till at long last we were led through to sit round a polished table bearing, in front of our host's chair, a large silver domed dish. Ali lifted the lid to reveal a succulent looking, slightly overcooked leg of mutton crisply brown on the outside.

Taking up a carver and steel, Mr Briggs, with a flourish, proceeded to sharpen the blunt side of the knife, leaving the blade untouched. Feeling this blunt edge and, apparently satisfied, he applied it to the joint which, not surprisingly from the long delay, was loose from the bone. Soon a large hunk of meat became dislodged; our host, suddenly lacking resistance to his furious hacking, sat sharply down leaving the carver to clatter into the corner from where Ali solemnly retrieved it before helping his master back on to his feet. Soon the polished table and floor were littered with juicy chunks of meat. In despair, Chief and I exchanged glances. The joint had smelt and looked so delicious, such a welcome change from the often all too familiar submarine corned beef. Eventually the almost bare bone skidded off the dish and rolled under my chair.

"I'm sorry, I am afraid the mutton was off."

Without instruction, Ali removed the empty dish and hot plates, soon reappearing with four others on each of which sat an unappetising slice of corned beef. At least no carving was needed and we enjoyed the accompanying vegetables. Of the ice cream which followed, quite a proportion slid off Mr Briggs' spoon down his shirt front, which he calmly claimed he found a good way to keep cool.

After coffee, Rob suggested we accompany him to the Sergeants' Mess sing-song where he was expected to put in a brief appearance. Leaving his co-owner slumped comatose in an easy chair, he led us outside to a garage with one of its double doors unhinged and leaning drunkenly out. "Charles sometimes forgets to notice whether the doors are open or not before driving in," explained Rob. From the shape of the car's front wings it was clear that Mr Briggs was in the habit of entering his garage at some speed.

"Sorry about the meat at dinner. I'm afraid it quite often happens. Ali always has corned beef ready in reserve. I find the only answer is to leave Charles to carve. He gets so upset if I offer to do it," explained Rob in a matter of fact voice, as if there was nothing unusual about it.

The climb up the long hill to the Sergeants' Mess in the cool evening air was magical. A narrow corridor of reflected brilliance along the sea far below led to a three-quarter moon lighting outlandish shaped rocks towering larger than life beside the winding tarmac.

Descending once more, following the sing-song, the car's tyres screeched as Rob negotiated the contours of the hill at speed. It seemed wise to avert one's eyes from the sheer drop from each right hand bend almost vertically down to the glistening sea several hundred feet below. Alarming enough as was being driven fast down by the capable Rob, the thought that it could have been Mr Briggs driving conjured up the nightmare of finding ourselves unwilling passengers of an inebriated Mr Toad at the wheel.

Safely delivered back to the villa, Chief and I, after declining a nightcap, were shown up to the bedroom Bill had described. On unzipping his overnight bag Chief discovered that he had by mistake collected one containing books and dirty starched collars in place of the one he had packed with pyjamas and washing gear.

"Never worry, Chief," Rob breezily assured, "I'll soon get you a pair of pyjamas and a razor."

We heard sounds of drawers being opened and shut in another room before he returned bearing a pair of striped pyjamas and a safety razor. Holding the pyjama trousers alongside Chief it was clear they were made for a taller man. "Don't seem to fit awfully well, Chief," he commented. "Still we'll soon fix that." With several sharp snips with a large pair of scissors he proceeded, before Chief had time to protest, to snip off the bottom four inches. With a happy grin Rob explained he need not worry, they were a pair of Charles' pyjamas and he'd probably never notice. A sound sleeper, I missed the next episode: chief at one in the morning became suddenly aware the bedroom light was on.

Chief viewed a pyjama clad Mr Briggs in the large area beyond the beds indulging in strange contortions, legs well apart, arms straight with hands together he swayed to and fro from the waist. Raising arms above his head and swivelling on toe and heel he swung down and round, narrowly avoiding falling over. When Chief heard him mutter, "Blast that bloody bunker," he sat up in bed to enquire, "Hallo, Sir, can't you sleep?'

"Sorry to awaken you, Mr Herbert, I was just practising one or two golf shots. I actually came in to bring you a new razor blade. I threw the old one out." He wandered off.

With morning sun flooding in through the shutters, Ali awakened us with tea. As Chief was pouring, Rob poked a head round the door. "Morning chaps. I say, Chief, I was afraid your razor blade might be blunt so I've changed it." Regretting the absence of a broker to instruct to buy Gillette shares, we rose, breakfasted, bade Rob goodbye and returned down the hill to *Stoic*'s berth.

Prosper, who had been duty officer, was on the fore casing to greet us. He seemed much less interested in hearing of our experiences than in telling of his own. Soon after his solitary supper, the other two having gone ashore, the trot sentry had knocked on the wardroom bulkhead to announce that there was a lieutenant-commander on the jetty who had asked to speak to the duty officer.

He discovered a forlorn figure wearing Great War campaign medals who, invited down, refused a drink and began to list his woes: how, after he had built splendid bathrooms for the stokers on his staff, they still remained unused; how the impossible Boom Defence Officer even refused him entry to the Boom Depot; how he hated Aden where no one understood him; how beautiful were his baths; how he'd been so long away from home, he sometimes forgot the address of the house they'd owned for twenty years when writing to his wife and, coming at last to the point after several further miseries, how welcome any *Stoic* officers would be were they able to spare the time to visit his baths which, unfortunately, were not in use because that idiot Parkins, claiming a water shortage, had refused him permission to connect them to the water main; hardly anybody had come to see them and the Commodore always claimed to be too busy. Prosper promised we would try to pay the baths a visit before we sailed. Pathetically grateful, his guest left.

Subby and Joe seemed disappointed that their run ashore had proved uneventful.

It was almost eleven under a remorseless sun, when the sentry came down to report that the Captain was returning along the jetty, having dined and spent the night staying with the Commodore. His brow was furrowed as he crossed the plank, complaining that there was a loose rope end over the saddle tanks and asking why the ensign halyards were slack, before descending gruffly below. It was only later, after a lunch time gin, that he began to thaw and tell us of his night ashore.

Apparently, following a convivial evening with the Commodore and other guests, he had descended late for breakfast after his host had left for his office. It had been a heavy night and he was pouring himself a much needed cup of coffee when he thought he saw a tiny antelope silently enter the room then walk round the breakfast table and out on to the veranda for all the world like a Walt Disney character with the sound switched off. After a meagre breakfast but fortified by two more cups of strong black coffee and, still uncertain if DTs had struck, he returned upstairs to pack. On looking out to the garden, to his intense relief he observed one of the Commodore's servants feeding the animal. Our lack of reaction seemed to disappoint Sam till he had heard of our experiences.

Before leaving Aden, most of us visited the Crater City market and bought cheap watches and sandals, noted with surprise carts pulled in the streets by camels, and even paid a visit to the waterless baths on the Boom Jetty to overwhelming gratitude from their architect.

Convinced that the rumour questioning the sanity of those posted to Aden not ill-founded, *Stoic*, allowed a trawler escort till clear of Socotra and the Gulf of Aden, proceeded east, zigzagging to confuse any lurking German or Japanese submarines known to be operating in the area.

While enjoying bright midday sunshine on watch next day, the port lookout beside me on the bridge shouted that a splash had appeared several miles on the beam. As I swung my binoculars on the bearing, the sound of an explosion reached us. Despite inability to see anything, I called the Captain to the bridge as a precaution. then as we all peered to port, a vast black object like a V bomber leapt from the sea's surface, to belly flop back with a great splash, followed seconds later by a bang: a manta ray often described as a sea bat was leaping in the air, perhaps to rid itself of vermin. Sadly there was no repeat performance.

The following night an off watch stoker asleep in the stern was awakened by a thump as if something solid had jarred the rudder. Only when the starboard shaft bearings began to heat and the propeller to sing did he report what he had felt. Soon the bearing grew so hot that we were forced to stop the starboard diesel and continue for a few hours on the port alone before trying once more with both: it was no use so, to avoid further damage, we continued our course across the Arabian Sea through the gap between the Maldive and Laccadive Islands to Colombo on one screw. Favourable tides allowed our arrival when expected to sight in clear visibility the faint pale blue outline of Adam's Peak, sixty miles inland. It seemed to float in the air above the heat haze over low lying land round the port.

An order flashed from shore that we were to berth alongside *Plancius* moored in harbour inside the breakwater. By the Dutch submarine berthed alongside, we identified the KLM liner with one tall funnel which had been modified as a submarine depot ship. Among a huge wodge of signals delivered after we secured was one asking the Captain to call on the Senior Submarine Officer in Room 195 of the Great Oriental Hotel, which had been requisitioned as Naval Headquarters. Once he had left in a motor boat for the shore, the Coxswain and I crossed over to *Plancius* to investigate arrangements for accommodation and supplies. As a passenger/cargo liner she afforded sufficient cabins to allow chief and petty officers to share double cabins rather than be crammed together in one mess, while the junior ratings were messed in her converted cargo holds. While living aboard, everyone would be fed in the luxurious style expected by peacetime KLM passengers.

The arrangements for submarines to draw food rations were equally acceptable. The 'Swain was told to order whatever he wanted and they would try to make it available. As the Dutch merchant navy officer pointed out, KLM would charge the Dutch Navy, who would then charge the British flotilla victualling officer, and whoever it was who finally paid it would be neither him nor us. As *Maidstone*, our future depot ship, was still in the Mediterranean and we were temporarily attached to *Adamant*, depot ship of a flotilla of T-class submarines in Trincomalee on the eastern side of Ceylon, it was likely to be many months before a claim arrived in any case.

Sam returned with the news that we were to enter dry dock next morning, sharing it with a T-class boat already on passage from Trinco. While in dock, one watch would sleep in the boat each night and the other two would live in *Plancius*. The dry dock lay to the north of Colombo between a warehouse area on one side and open jungle on the other. He had been warned that the native labour working aboard would pinch any loose objects they could lay hands on, so it would be the duty of the gangway sentry to search everyone leaving the boat after working aboard.

Once the two submarines in line were squared on the blocks in the centre of the dock, the Pump House chimney beside the dock gate began to belch black smoke, the pumps to hum and the water level inside the dock to sink. Shores of timber having been hammered tight to make sure neither boat would fall over, at last the water level began to drop on our hulls. Crews of Sinhalese on rafts were busy scraping weed off the sides of the saddle tanks as they were exposed. At last the top of the rudder broke surface, followed by the blades of the screws. The edge of one blade on the singing starboard propeller was turned over and a large chunk was missing. Clearly we had hit something solid on passage. Eventually, the after hydroplanes were awash and gurgling sounds rumbled out of the ballast tanks as each in turn emptied into the dock till, at last, with the dock dry, we were able to climb down for closer inspection. It was clear the starboard propeller would need replacing, while minor distortions on that to port were repairable. Dockyard maties were chipping away at clusters of barnacles along the bottom, where some of the boot-topping paint had washed off to reveal bare patches of rust. Already a stale fish-decaying smell was beginning to assail our noses.

A white overseer came down with the Base Engineer Officer to discuss what work was to be done. Apart from the screw replacement, the starboard shaft would have to be removed, heated up and straightened and all the routine inspections of underwater valves and fittings and any necessary repairs carried out before, to our sadness, our striking blue paint on conning tower and casing was to be painted over with pale, rather wishy-washy, light green paint.

The hubbub and clatter continued till late on the first night I was aboard in dock. No longer insulated by cool sea water and despite ventilating fans, the thick steel hull radiated heat like an oven leaving all aboard dripping with sweat and finding it hard to sleep. Fortunately, there were few internal repairs needed apart from the removal of the propeller shaft, so that checking for pilfering was not too difficult. Nevertheless, we were glad to undock after ten days. Conditions aboard had been unpleasant, not improved by lack of boats for moving watch-keepers, their kit and provisions daily, so that it was refreshing to sail south and then up the east coast of Ceylon bound for Trinco, our future base, where lay warships of the Eastern Fleet with attendant tankers, supply and hospital ships as well as our temporary depot ship *Adamant* and her flotilla.

Landfalls at Trinco were difficult. Off the low lying land there would often be a haze obscuring Foul Point Lighthouse at the entrance. It was then necessary to look for a buoy some miles offshore before setting course for the gap in the boom at the harbour entrance.

Once we had passed the gate vessel, *Adamant* appeared from behind a low hill in Battenburg Bay to port. Ordered to berth on her starboard side, we found after rounding her stern, several submarines alongside. In addition to her larger T-boats, she was also caring for three S-boats of our future flotilla till *Maidstone* arrived from the Mediterranean.

During our week alongside preparing for our first Malacca Strait patrol, I was involved in a row with the spare crew CO, nicknamed Horizontal Horace, who ordered me to embark the stern torpedo in a position which appeared dangerous. After I refused, he complained that I was uncooperative and obstructing the smooth running of the flotilla. Sam, in a bad temper, was summoned to settle the dispute and, to Horace's sullen anoyance, agreed with me. I was grateful that we were only temporarily part of *Adamant*'s flotilla. Whenever crew replacements were needed, they were chosen by the spare crew CO, who could easily see that less desirable men were chosen to join a submarine he disliked.

CHAPTER 14

First Malacca Strait Patrol

AT LAST, IN EARLY MARCH 1944, *Stoic* left Trinco, escorted till thirty miles offshore by the trawler *Magnolia*, which then turned back, leaving us to sail eastwards to disturb the gently undulating green mirror of the Indian Ocean alone. In bright sunlight flying fish would take off ahead to glide effortlessly for ten or fifteen yards, gradually losing height till their rapid tail beats, leaving a wavy wake behind, drove them a further few yards before re-entering their natural element with a sharp plop. That night, possibly attempting an altitude record, one landed beside me on the bridge fifteen feet above the water surface. Having learned in the West Indies what a delicacy lightly fried flying fish could be, I sent it down to the chef to be cooked for my breakfast.

Our orders were to patrol Area A, the coast of Malaya south of Penang, one of several areas into which the Malacca Strait between Sumatra and the Malay Peninsula were divided. We were to observe, report, but not molest the coastal traffic in junks and motor sampans. Having passed south of Great Nicobar in the forenoon, by evening we had travelled well within the Strait. Then life became uncomfortable.

All we carried at the time was an air-warning radar mounted abaft the periscope standards on the bridge. The radar operators, young and in their first operational submarine since their training, kept reporting echoes, many dismissed as false. It was well nigh impossible to distinguish between genuine and false echoes and soon one appeared at seven miles. Diving stations were ordered and a plot started. Prosper on the plot eventually suggested, and later confirmed, an enemy course roughly opposite ours with a speed of 12 knots. Then it was reported that the ship, if ship it were, had turned towards us and was closing rapidly. Yet in the very clear visibility the officer of the watch and lookouts on the bridge could find nothing. After the range had closed to two miles with still nothing in sight, Sam decided it must be yet another false echo.

These false echoes became the bane of our existence. Many behaved realistically as if from a ship. Time after time, hours were spent closed up at diving stations over these deceptively realistic echoes. Indeed, some submarine COs on patrol in the Straits refused to use their radar at night because of the

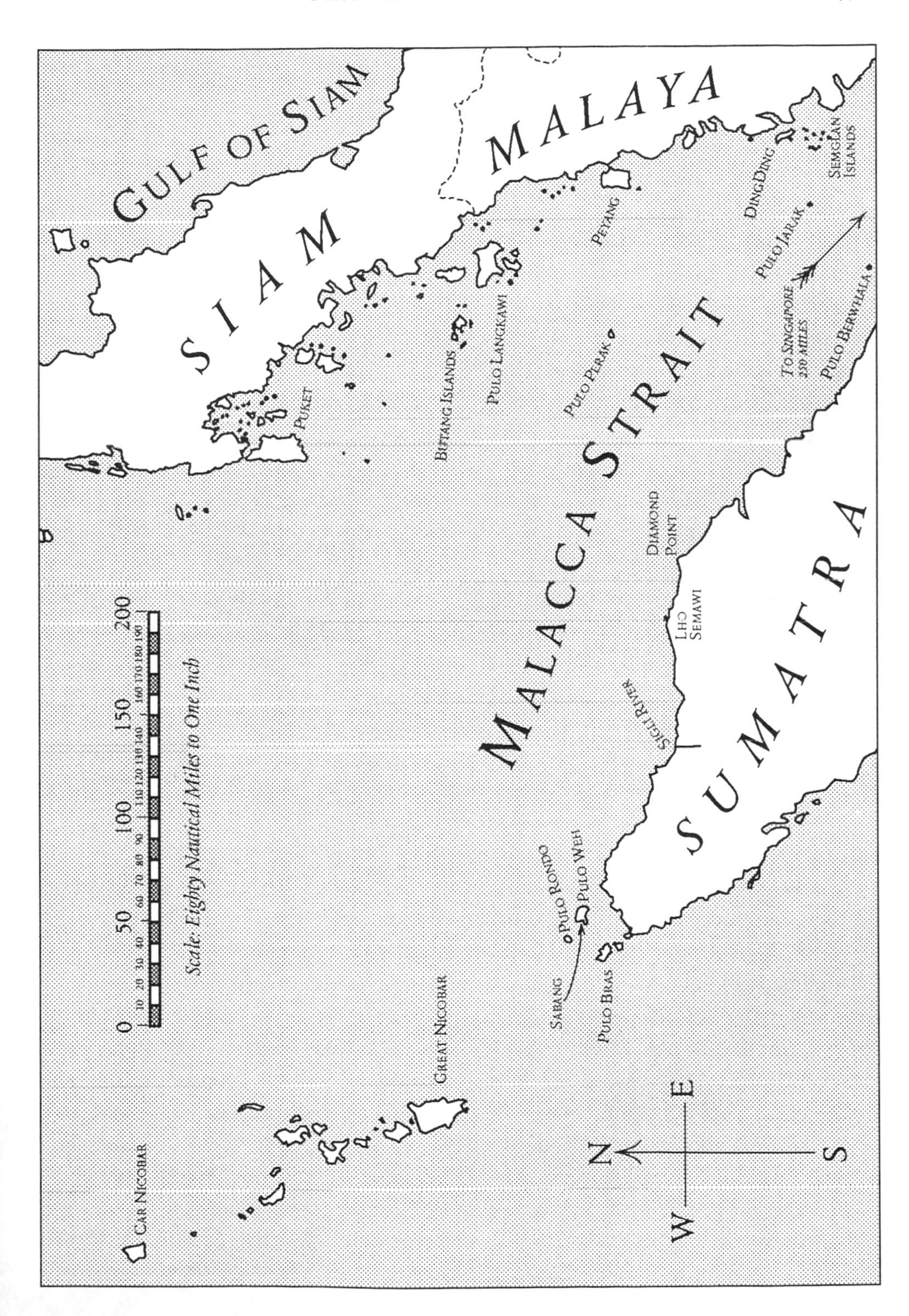
Gulf of Siam
Siam
Malaya
Malacca Strait
Sumatra
DingDing
Semgian Islands
Pulo Jarak
To Singapore 250 miles
Pulo Berwhala
Peyang
Pulo Perak
Pulo Langkawi
Bittang Islands
Puket
Diamond Point
Lho Semawi
Sigli River
Pulo Rondo
Pulo Weh
Sabang
Pulo Bras
Great Nicobar
Car Nicobar
0 50 100 150 200
10 20 30 40 60 70 80 90 110 120 130 140 160 170 180 190
Scale: Eighty Nautical Miles to One Inch
N
S
E
W

disturbance it caused their crews. Yet early warning of a target and an opportunity to reach a good torpedo firing position could thereby be sacrificed.

We continued to operate our radar and, as the radar operators gained experience in detecting false echoes, our nights became less disturbed. The radar was useful for navigation and during that first morning watch detected Pulo Jarak, a large lump of vegetation-covered rock about 500 feet high in the centre of the Strait. There were two of these Ailsa Craig-like islands 100 miles apart; the other, called Pulo Perak, was treeless and white from gulls and their droppings. About forty miles off the Malayan shore both were most useful for navigation. It was rumoured, and subsequently disproved, that a Japanese lookout post was hidden in Jarak's vegetation.

At daybreak, *Stoic* dived in position just south of the port of Dingding, about fifteen miles from the Sembilan Islands, which, as we approached closer, were revealed as bluff lumps of land with jagged rocks offshore interspersed by white sandy beaches. All were coated in dense, dark green jungle which seemed even darker when contrasted with the pale blue-green water. We steered to pass between two groups of islands.

Submarine navigation inshore entailed using a periscope bearing and either adding or subtracting it from the ship's head to obtain a true compass bearing, the control room messenger noting the bearings and writing them down.

The islands among which we were patrolling were Pulo Nipis, which rose from each side to a large tree on its highest point; Pulo Rumbia, long with a pair of rounded peaks not unlike the Paps of Jura; Pulo Buluh, a tall flat-topped isle featuring an extraordinary white rock standing as a jagged pillar thirty-five feet high, and the triangular Pulo Agas. For simplicity these were named Nipple Island, Rumbles, Elephant Island (from Pulo Buluh's shape) and Aggie (after the Aggie Weston Sailors' Home in Portsmouth) and these quickly became familiar and avoided any muddle over pronunciation when noting bearings.

Soon a junk was reported in sight, small with a ramshackle cabin, its red slatted sail full of holes. In brief periscope looks we watched the helmsman lazily steering with its long pole of a helm resting under one armpit. More and more junks were sighted till, when we had closed the shore to look along the channel inside Dingding Island, a whole squadron came in view, some mere overgrown sampans, some with twin sails and a makeshift cabin, while one or two trading junks featured raised forecastles, two holds, twin masts and a higher stern. Some sails were of canvas but most used woven palm leaves, stiffened and kept in place and shape between several pliable rattan canes.

Later in the afternoon we were able to watch fascinated while a great bull-mastiff of a junk sailed close past on her way into harbour. Under a Japanese flag flying from the mizzen yard, her decks were piled high with a cargo of boxes and timber, while her stern castle was decorated with a carved wooden balustrade over which leaned several passengers. Shaped like a Spanish galleon, she must had displaced a couple of hundred tons. Soon after their passing, the Asdic operator reported fast running HE (hydrophone effect) and chugging out of Dingding on the reported bearing appeared a small motor boat flying a Japanese flag considerably bigger than itself. After coming alongside, a pilot climbed over the junk's side before both made their way into harbour.

Charging batteries on the surface that night, there were occasional alarms for sighting unlit vessels, identified by stopping engines to listen on Asdic for HE as junks' lack of HE indicated a sailing vessel allowing the battery charge to recommence. Around midnight, after several hours of this charging, breaking the charge to listen and then restarting the charge, yet another darkened shape was reported from the bridge. This time, after stopping to make sure it was yet another junk, the Asdic operator reported, "HE bearing red 30°, 120 revolutions". The vessel, whatever it was, seemed too small to be a worthwhile target. As a precaution, the Captain dived the boat to sixty feet to listen out. Still hearing HE on changing bearings after an hour listening, it seemed likely that we were in contact with a submarine chaser.

The batteries, because of earlier disturbances, were only half charged, undesirable for the day's dived patrol so, if at all possible, the Captain was keen for a further two hours' charge before diving at dawn. He therefore decided to risk coming up for a quick look round.

Surfacing at night in enemy waters is always tense. Using the periscope in the dark without breaking surface is impractical, so there is no alternative to coming straight up to the surface from deep. From the control room dimly lit with red light, the lower hatch is opened and Captain and Signalman climb the conning tower ladder to below the top hatch. Then the order to surface is quietly given.

Air hisses into the ballast thanks and the bubble moves forward as the bow starts to rise. With the Signalman firmly grasping the Captain's legs to the ladder, the depth needle creeps back with increasing momentum showing 58-56-52-40-30-15 feet when the bridge breaks surface, the lid thumps open, ears pop, Number One orders, "Stop blowing; flood Q," water gurgles as the voice pipe is drained, leaving water lapping the saddle tanks the only remaining sound. Meanwhile, on the bridge, Captain and Signalman sweep the horizon through their binoculars, first a quick sweep, then a more careful look all round.

"Nothing in sight; tell the First Lieutenant to start the charge" comes Sam's cheerful voice down the voice pipe. The tension relaxes, a burble of conversation breaks out, telegraphs clang and, after engine clutches are engaged, the diesels thump into action.

Sometimes, however, before Q tank is even fully flooded, there is a clatter, two compelling Klaxon blasts and a crash as the Signalman lands breathless below while the Captain, clipping the hatch orders, "Sixty feet, Number One, there's an escort on the port beam, shut off for depth charging."

That night the charge remained unbroken despite again sighting the chaser in the distance. However, off Dingding, we soon had to come to terms with the greatest problems of a submarine patrolling enemy waters close to the Equator: heat and humidity.

Stoic was fortunate in being built late enough to be equipped with an air conditioning plant. This was noisy and its use in contact with Japanese submarine chasers a risk. These small vessels, fitted with a gun forward, a score of depth charges and some sort of listening device for detection of their prey, often proved ubiquitous. Kept down by their presence, it would prove impossible to recharge fully the 150 tons of battery on which we depended to manoeuvre by day. Charging at a high rate raised its temperature till the deck above it, over which we lived and moved, would blister bare feet and even slowly fry an egg. Running the battery ventilation system, making a noise like the air conditioning plant, to keep it cool and remove the gas above the lead-acid cells, risked detection if used in the presence of a submarine chaser. Yet the battery handbook suggested risk of an explosion at temperatures over 142°F and ours several times approached this dangerous level.

Within the Malacca Strait, reputed to be the world's warmest patch of sea water, the air conditioning plant, if it could be kept running continuously, would collect seventy gallons of water daily, useful for washing, cooking and even drinking what was partly the crew's own sweat. When enemy presence precluded its use, temperature and humidity rose to sweltering heights and outbreaks of prickly heat and crotch rot caused discomfort. *Surf*, a boat in our flotilla built without air conditioning, suffered such serious health problems that her patrols had to be so curtailed as to limit her usefulness.

Following several more disturbed nights going up and down like a department store lift and with never a worthwhile target in sight, Sam decided that the next evening he would leave the area for a couple of nights' peace to sleep and cool down the battery. However, before that, dived slightly to seaward of the position we had previously maintained, there was a shout soon after breakfast from the officer of the watch at the periscope that smoke was in sight to seaward. Despite the usual few junks around, Sam ordered the boat to twenty-eight feet and then, with a full eight feet of periscope above the surface, had a good look to discover below the smoke a large white painted ship still some fifteen miles distant. After studying the chart he decided it was likely to pass outside Dingding Island making us too far inshore.

Diving deep he used a long burst of speed to move closer to the target's likely course. On return to periscope depth, the ship was closer but the bearing still further to seaward. In addition he spotted a small destroyer ahead well out on her port bow. As all torpedo tubes were brought to the ready, Sam estimated an enemy speed of 14 knots and noted she was zigzagging while the destroyer ahead followed an independent zigzag. Still well off her track, there was no alternative to going deep for a further burst of speed.

When next up, as the LTO anxiously checked temperature and acid density of the battery, Sam peered through the periscope, found the target, muttered to himself, called me from the trimming panel and said, "Here, number one, come and look at this."

The distant ship, a fine modern 10,000-ton cargo vessel with four holds and powerful derricks, was painted in Geneva Convention Hospital Ship colours. Around the hull was a green line broken by red crosses. Escort by a destroyer was in contravention of Geneva, yet it was against all British ethic to attack a hospital ship. What an appalling dilemma for our Captain.

Deciding to attempt to sink her after a long pause for thought, he raised the periscope once more only to find she had zigged away from us increasing the range and putting us on her beam; Oh, for the German or American angled torpedoes!

Risking being sighted, Sam surfaced, put in engine clutches and with the rattle of diesel engines rising to a roar, belted after the retreating vessel five miles distant. In bright sunlight we cut the green waters at our maximum speed leaving a creamy wake behind. Passing close to a junk, whose Chinese crew stared mulishly at us till forced to hang on as our bow wave lifted their craft bodily to roll heavily in our wake, Sam decided to chance a long range torpedo attack from astern, with success doubtful, particularly should the target zigzag after firing. Sent down to the control room from the bridge, I was ordered to supervise the firing of a full salvo of six torpedoes at six second intervals.

Just before firing, Sam ordered a small course alteration. Unhappy at the coxswain's slow reaction, I grabbed the wheel and pushed it over, we swung too far and the first two torpedoes of the salvo were off course. I knew from the pained look on CPO Wales' face that I would bear his blame for our resulting failure to secure any hits. Despite being in full view at only four miles range, neither target nor destroyer escort gave any indication of awareness of us or our failed attack and, adhering to the plan to allow the battery to cool by a slow and deliberate charge off Pulo Jarak, we slowly closed it on one engine, charging batteries on the other. Running fans at full blast all night, we had reduced battery temperature by the time we dived at dawn to reload torpedo tubes next day.

Pulo Jarak being close to the trade route from Singapore to Penang, our Captain decided to continue patrolling there instead of returning to attack possible coast-crawling shipping inshore. The north east monsoon was dying down, leaving the weather hot, heavy and sticky when we surfaced at darkening. The sky was clear but the barometer was rising fast. During my watch lasting from surface time till eight-thirty, the radar kept reporting more than the usual number of false echoes.

Conditions seemed right for a "Sumatra", described in the Pilot as a strong SW. wind which rises soon after sunset, blows with violence for a few hours and then drops as quickly as it rises. On the bridge we watched heavy clouds gather to the southeast where flashes of lightning jagged from them into the sea. Despite a clear sky and an eerily still night, the storm was rumbling away further up the Strait. As it seemed to be moving closer with the air feeling heavy, I shouted down to inform my relief he might need an oilskin.

Hardly had I sat down to my supper before the night alarm sounded its insistent series of short buzzes. A darkened ship was reported in sight. The newly reloaded torpedo tubes were brought to the ready once more, engines stopped and clutches disengaged as the Captain watched the ship. Asdic reported "HE, 210 revolutions" in the direction and when a separate similar HE was reported on a different bearing the Captain surmised that these could be escort vessels, but what were they escorting?

With a resounding crash of thunder, the storm was upon us and those on the bridge were unable to see anything through the hissing rain. In the control room gloom of dim red light, we waited expectantly. A clatter of heels down the conning tower ladder prepared us for the klaxon which immediately followed. Unable to see up top, Sam had decided to dive, slow down and listen for HE on the Asdic. Already the plot started after the night alarm was beginning to picture the movements of the two contacts; then another contact was made further away and, to try to differentiate between them, Prosper took names from Snow White and the Seven Dwarfs.

"Bearing of Dopey?" elicited a prompt reply from Jock on the Asdics, "030, sir". Assuming the escorts to be destroyers, it appeared likely that 210 revolutions would correspond to 21 knots – no slow target this. Soon a picture of the enemy's movements and zigzag built up by which time Dopey, Happy, Sleepy, Sneezy and Grumpy were all being plotted. Then came the report, "HE bearing

040, 150 revs:" the big ship at last. All was quiet below as *Stoic* slid inside the screen between Dopey and Happy. Plotting officer and Asdics were instructed to concentrate on Snow White as Sam hopped from plot to Asdic to fruit machine and back again trying to decide on an attacking course. The target's irregular zigzag alterations seemed to follow no clear pattern, defying intelligent anticipation.

"Surface, Number One, use plenty of air. I'm going up for a look. Be ready to dive again at once." Seconds after breaking surface, Sam and signalman were on the bridge as I stopped blowing and flooded Q to wait tensely for orders.

As the large second hand of the control room clock crept slowly round, a resounding earsplitting bang assaulted our ears following a violent flash. "Good Lord, they've opened fire on us," muttered the second coxswain.

Still no orders from up top.

I shouted up the voice pipe to the bridge that the Asdic bearing of Snow White approached the firing bearing.

Again the klaxon sounded and we dived, losing Asdic contact in the disturbance. On regaining contact, the enemy had passed the firing bearing.

"Hard a port. Full ahead starboard," Sam ordered to turn to a new firing course; then as soon as the bow steadied, he fired off two torpedoes in quick succession.

By now we knew from the plot that the enemy was two and a half miles distant. As long as she did not alter course there was a chance of a hit. Sadly, before the fish could reach their target, the Asdic bearings indicated an alteration of course away.

Poor Sam, success in war so depends on luck as well as skill.

In reply to my query whether we had been fired on, I was told the terrifying bang was caused by lightning hitting the sea a mere hundred yards on the beam. Blinded and semi-stunned on the bridge, he decided to dive and fire on Asdic bearing. Yet only half an hour later when we surfaced, the sky was clear, the sea calm and only lightning flashes to the north west marked the passed storm. An immediate enemy report was transmitted. Later, on return to harbour, we were told that intelligence had reported the enemy's safe arrival in Penang.

Left with four torpedoes forward and one aft, we returned to patrol to be disturbed by submarine chasers for several more days off Dingding before deciphering a signal ordering us to proceed to an area off Sabang, the northern tip of Sumatra, where there was the possibility of contact with a Japanese submarine returning from an Indian Ocean patrol.

Two days later we were in position close to Pulo Rondo, another rounded but heavily wooded Ailsa Craig look-alike island where we began several more days' patrol till, during an all round periscope sweep, I spotted what looked like a small motor boat appearing and disappearing in the long swell rolling in from the north. The Captain, when called, told me to bring the boat up from thirty-two to twenty-seven feet, and then, showing several feet of periscope, he saw what appeared to be a square box with light smoke near it. He could not make it out but decided that whatever it was, it would pass well to the south of Pulo Rondo where we were. As it seemed to be coming out of the west, he took us deep to steer south at high speed for twelve minutes.

At his next look after our return to periscope depth the Captain identified the long hull and conning tower of a submarine. Still far to the north of her track, we went down for a further burst of speed. All four bow tube lights glowed "READY". At his next look, the target was two miles away and in a position to allow us to fire on the best possible firing course. The four remaining torpedoes were set to run as deep as possible without a risk of passing under her. When she reached the firing bearing, a carefully aimed salvo was fired. The stop watch was started and we all awaited results with confidence. When the torpedoes should have been about 1,000 yards off her, the Captain raised the attack periscope. As he watched he cursed, "She has turned away and is making huge clouds of black smoke."

Somehow she had seen the tracks or detected the torpedo engines. Disgusted at an attack proving abortive once again, Sam returned next door to the wardroom, telling me to resume watch diving and fall out diving stations. With empty torpedo tubes we sailed back to Trinco that night. Sam added to the signal reporting our activities, "Returning with no torpedoes, no hits and no decorations." The signal was not well received.

Maidstone, our depot ship, had arrived and we were happy to secure alongside her on return. Always reputed to be a happy ship, we liked her as much as we had disliked *Adamant* and were proud to belong to the 8th Submarine Flotilla.

Exposure to high temperature and humidity had made worse our Navigator, Subby Pratt's earlier skin condition so that, instead of taking his turn for leave, he was despatched to a hospital ship for treatment to try to get him fit for the next patrol.

Chief opted for the rest camp high in the hills near Nuwara Eliya, which we learned to pronounce Newralia, leaving me to travel alone to stay with a tea planter above Kandy. To be awakened after a full night's sleep by a bearer with half a paupau and delicious fresh tea and floating slice of lime seemed the height of bliss, to be followed by peaceful wanders along the winding tracks clinging to steep slopes through the tea gardens.

Three days later, fully refreshed, after inveigling my way aboard SEAC Special, a train reserved for the staff of Lord Louis Mountbatten based in Kandy, I enjoyed one of the world's most breathtaking journeys round the edge of the mountains, plunging through tunnels to emerge, as if flying, and looking down a 1,000 foot drop to the valley below. Carriages rattled and grunted round steep curves, swaying startlingly, with the engine's brakes constantly screeching till, at last down on the plain below, the single track doubled to cross the cultivated patchwork of crops and paddy where patient water buffaloes plodded pulling wooden implements through the flooded fields. Cars and donkey carts waited at level crossings till we passed through palm clad suburbs into Colombo.

While Wren friends from home worked, there was time to enjoy the Indian market, bargain for sapphires locally mined and buy brightly coloured sarongs, so much more comfortable than khaki shorts in the hot humid atmosphere of the boat, till we could join up to swim at Mount Lavinia and eat out of doors below the fluttering flying foxes in the cool evening before dancing at the one and only night club.

Reinvigorated, I managed to get the job of King's Courier for the night train trip back to Trinco. This entitled one to a first class sleeper to oneself, so much better than being Officer in Charge of Train responsible for supervision and safe arrival of ratings travelling.

On return, *Stoic* was almost ready for sea once more. Sam and Joe, who would be due leave after the next patrol, had met two VADs and, before sailing, we all five took a whaler for a sailing picnic, only to be forced to beat a hasty retreat from the beach where we had landed for tea when a swarm of black ants, each about an inch ling, emerged from the jungle to advance on us in a black line. The girls, who lived in a large cottage with its own pier, invited us to visit after our patrol and to bathe with them on their special beach. With over 5,000 men and only 50 women at Trinco, perhaps *Stoic*, unlucky in its first war patrol, might prove lucky in love.

CHAPTER 15

Special Operation Off Sumatra

BEFORE SAILING on our second tropical patrol soon after my twenty-third birthday, we revised the skills learned off Campbeltown with COPP 10 six months earlier, both in harbour and later at sea with COPP 8. Once more we worked to save seconds off the time taken to open the fore hatch, heave up and launch folboats and dive to the bottom again. With only cruisers and larger Japanese warships as permitted targets till our beach survey off the small town of Lho Semawi on the north coast of Sumatra was complete, *Stoic* sailed under grey and overcast skies to roll queasily on the long swell built up by the south west monsoon. It was a pleasant relief to reach the Strait and enter calmer water.

We had taken considerable trouble to explain to our visitors, one regular and one RNVR officer, the mechanics of the heads. A submarine lavatory is a complicated mechanism with valves, vents, gauges and a blow enabling it to be flushed even when deep under water. It was most important to follow the correct procedure to avoid that disconcerting event known as "getting one's own back" propelled by a firm charge of compressed air.

After three days at sea one of our visitors, Sub-Lieutenant Peacock RNVR, was observed to look green, off colour and lacking in appetite. Despite his protest that he felt fine, he had a temperature and only on the fourth day, when we were becoming seriously worried, did we discover that, being so anxious about the danger of flooding the boat unintentionally, he had refrained from attempting a visit to the heads. Following a further demonstration of the procedure, a dose of No.9s and a successful visit next morning, he was soon as right as rain.

To save compressed air, there was a small funnel at the side of the bridge with a pipe leading to the sea known as the Pig's Ear, for use by those only needing a pee, hence requests up the voice pipe to the bridge, "Permission for one hand on the bridge to use the Pig's Ear" affording stokers, telegraphists and some seamen their sole opportunity for a breath of fresh air.

Ten miles off Lho Semawi, we dived to close the coast carefully at periscope depth. With distant 10,000-foot mountains silhouetted by the newly-risen sun, we could pick out a sandy shore with dark green clumps of casuarina trees dotted against palms, aloes and swamp vegetation. Only a few native palm-fronded huts indicated a town out of sight round the low foothills.

During the day familiarising ourselves and the pilotage party with the limited features to help fix their position, the officer of the watch in mid afternoon watched an old and dilapidated cargo steamer emerge round Semawi Island to the South East. Her tall funnel belched black smoke. Sam closed up the attack team to practise a torpedo attack, manoeuvring to an ideal attacking position 800 yards on her beam, and then watched in frustration as she steamed past with two of the Chinese crew lolling lazily over the stern guard rail, staring vacantly to sea.

With a light breeze, conditions seemed ideal for the night's special operation. The few fishing praus had returned early to the shore and only the odd pedestrian and an occasional cyclist travelled the road close to the beach. Ponsonby, a qualified navigating officer, and the fully recovered Peacock, with blackened faces, were dressed in good time before, so close inshore that we could hear a chatter of native voices, their folboats were launched with what seemed a loud splash before disappearing into the dark, loaded with crew, instruments and paddles, allowing us to clear the coast and recharge batteries. It seemed no time before I was awakened in my bunk to be told we were returning inshore once more.

On arrival at the rendezvous position, Sam on the bridge sent for a pair of officers to reinforce the two lookouts on watch. We peered inshore to sight any light flash from the returning canoes. After two hours' fruitless search, *Stoic* slowly sailed a few hundred yards up the coast and back before the eastern sky lightened and, still without sign of COPP 8, it was time to move; it had been arranged that, after dawn, they would paddle out to sea, returning to the rendezvous again after dark.

With heavy hearts, still straining eyes in a last desperate effort to sight them, we left the coast and, four miles clear, prepared to dive. Then, at the very last moment a lookout shouted, "Canoes in sight". There they were, low on the waves and difficult to see, paddling away from us. As we turned to follow them, they spotted us, waved, turned towards us and in a few minutes, they and we were down below.

They had been disturbed by passers-by on the road, a dog had barked furiously, but, survey completed in good time and having paddled away from the shore, they discovered lapping waves made it difficult to see far ahead. From time to time they had stopped to flash without result till, deciding they must be too close inshore, they had paddled away from it for twenty minutes thus somehow getting themselves to seaward of us till, as it began to get light, they were forced to steer out to sea. After a hearty breakfast, they slept till late afternoon while we patrolled the coast to return, after a night's charge, off the Sigli River where, the Pilot informed us, the Dutch had manned military posts either side of the combined road and rail bridge. From close to its mouth we watched an occasional car drive across the bridge.

Peacock requested permission to use his folboat to place demolition charges against the bridge supports that night, firmly to be told, both by his fellow COPP and our Captain, not to be ridiculous. We had, however, identified Sigli Bridge as a possible bombardment target before we steered west that evening, diving at dawn next day five miles off the Port of Sabang and aiming into the long bay, to the left of which the town, wharves, cranes and a white painted flagstaff stood out in sharp contrast to the lush surrounding jungle.

Close inshore, at the head of the bay, could be seen a medium sized cargo ship. Sam, after some thought, decided that she warranted a torpedo attack, hoping to break our duck. Thus, as we passed close to the harbour entrance, three torpedoes spread over her length were fired. Once the third torpedo had left its tube, the Captain swung the periscope for a quick all round look, only to spot a fast moving vessel closing rapidly out of the narrow entrance, pointing straight at us. Snapping up the periscope handles for it to be lowered, he ordered sharply with an oath, "Starboard 15; sixty feet; shut off the depth charging."

As watertight doors were clanged shut, but before even reaching the ordered depth, the sharp rattle of a fast revolving propeller could be heard passing over the top followed shortly after by a great explosion which thumped the hull, causing lights to flicker and a shower of cork to fall. Everyone hung on as a second depth charge exploded. Increasing speed, the Captain made for deeper water ordering the bathy-thermograph to be switched on. This barograph-like instrument, newly fitted after our first patrol, recorded on a paper roll temperature of the water against depth. Because the density and salinity of sea water is not even, its temperature can be used to identify layers of varying density. These layers will bend sound in the same way that a lens or prism will bend light, thus offering possible opportunities for escaping detection by surface transmissions or listening devices.

Once we had slowed down on reaching deeper water, Jock, listening out on the Asdic, regained contact both with our recent assailant and with a second vessel which had joined her. Clearly the enemy had been alerted and were aware of our presence even before we fired torpedoes.

Both vessels were moving slowly; then one was heard to increase speed towards us, followed by another four depth charge explosions, none close enough to cause damage. I was told to take the boat down to 200 feet but stuck at

120 feet despite fore and after planes at full dive as if sitting on the bottom: we had found a layer of denser water. Only after more water had been flooded into the midship trimming tanks did we manage to sink deeper once more. As we did so, Jock, who had clearly heard the propeller noises till then, reported their becoming fainter and fainter till he lost contact altogether. The graph of this temperature charge, together with a few sharp peaks when depth charges earlier on had caused the needle to jump, showed clearly on the bathy-thermograph roll.

Apart from sounds of several more distant explosions all was peace and quiet down at 200 feet. After waiting several hours hoping the opposition would have returned to port, it was time to risk coming back to periscope depth. To do this the pump had to be started to remove the water which had taken us through the denser layer, otherwise we would be too heavy. The pump sounded exceedingly noisy breaking the comparative silence down deep. Once the Captain was able to raise the periscope and look round, there was sign neither of the submarine chasers nor of any damage to the ship we had tried to torpedo, which we later discovered was protected by anti-torpedo netting. Even more irritating was the discovery on return to Trinco that *Sea Rover*, the preceding boat in the area, had happily bombarded Lho Semawi only days before our special operation: so much for not attacking ships for fear of betraying the presence of British submarines.

Describing their trip, Freddie Ponsonby wrote as follows in the COPP diary:

> We are getting a little jumbled up with dates but I feel that a personal note or two on our recent trip is called for in addition to the official narrative which is but a bald statement of facts. This is what I wrote in the *Stoic*'s visitors' book when we left:
>
> To merely goof at sea and swell
> For you one knows is perfect Hell
> But we expecting several hits,
> Had failed to cater for a blitz,
> Which frankly shook us to the tits.
>
> Regret we sat and drank your Beer,
> And also cost one fish, I fear,
> But you made comfort every way
> To see that we enjoyed our stay.
> Our thanks, Good Luck, Godspeed, Good Day!
>
> Meet Lt. P.B. Marriott DSO RN, Skipper of *Stoic*, and Sam to his friends.

A sound type. Not particularly brainy perhaps but the typical country gentleman and a horseman. With an inexperienced crew, what a life. Chasing around most of the 24 hours. He can have it. No. 1 a Lt. RN, one Durham, a pleasant type but pretty scatterbrained. All for the wildest scheme and he scared me. Age will perhaps bring him discretion or he will lose his skin. Tempered with his enthusiasm he may one day be a good C.O. Anyway he looked after us damned well which is the main thing. Next Pratt, Lt. R.N.R. a goodly type. Torpedo officer and worker of the fruit machine. Charming to us, but suffered from complaints on the trip which distressed him. Next the youngsters, both married and both subs. The first R.N., and 2nd R.N.R., poles apart in character. Perowne, the gash hand, fleshy, happy and extremely simple. Dowden the navigator an enthusiastic and capable one, quiet and literary minded. Both good companions in their own way. Lastly Chiefy Herbert the warrant engineer. The ablest man in the boat, the longest in submarines, and the one who had seen most action in this war. A good type but justly irritated for he was never allowed to be right about his own engines which he knew backwards. A jewel to me because he disliked sleeping in his bunk at night, and pressed me to take it. Suited me all right.

Those were the chaps and now just one or two short sketches of us in the wardroom. Can you see us? Mike sleeping on the deck under the table, over the top of the batteries which had a temperature of 110 degrees. I hoped at least that this would reduce him in fat but it didn't. General post at meals. Five pews and eight bodies. Magnificent give and take over this really. Meals always passed off without trouble ably assisted by Murray the wardroom messman who was a peach. Luckily, the chair situation did not arise most of the day as the submariners leapt into bed for a drop of shuteye at ever opportunity. After tea all were awake. Uckers time was upon us. Out came the pack of cards for a poker hand to see who should play. The unlucky ones spectated and for two hours the dice rattled. This game was on in earnest and with cheating and chinking made its progress. These games were always a joy. Our other pastime was cards. The two very cheap packs we took with us certainly served their purpose. Games of patience were in progress nearly all day. How many times the Captain, Mike and I laid out our packs on that trip I don't know, but we occasionally got one out without cheating.

Last picture of life in the mess. Surfacing hour. 14 hours underwater and the blessed hour was upon us. Who shall dare to describe the joy of that first cigarette, and on the lucky nights something more. 36 bottles of beer we took with us, and it was at this time that we had it off the ice. What nectar. Never has such beer been served before in all the pubs of England.

A final glimpse of life for you, the life in battle and not so pleasant. Mike and I sitting in the wardroom alone. Next door many minds are concentrated. We are at 300 feet. All the machinery in the boat is stopped. Only one of the motors is running dead slow. It is deathly silent. We play patience to pass the time. The sweat drips off. The fans are all off. It is horribly hot, damp and sticky. Then crump, crump they fall and explode. The depth charges. There is no warning it just suddenly comes. First the noise and then the sound of water swishing against the casing outside. The pattern has just finished, perhaps it was one, perhaps three, perhaps five. now it is over and all there is to do is wait for the next dose. 15 depth charges and three hours of hunting we put up with from the two chasers. Then perhaps they lost us, or maybe were just fed up, and they went home. At that moment my patience came out.

On return to Trinco, worsened by the damp sweltering heat on patrol, Subby Pratt's skin complaint sadly made it impossible for him to remain third hand. Discharged to hospital, his place was taken by Peter Fickling, a young sub-lieutenant of fine tenor voice and infectious sense of humour fresh from submarine training in the UK. Sam and Joe whose turn it was for leave, hitched a lift in a service lorry to reach a ford across the Mahawelli Ganga, Ceylon's largest river, a few miles downstream from Kandy. From there, accompanied by a commando friend, they planned to descend the river by canoe to its mouth near Trinco. Full of envy we saw them off, loaded with hammocks, service rifles, shotgun and revolver, kit bags containing mosquito nets, quinine, food and drink, all in addition to two folboats.

Meanwhile, while preparing for the next patrol and awaiting their return, bathing expedition with the Temple Cottage VADs, shooting expeditions in the flotilla jeep, sailing picnics, guest nights and evenings of bridge or poker followed by the bliss of undisturbed nights' sleep soon recharged our human batteries. Eventually, the safari party was sighted paddling back alongside *Maidstone*. Deeply tanned and half bearded they unloaded before coming up to the mess to tell of their experiences over a cool drink.

Each night leopards or some other jungle cats had prowled round their camp; they had shot one of the hundreds of muggers, the local crocodiles, on the river bank and then been sick at the ghastly stench when they tried to skin it.

One memorable night Sam and the soldier who, unlike Joe fifty yards away upstream, had slung their hammocks between trees close to their camp fire to awaken at daybreak in time to watch and photograph, in the half light, a herd of about seventy elephants, some with young calves at foot, starting to cross the river just beyond the sleeping Joe's hammock until they scented him when, trumpeting and stampeding, the whole herd lashed the river to foam as they followed a large bull elephant out on to the far bank. At this point Joe woke up only in time to observe their rapidly departing rears disappearing into dense jungle.

Rapids had delayed their progress downstream, forcing each canoe to be separately drifted down at the end of a long rope guided by its occupant waist deep in the swirling water; nevertheless they had safely completed the trip, returning well pleased with themselves on the arranged day.

It was time to sail once more.

CHAPTER 16

A Chase Off Penang

JUST BEFORE SAILING EAST ONCE MORE, I was depressed to hear the BBC announce the sinking of *Laforey* off Anzio with serious loss of life. Sadly, I was later to discover that my friend Walter Gath, who had taken over my job as gunnery control officer, was killed, together with the rest of the director's crew and many other ex-shipmates.

For this patrol, in place of four torpedoes we had embarked eight magnetic mines. As a result of British submarines' fruitful campaign waged against traffic supplying their army in Burma, the Japanese, for lack of freighters, had been forced to make use of junks, so these had now been added to the list of permissible targets. The monsoon was blowing hard as we crossed the Bay of Bengal, but often at sunset the sky would clear. The following description by Lin Yutang graphically describes a typical sunset:

> The best "spectacle" I ever saw took place one evening on the Indian ocean. It was truly immense. The stage was a hundred miles wide and three miles high, and on it nature enacted a drama lasting half an hour, now with great dragons, dinosaurs and lions moving across the sky – how the lions' heads swelled and their manes spread and how the dragons' backs bent and wriggled and curled! – now showing armies of white clad and grey uniformed soldiers and officers with golden epaulettes, marching and counter-marching and united in combat and retreating again. As the battle and chase was going on, the stage lights changed, and the soldiers in white uniform burst out in orange and the soldiers in grey uniform seemed to don purple while the backdrop was a flaming iridescent gold. Then as nature's stage technicians gradually dimmed the lights the purple overcame and swallowed up the orange, and changed into deeper and deeper mauve and grey, presenting for the last five minutes a spectacle of unspeakable tragedy and black disaster before the lights went out. And I did not pay a single cent to watch the grandest show of my life.

Because torpedoes were loaded ready for firing in only four of the six tubes two were empty and available for our planned lay across the main sea lane inside the Langkawi Islands north of Penang. Once two mines close together in shallow water had been laid, tubes were drained down and reloaded allowing two more in continuation of the line to be dropped. Then, next day, the performance was repeated nearby, allowing us to reload the two empty mine laying tubes with torpedoes.

Joe, who had earlier complained of feeling unwell, was discovered to have a high temperature. We did carry quinine tablets for the treatment of malaria and, aware that his Mahawelli Ganga trip had passed through mosquito infested jungle, the coxswain and I diagnosed that he was most likely suffering from a malaria attack. However, as watches had to be re-organised while he was sick, the Captain was consulted. He, firmly dismissing our diagnosis as nonsense, stated these were clearly symptoms of jaundice, an illness he had recently suffered. We were firmly instructed that the patient was to be dosed, not with quinine but with M & B, the most up to date wonder drug that we carried in the medicine chest.

Following a miserable night of tossing and turning with alternate bouts of profuse sweating and violent shivering, our patient next day looked even more ill with the remarkable temperature reading of 105°F. This faced Sam with the difficult decision whether, if Joe's life was threatened, he ought to abandon the patrol and return to Ceylon for medical assistance. Unknown to him, and in flagrant contravention of his orders, the coxswain and I had already began to dose Joe with quinine.

Sam eventually decided to remain in the Malacca Strait. That day, north of Penang Island, fishing sampans, distant junks close inshore, a motor launch and a patrolling aircraft were all sighted in the periscope but no possible target. After being disturbed, but not detected, by a submarine chaser during the night's battery charge, the Captain decided to wait one more day before moving to seek prey elsewhere.

However, after diving, we were rewarded by sighting two junks, one of about 60 tons, the other smaller. Sailing along at 3 knots they were heeling over as we followed till, after allowing the crew to finish breakfast, Sam ordered, "Stand by gun action stations." With the wardroom table cleared away, the gun tower ladder replaced it over the dozing Joe's bunk, while the magazine was opened allowing shells to be piled up at the foot of the ladder. Through the periscope the gun layer and trainer were shown their target and given their point of aim. Range was estimated at 1,500 yards and deflection at five right.

When all was ready Prosper took over the trimming while I climbed the conning tower ladder before the order to surface was given. When the bridge was heard breaking surface a whistle was blown, the signal to open both conning and gun tower hatches. Our eyes were dazzled by the bright sparkling sunshine as we climbed out. There, apparently unaware of the submarine treading on her tail, the junk sailed serenely on while our gun was trained round, telescopes were shipped, the sight setter wound on the range and deflection and shells were heaved up out of the hatch opening. I was able to follow the trajectory of the first shot across her bows till it burst in the water in front of her provoking feverish signs of crew activity. The helmsman having abandoned the helm, she came up into the wind sails flapping and while some men moved to the halyards, others made to launch the boat stowed on deck; one had even climbed down on to the top of the rudder where he clung on desperately as it idly swung to and fro.

Soon, after retrieving their comrade who had fallen off his precarious perch, the crew in the boat pulled clear, allowing the gun to aim directly at their abandoned craft. The second shell, with a vivid flash, scattered pieces of wood from the puff of black smoke where it hit. Finally, after a few more hits on the waterline, a direct hit on the mast caused it to fall overboard still held by a tangle of rigging. As we put in engine clutches to chase the other, the first junk sank leaving a flotsam of planks and other debris floating.

We steered to close the other which, to no avail, had piled on all sail in an attempt to escape. Fired from two miles off, the third shell hit her side, but it was not till her mast was brought down several shots later that she slowed and her crew of three were seen to leap overboard. Once they had swum well clear, we were able to work along her waterline with a series of hits from close range, each bursting with a sharp crack till eventually she rolled over on her side. Only then, to our Captain's especial horror, from below emerged three more men, their faces blackened and bleeding. Sam turned towards them intending to pick them up and dress their wounds but the sighting of an aircraft thwarted this intention, forcing us to dive.

Down below, seated round the wardroom table, we agreed that it was all very well sinking junks to deny their use to the enemy; the wounding and even risking killing their defenceless crews was quite another matter, seeming neither fair nor justifiable; we believed some other way would need to be found.

As we moved away, the officer of the watch saw through the periscope the first junk's boat hauling the swimmers aboard.

All this time, Joe had lain in his bunk shaken by each firing of the gun overhead; but claiming to feel no worse as a result of this experience: it was clearly not the ideal treatment for a seriously ill patient: in Sam's absence more quinine was smuggled to him. Without daylight it was not possible to show his lack of the typical yellow skin or white of eye likely from Sam's diagnosis.

Having betrayed our presence, it appeared prudent to move to south of

Penang Island where, over the next few days, several more junks were sighted. Sam's excuse for not surfacing to sink them was his unwillingness to betray our position though we suspected the real reason was to avoid any risk of repeating the crew injuries we had inflicted in our last gun action. Meanwhile, Joe who had begun to eat again, seemed somewhat recovered and was allowed to keep a dived periscope watch. Sam smugly claimed his improvement to be clear confirmation of the jaundice diagnosis and only sourly accepted my fiver bet that a blood test on return to harbour would confirm he had suffered an attack of malaria; we continued to smuggle quinine to him.

A small coaster hugging the shore was sighted. Unless we were prepared to venture into water too shallow to allow us to dive, an unjustifiable risk for so small a vessel, our only chance was gun action from the extreme range of our 3-inch gun. Once *Stoic* had surfaced to open fire at 6,000 yards, the ship turned away stern on to steer into even more shallow water. Despite our achieving three hits out of about forty shells fired, she continued to weave away till finally out of range.

Ceasing fire, our frustrated attention turned to a nearby junk whose crew had already launched a boat to abandon ship even before we opened fire. After sinking her with a dozen well aimed shells, all of which hit the waterline, we moved to repeat the operation on another further offshore before hearing that evening, as we moved back north of Penang once more, the BBC news announcement of Allied landings in Normandy. "Better them than us," contemplatively murmured Chief in the wardroom.

Using the big periscope with its binocular vision and high magnification during a regular sweep of the horizon, I noticed one forenoon an ominous black cloud from which heavy rain was falling; on a subsequent sweep a few minutes later, I was amazed to sight a moving black line leading from the surface up into the cloud where I watched it alter its position and density before fading into torrential rain once more. Studying the Pilot's warnings about water spouts, of which we were to see several more, mariners are warned to try to steer clear of them because of their ability to lift quite substantial and solid objects in their path.

Our periscope watches were seldom without interest, often with leaping shoals of Spanish mackerel and tuna above our submerged bow, with occasional sharks coming to look at us, while numerous brown boobies, like gannets with a silvery grey beak, would drift past, perched on floating rafts of debris washed down by rivers in flood, quite unaware of being watched, preening and flirting with each other; overhead, trailing tails three times the length of their bodies, tern-like tropic birds danced over the surface of the water sometimes disturbed by the sweep of a piratical frigate bird.

Joe, suffering a relapse, was back once more under the blankets shivering in misery despite the heat in the boat. His evening temperature rose to 102°F only to fall to well below normal next morning before a further bout of sweating.

At last, after breakfast on 11th June, in poor visibility, a ship making her way up the coast from Penang through heavy rain came in sight. Already abaft her beam and in no position for a torpedo attack, after we had watched her safely pass over the area where we had laid mines ten days earlier, we just had time to estimate her speed as 13½ knots before she passed from sight inside the island of Pulo Langkawi.

Poring over the chart it was estimated she would be making either straight up to Rangoon or maybe for Puket (which we pronounced Puck-it to rhyme with the sailors' favourite epithet rather than Poo-ket as we later learned to be correct) 130 miles up the coast. Our maximum speed being only 15 knots, there was no time to be lost in giving chase. While the ship was able to pass inside the Langkawi Islands, we would have to steer round them before we could set off north in pursuit.

Once surfaced, the diesels soon worked up to their recommended maximum 400 revolutions and then Chief risked a further 20 for good luck. We could only hope the haze would shield our long white line of wake across the smooth grey surface of the sea from the prying eyes of any patrolling aircraft. Ranges of the land by the radar assisted navigation. We calculated that the distance we would need to cover to reach Puket would be similar to that covered by the coast crawling ship and thus, assuming she already had a ten mile lead, we could hope to be level with her by five in the afternoon and still have a reasonable chance to reach a firing position for a night torpedo attack should she continue north instead of putting in to Puket.

Breaking radio silence to announce our move out of our allotted area and seek guidance on the ship's likely destination, we received Puket as a reply. Cheered by the frenzy of excitement over the chase, Joe extracted a promise that he would be allowed to vacate his bunk to work the fruit machine should we start a torpedo attack.

The cloud having lifted, it was bright and sunny when I took over the watch on the bridge in the afternoon. Astern lay the Langkawi and Batang Islands while, assuming our calculations to be correct, twenty miles to starboard should be our ship on a converging course. What a pleasure it was to be keeping watch on the surface cooled by a light offshore breeze, instead of peering through a periscope eyepiece, constantly wiping off the sweat dripping from one's brow and adjusting the waist of a soaking sarong.

To gain extra visibility, the officer of the watch could perch up on the periscope standard eight feet above the lookouts on the bridge below. It was from here that, at long last, the tops of the two masts appeared above the horizon abaft our beam: we were doing even better than expected. By the time my relief arrived to take over, it was just possible to see the top of a funnel between the two mast tips, while the bearing had moved two degrees further aft: we were gaining on her.

Just before sunset, with the enemy's bridge then in sight twelve miles off and thirty degrees abaft our beam, the Captain decided we should take up position close to the south east corner of Puket Island, well placed to fire torpedoes should she not enter harbour there. Returning up top to relieve Peter after supper, I found *Stoic* patrolling two miles offshore, torpedo tubes flooded and ready. Though the night was dark, the shape of Puket Island, with some flames flickering from a bonfire ashore, was clearly visible to the naked eye as we moved up and down the coast. Below, after Prosper had taken over the watch, I found Sam huddled in dim red light poring over the chart table. On the large scale chart he showed me the winding channel between shallow sandbanks leading into the Puket anchorage. "It will be difficult to attack her in harbour, Number One, we may have to wait till she leaves."

Back on watch after three hours' sleep, the only change was that the risen moon lit the shore, causing it to stand out as if it were even closer. Nothing stirred over the two hours till I could return once more to my bunk, only to awaken later to the sound of compass bearing and alterations of course being shouted down the voice pipe from the bridge. Before long, just before six, we dived to sixty feet to wait for it to get light.

On our return to periscope depth in a position four miles off the harbour entrance Sam, after a sweep round, announced, "I can see her," and took a careful bearing to be plotted. Between us and her was a mile of sandbanks, some marked on the chart as drying at low water, others covered by only a few feet of water. Fortunately, because it was high tide, most of the banks should be covered by around six feet of water.

There is a risk that shallow set torpedoes will porpoise and veer off course but Sam eventually decided to chance firing a salvo of three spread over the ship's length and set to run two feet under water, in the hope that they would safely cross the shallows. He decided to fire on the watch, thereby avoiding any risk of upsetting the trim, calling out only Coxswain, second coxswain and TI to join those on duty.

After Prosper had turned trimming over to me, he positioned himself at the plot. Tubes One, Three and Five having been made ready, Prosper was soon able to report to the Captain, "One mile to go, Sir." The sounding machine reading of eleven fathoms gave a clear six below us. At his next look with only half a mile to go Sam announced he could see her unloading cargo into a lighter alongside.

"Up periscope."

The periscope hissed up till the Captain could reach and pull down the handles then slowly to rise with it. Once it broke surface a gesture stopped it being hoisted higher, thus allowing him to swing round till its cross wire rested on the target's centre one degree on our port bow, with only a few inches breaking surface. Centring the periscope he looked at the fore hold. Ordering, "Fire One; port five," he followed the first shot with two more, one aimed amidship and the last aft. Slapping up the handles for the periscope to be lowered he requested, "Let me know when torpedoes have run 2,000 yards. Number One, try to get a rough trim to allow me a look."

On my assurance I could hold depth at our present speed, Sam ordered a turn away and then, just after rehoisting the periscope for a look, a loud banging thud thumped the hull, followed seconds later by another. Dancing at the periscope, he announced, "We've got her; she has broken in half," then motioned first me and then the coxswain to take a brief look.

All I could discern was smoke, descending spray and the blurred outline of funnel and bridge. As we made off while still in too shallow water to dive deep, Jock reported HE ahead and Sam, looking out on the bearing, sighted a pair of trawlers which seemed to making for Puket at speed; they passed half a mile off, allowing us a peaceful departure from the area.

There was a cheerful buzz of conversation as the crew made a late breakfast; one or two who had slept through the attack were unable to believe it had taken place. While the fore-end men reloaded torpedoes, I made my daily visit to the chief and petty officers' Mess to witness the day's issue of rum, only to observe them preparing a skull and crossbones black flag mounting a white bar for the torpedoing, four stars for gun action and a dagger for last patrol's special operation: our Jolly Roger to fly at last.

Once clear of the coast, we surfaced to transmit a cipher requesting permission to move to Area D, containing the bridge seen on the last patrol. Permission granted, we dived five miles from Sigli on the Sumatran coast at dawn next day to prepare to destroy the bridge. Closing the shore, Peter on watch was forced to use the small periscope with extreme care to avoid detection while trying to weave between a fleet of sailing praus and sampans busy netting fish. By the time I relieved him, we had safely reached a point in sight of the wooden bridge which crossed the Sigli River between dense bamboo groves on either bank. Orders were to observe and report road and rail traffic using it before surfacing to attack and be well clear by sunset. Later we began to hear occasional dull metallic thuds, perhaps grenades intended to stun fish or maybe from quarry blasting ashore, while the praus began to return to the beach.

When I spotted a plume of white smoke rising from behind the palms and bamboos and moving towards the bridge I called the Captain in time for him to watch an engine cross it. Although gun action stations were ordered, by the time everything was ready it had been lost to view. I was told immediately to order gun action should another train come in sight, but all I saw was a fat man in white uniform cycling across before Prosper took over. He later ordered "gun action stations" and everyone rushed to close up ready for the boat to surface. A train from the opposite direction was approaching the bridge but, once again, had vanished before there was time to surface. Determined not to be caught out a third time, Sam instructed the officer of the watch to surface the boat immediately he sighted another train as a signal that the guns' crew were at once to climb up and open fire. It seemed to be a very busy railway line.

Sure enough, before long main ballast tanks were blown, accompanied by a further rush aft to begin gun action once the whistle blew for the guns' crew to leap out of the gun tower ready to open fire. It seemed dazzlingly bright and the guns' crew were unable at first to distinguish their target. I shouted down to pinpoint it, when there was a whine overhead and, as I was shouting instructions from the bridge, a puff of smoke in the western plantation was followed by a bang.

Just as I ordered, "Shoot" to the guns' crew, Sam beside me shouted, "Down below." The startled guns' crew paused for a second to grasp this unexpected order before piling below once more just as a shell burst alongside. *Stoic* was the hunted not the hunter.

"So much for your ten minutes uninterrupted bombardment," wryly muttered Sam as he climbed down after me, shutting the hatch.

As the boat dived, we heard another of the bangs that had so mystified us. A shore battery seemed to have been sighting on and firing at our periscope before using a train to steam to and fro to tempt us up. Their first shell passed over us, the second fell just short; we had had enough, so no one saw where the last shell burst. The shore battery must have enjoyed their unexpected target practice and we wondered if the engine driver received danger money.

It was as well the Captain steered clear of the coast because two hours later we watched a destroyer arrive from the direction of Sabang to hunt for us off the river mouth.

We returned home entering harbour proudly flying a Jolly Roger. A boat took Joe across to the hospital ship *Tjitjalenka* which treated him for blackwater fever, a serious malarial fever. That would teach him not to be careless with anti-malaria medication. It seemed too sore a point to claim my bet and the subject was never again raised with Sam.

CHAPTER 17

The Captain's Trilby Hat

I RETURNED FROM LEAVE TO DISCOVER *Stoic* sporting an experimental camouflage, with three triangles of darker green paint, smaller ones on fore and aft casing and a bolder one with its apex at the top of the conning tower, suggested and designed by the artistic third hand of *Surf*. An exercise to test its effect had been planned for next day.

Dived five miles offshore, we carried out a practice attack on *Storm*, similarly camouflaged, finding her silhouette so broken as to make estimation of her course far more difficult. We then surfaced to allow her to repeat the exercise. On return, a decision was made to adopt this camouflage, which proved even more effective at night, on all the boats in the flotilla.

Before sailing on what was to be our last Malacca Strait trip, *Spiteful*, who had relieved us in the Puket area, returned with news gathered from the captured captain of a junk who had been there at the time of our attack. The 1,130-ton Kainan Maru had brought stores and a relief for the local garrison from Penang. On arrival, they began to unload stores by arc light and next morning were visited by the Japanese Military Commander of the area to inspect the new draft of troops. Hardly had his boat left the ship to return ashore, when our two torpedoes exploded, killing at least twenty of the soldiers aboard and wounding others in the sinking of the ship, which caused consternation in the harbour. The unexploded third torpedo ran beyond to ground on the shore where the Japanese succeeded in salvaging it without blowing themselves up.

Sent once more to the Penang area, after successfully sinking a 70-ton landing barge by gun fire, we were able to try out the technique developed by another boat for junk destruction, making use of demolition charges.

A hosepipe packed with explosive wrapped round the foot of its mast attached to a six minute fuse would, when exploded, cause the mast to descend through the keel of the junk making repair impossible even should it remain afloat.

Approaching our junk dived, we surfaced nearby and, in case she failed to heave to, manned, trained and laid the gun on her mast. As we made to come alongside, to the Captain's and my extreme irritation, our wretched gun layer pressed his trigger, firing a shell which dropped her sail and wounded her captain.

Roundly sworn at and told he would appear as a defaulter later, we gently came alongside the junk. Her crew all descended below deck when the boarding party leapt aboard, led by Peter, revolver in hand, followed by Leading Seaman Robinson wielding a crowbar as if it were a cutlass, his bare muscular tattooed torso crowned by a piratical black beard. Seconds after the ferocious looking Robinson had dropped below deck, out popped the Chinese crew for all the world like rabbits fleeing a ferret while, perched on the fallen sail, a scraggy hen, alarmed by the commotion, clucked anxiously.

Last up was their captain, his face and forearm bleeding from shell splinters. After discovering that he spoke good pidgin English, he was deemed a suitable prisoner to take back with us to Trinco. His crew, once they had been sent below to collect their belongings in suitcases, were ordered to launch their boat and climb aboard. After loading a cask of fresh water and a large tin of ship's biscuits they pulled clear, four oars flailing out of time with each other causing the boat to rock uncomfortably.

Meanwhile, from inside the junk emerged two other members of our boarding party bearing such useless souvenirs as an alarm clock with only one hand, a broken china jug, a cotton sarong and a pair of scissors as large as garden shears, to be followed up by Leading Seaman Robinson wielding an axe with a curved blade in true Lord High Executioner style which he had clearly decided was a far more suitable weapon for a self respecting member of a boarding party than any crowbar. Peter had contented himself by collecting a stalk of bananas and a box of black hairy pills which he thought to be opium. He had discovered that the junk's cargo stowed below consisted of sawn timber.

Johnny Chinaman, proudly wearing the trilby that we discovered to be his badge of office as Captain, was led below for the coxswain to dress and plaster his mainly superficial wounds, leaving the TI to light his fuse and, after capturing the hen, climb back onto the casing.

Once the charge had exploded, lifting the junk and collapsing its mast, we set off to chase a second junk for similar treatment. Whilst alongside her, a distant aircraft was sighted and the boarding party was warned that we might be forced to dive but would return later to collect them. However, the plane approached no closer than five miles, so this was unnecessary and the demolition was able to proceed undeterred.

Underwater once more, Johnny, whose own clothes were blood spattered, was fitted out with new khaki shirt and shorts. He remained wearing his hat and it was rumoured in the stokers' mess aft, known as the duck's arse, where he was accommodated, that he even slept in this mark of his authority. A friendly and co-operative elderly man, when interrogated in the wardroom he freely answered our questions about how the Japanese, who had ordered him to cross to Lho Semawi, controlled junk traffic. That night after we had surfaced, he was brought along to the control room for a breath of fresh air. "Carry on smoking" had just been passed and several of our crew were lighting up cigarettes; with a diffident smile Johnny asked for one which he lit and puffed in a contented self assured manner. We were getting to like our prisoner who seemed to have settled into submarine life with such dignity. The hen, our other prisoner, had also settled down in a box under the torpedo tubes in the fore ends and an egg was hoped for.

Next day, soon after diving, the forward hydroplane started to stick and, on examination, pressure could be heard leaking from the hydraulic control valve. Chief asked the Captain to allow him about an hour to strip it down to find out what had gone wrong. This would necessitate sitting on the sea bed while the work was done.

Sand or shingle are best for bottoming but the chart marked mud at ninety feet in our position so, lacking any choice, we descended very slowly and gently, almost stopped and only a few gallons heavy, till we settled with the bubble one degree aft. With much heavy hammering the defective unit was stripped down, to discover that a worn leather cup on the plunger was allowing fluid to escape. Fortunately, we carried a spare so after the repair was complete with planes tested working normally once more, we were all ready to return to periscope depth.

In the control room with hydroplanes set hard at rise the Captain ordered half speed ahead. While the boat shuddered with vibration, it failed to lift. After increasing motor speed to full, the pump was started in an endeavour to pump water out of the trimming tanks, but this proved ineffective because its outlet seemed to be blocked by mud. The only remaining solution appeared to be to blow main ballast tanks, accepting the vast disturbance which would bubble up on the surface of the sea when, once clear of the mud, main vents were opened.

First of all forward ballast tanks were blown resulting in a slight lift of the bow; next it was the turn of midship tanks, while the whole boat juddered to the thudding of propeller blades yet still we seemed stuck. First full ahead then full astern blowing more air forward was tried, without result; with supplies of compressed air fast reducing, our predicament was obviously a worry but there seemed no alternative to continuing to blow the forward tank. At long last, following a further burst of full astern, the bow rose as *Stoic* tore herself free of the mud.

Despite the immediate opening of main vents, I watched helplessly while the depth gauge needle swung up and the bubble moved right till the boat finished fifteen degrees bow up, with people and lockers slithering aft to the sound of smashing crockery. Though we had flooded Q tank the bow still surged up to break surface before it and the boat began a rapid descent back towards the mud as we blew Q and gradually began to achieve control over our bucking steed, regain trim, and allow the Captain a good periscope look round. To his relief nothing except a large swirl of wake and escaping bubbles was in sight. It had been an unhappy quarter of an hour.

We grew increasingly fond of Johnny, who spent hours in the control room seeming to enjoy the company. One day on watch I made my usual gesture for the periscope to be raised. The duty stoker's attention was elsewhere but, noticing, Johnny went straight to the control lever to raise it for me. After an all round sweep I called him over to the eye piece for a look and watched him swing it round, putting it in and out of high and low power as if he'd been doing it all his life. To save his having to beg cigarettes on the surface, he was given a packet of his own, which he gravely offered round that night on surfacing. One afternoon in the after ends he watched two stokers play chess, then challenged the winner, who met early defeat. We also discovered him to be a linguist speaking Malay, two Chinese dialects, Dutch and pidgin English, altogether a remarkably intelligent prisoner.

One dark night, a suddenly sighted submarine chaser only a few hundred yards away caused the officer of the watch to dive directly to sixty feet, ordering the boat shut off for depth charging as it descended. All below was silent as Jock reported the vessel getting closer; then we all heard its propeller noise as it passed over the top. Everyone was listening intently for the sound of dropped depth charges hitting the water surface when, from the fore ends, the silence was broken by a loud clucking sound: our hen had at last decided to lay. With a squawk she avoided the TI's attempt at capture, taking wing to the top of a torpedo tube clucking defiance: imagination boggled at what a Japanese hydroplane operator above might be hearing. Meanwhile, as the others in the tube space attempted to divert her attention, Robinson, bearing a large spanner, eventually succeeded in striking the wretched fowl stone dead with an almighty swipe. By this time Jock had reported HE again getting louder, an indication the ship had turned and was coming towards us. We waited with apprehension but the expected attack never took place and she passed clear down one side and eventually out of Asdic contact, quite possibly unaware of underwater poultry-keeping throughout.

Joe, on watch at night crossing the channel between Great Nicobar and Sumatra, sighted a dark shape on the port beam and sounded the night alarm.

Sam, on his arrival up top, could not see it, but by then Joe had decided it was a submarine on the surface. He was told to turn and fire torpedoes at it and the night sight was set to an estimated firing angle.

After ordering port helm to turn on to a course to fire, he gave the order to steady on the firing course, yet still the boat continued to swing with the helmsman shouting up the voice pipe from below that the rudder seemed jammed. It was not till after *Stoic* had completed a full circle that it responded by which time the target was fast disappearing out of sight ahead. Chief, sent to investigate, could discover no defect in the steering.

Breaking radio silence our enemy report of a U-boat travelling west was transmitted. The reply when deciphered was marked "immediate" to prohibit any night attack on submarines in the Bay of Bengal.

It transpired that *Surf*, without air conditioning and thus limited to short patrols, having completed a special operation earlier than anticipated, had signalled an intention to return to Ceylon early. To her extreme danger, our operating authority had failed to notify her change of plan to other boats at sea. It seemed likely that forty-four men's lives at serious risk had been preserved by our inexplicable rudder jam: was it a coincidence or could it have been divine intervention? Whichever, as a result, there was an almighty row over the failure to broadcast the change of plan.

On our return, we discovered a large floating dock, which had been built to American design in sections in Bombay and then towed to Trinco, secured in a position close to *Maidstone* in Battenburg Bay. From the back of the bridge Johnny had been allowed to watch our return to berth outside two other boats. He had been presented from the canteen fund with two new pairs of khaki shorts and a packet of 200 cigarettes as a parting gift.

Once the plank was out and the Captain had crossed to *Maidstone* to report, a sergeant accompanied by three privates crossed. He came to attention with a stamp which made the forecasing ring, to salute me and announce, "Escort to the prisoner, Sir." Hovering behind were the three privates armed with tommy-guns.

Asking whether we had our Chinese prisoner blindfolded, the sergeant appeared non-plussed when told, "Good heavens no; he's down below saying goodbye."

"Orders, Sir, are for the prisoner to be blindfolded".

"For heavens sake, Sergeant, he was on the bridge watching us manoeuvre alongside; how on earth do you think he could cross the three planks between us and the depot ship blindfolded? Besides he has given us much useful information and unless he is sensibly treated he will be useless to any intelligence officer."

After serious consideration and a look that implied that naval discipline left a lot to be desired, he accepted. Up the hatch climbed Johnny, followed by half our crew, to bid farewell and shake hands with both the coxswain and me. Then, carrying his cigarette package and a suitcase of belongings, he crossed the plank, covered by the tommy-gun-at-the-ready toting privates, to farewell shouts and cheers from the men on the casing. Pausing to doff his trilby at us and totally disregarding his escort, he climbed the ladder to *Maidstone*, again politely removing his hat to the waiting quartermaster and officer of the watch on the gangway, before disappearing out of sight. We were fearful his cigarettes might be confiscated and Sam's later enquiry after his welfare remained unanswered.

When next ashore at Temple Cottage, the VADs enquired whether the rumours that *Maidstone* was soon to sail to Australia were true; we replied that it was news to us but indeed it did prove later to be correct. Returning from leave in Colombo, Sam, sharing a sleeper with a fellow CO, told him next morning of an extraordinarily vivid dream he had had that night, in which he had watched a floating dock containing a cruiser collapse, leaving the cruiser listing surrounded by debris. Only when their boat returned them to *Maidstone* did they discover that the newly arrived floating dock which had hoisted *Valiant* had indeed that very night split down the middle causing serious damage to the battleship below the waterline. His dream and premonition were the talk of the depot ship for days with much discussion of the theories of Professor J.W. Dunne in *An Experiment with Time.*

While *Maidstone* was crossing the line to reach Fremantle in Western Australia, *Stoic* returned to the dry dock in Colombo for a bottom scrape of the lush growth of weed accumulated over the previous six months. Before undocking to rejoin the flotilla in Fremantle, we helped the Dutch crew of *Plantius* celebrate Queen Wilhemina's birthday on 31st August.

Champagne flowed as we sat down to a remarkable rÿsttafel of some thirty individual dishes containing a curried mixture of chicken, meat of all sorts, prawns, lobster and all manner of vegetables to supplement great mounds of rice. During three hours of speechmaking and toasts to the Queen, Princess Juliana, Prince Bernhard and their children, then to the allied nations each in turn, and to Ceylon, followed by Churchill, Roosevelt, Stalin and Chiang Kai Chek, glasses were constantly refilled while Javanese boys circulated with yet more exotic dishes.

Barely able to stand from such an orgy of food and drink, we all rolled up the ladder to the lounge where tea, a birthday cake, and piles of cream cakes and meringues awaited us. There a procession of jubilant Dutchmen goose-stepped round the lounge singing lustily; defeated we withdrew to collapse bloatedly on our bunks to sleep till, fortified by black coffee, we sailed next day bound for Western Australia.

Perhaps due to our effective camouflage, we managed to creep south of the line for the first time to enter Fremantle harbour undisturbed by any visit from King Neptune and his Court.

After passing several American submarines tied to their depot ship we secured outside *Maidstone*, berthed opposite a vast grain warehouse. Now under American control as part of the 7th Fleet, it was necessary to learn their mode of operation and master the use of their cipher system, very different from ours. Their submarines, four times our size and half as fast again, able to traverse the vast spaces of the Pacific on three-month patrols, contained cabins for officers' showers, and they even held daily cinema shows in their fore ends at sea. Their most junior rating received a higher rate of pay than our most senior CO, a commander.

However, perhaps from several months' experience of our allies, the Western Australians were only too ready to welcome and make a fuss of their poorer Pom cousins. They threw open their homes and their hearts, gave parties and dances, made us honorary members of their clubs, arranged sailing races and sporting events, laid on cars and buses to transport sailors the twelve miles to Perth, that beautiful city built round the King's Park, or to one of the many bathing beaches and were in every way helpful, generous and understanding hosts.

We received twenty-five Australian shillings for each British pound sterling of our pay, were issued with clothes rations and found unrationed beer for only a shilling a pint. For the ratings, who had regarded Trinco as a tropical version of Scapa Flow, lacking girls, dances, cinemas, pubs or any of the other facilities to make a run ashore worthwhile, this was Paradise indeed.

What more could any seafarer demand?

In one unanimous voice they replied — more leave and less work.

The zest with which everyone set out to fight the Battle of Perth soon began to hazard the Battle of the Java Sea. Torpedoes failed to run straight, slapdash repairs led to serious breakdown at sea and the riot act had to be read. Once the depot ship's lower deck was cleared and everyone was mustered on deck, Captain S/M himself made clear that any repetition of this negligence, placing at risk the lives of the submariners they were there to serve, would result in the cancellation of all night leave, a disaster to be avoided at all costs.

Things rapidly improved.

CHAPTER 18

In The Java Sea

FOLLOWING A FORTNIGHT OF PREPARATION, swinging compasses, a practice shoot, torpedo attack exercise and enjoyment of the flesh-pots of Perth and Fremantle, *Stoic* sailed north, sharing an escort with the American submarine *Redfin*. That evening, as soon as the escort turned back, *Redfin*, with an exchange of farewells, disappeared ahead into the night at nearly twice our speed.

While steering up the coast of Western Australia, we watched a bush fire rage ashore before we reached Exmouth Gulf, a large empty bay 700 miles north of Fremantle and 1,000 short of the Lombok Strait entrance to the Java Sea. There we secured to a fuel barge to top up diesel fuel. To our amazement its American crew were bathing unconcernedly on the side opposite to where we were secured, while nearby the black fin of a cruising shark broke the surface. Their officer assured us the sharks were harmless, being well fed by waste from their camp ashore with the result that swimmers were unmolested.

The sun beat down to turn the hull into a baking oven and led to a request that our crew also might bathe. After exploding a grenade in the water and manning a machine-gun, permission was grudgingly granted, to the rather scornful amusement of the natives.

Exchanging greetings with a returning American submarine after sailing north fully fuelled once more, we resumed our zigzag as soon as the moon rose. Ahead lay the ordeal of passage through the anti-submarine patrolled Lombok Strait against the 5-knot tide which flows out of the Java Sea during October.

Following a practice deep dive to 300 feet, hours were spent at the chart table studying instructions in the Pilot before next day's dive to spend a day off the rugged south west coast of Lombok, only there to discover streaming tide rips where an offshore westerly set met the main southerly stream. Sam decided it would be best to try to slip through close to the Lombok shore. Before setting forth, however, he was determined to spend three hours charging the battery. Against a 5-knot current and assuming we were able to avoid being forced to dive, it would take over four hours at our maximum speed to reach the wider waters and comparative safety of the Java Sea. Already one of our

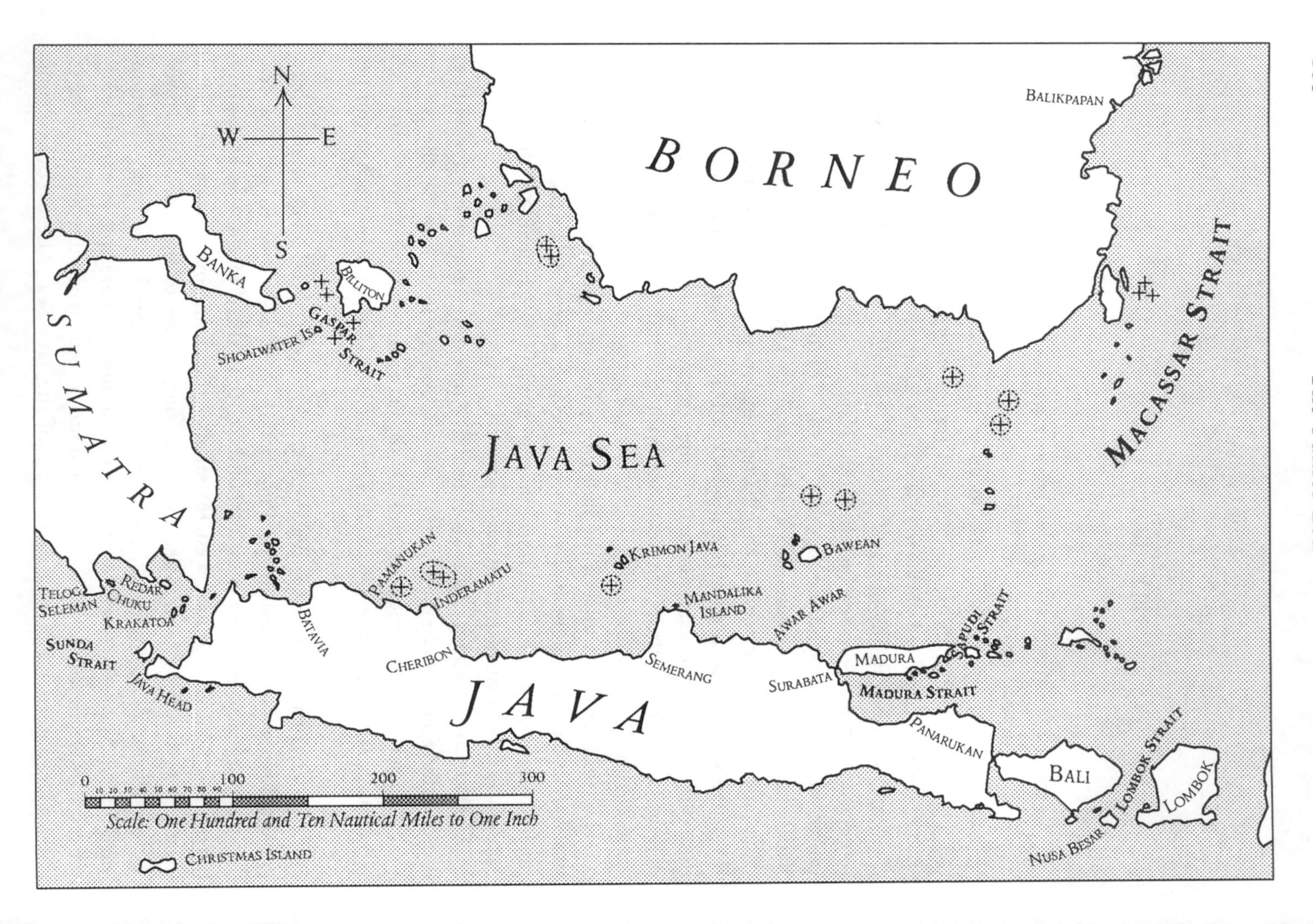
N
W
E
S
BORNEO
BALIKPAPAN
MACASSAR STRAIT
BANKA
BILLITON
GASPAR STRAIT
SHOALWATER IS.
SUMATRA
JAVA SEA
KRIMON JAVA
BAWEAN
PAMANUKAN
INDERAMAYU
MANDALIKA ISLAND
AWAR AWAR
SAPUDI STRAIT
MADURA
MADURA STRAIT
TELOG SELEMAN
REDAR
CHUKU
KRAKATOA
SUNDA STRAIT
JAVA HEAD
BATAVIA
CHERIBON
SEMERANG
SURABATA
JAVA
PANARUKAN
BALI
LOMBOK STRAIT
LOMBOK
NUSA BESAR
0
100
200
300
Scale: One Hundred and Ten Nautical Miles to One Inch
CHRISTMAS ISLAND

boats, driven down by the enemy, had been washed out of the Strait and forced to try again the next night.

Charge complete and with the moon obscured by cloud, *Stoic* set forth. All remained quiet for some time before a shout down from the officer of the watch reported that three vertical white lights, possibly on the shore, were in sight on the port quarter in the direction of Nusi Besar on the Balinese side of the Strait. Nothing disturbed our coast-crawling progress till, suddenly, a light seemingly not far off, flashed astern. Diving stations were closed up as a precaution whilst those on the bridge peered aft, still unable to find any ship.

Following several more alarms and excursions and one alteration of course away from a darkened vessel, it seemed safe to revert to normal cruising stations till, once clear of the narrows, we were able to reduce speed. To have escaped the anticipated harassment suffered by others making the same passage seemed rather an anti-climax.

There followed a frustrating fortnight roaming the Java Sea, mostly on the surface, but disturbed by unlit sailing vessels almost every night and often forced down by numerous patrolling aircraft by day. We visited the main ports of Semarang, Cheribon and Batavia, finding each empty, later again finding no Marus using the Jaspar Strait on the main route south from Singapore, where a lack of landmarks hindered safe navigation, and proximity to land made it prudent to remain dived by day.

Our wardroom life was enlivened by one incident. Before sailing from Colombo, Sam and I, after several bargaining sessions with separate Indian traders, had each bought a sapphire. Sam kept his in a cotton wool lined match box and was wont to take it out to admire on the wardroom table. That night after surfacing, once everything was settled down with the battery charging, I received the usual request: "Permission to ditch gash?" To avoid any risk of betraying the presence of a submarine, all rubbish, with tins punctured to be sure they would sink, remained stored in buckets till after dark when it was safe to dump it. Granting permission, I heard the usual clanking of buckets at the back of the bridge as each was passed up the conning tower, emptied and then lowered back down once more. Then, to my surprise the Captain's voice ordered up the voice pipe, "Stop ditching gash." Sometime later the remaining buckets were hoisted up and the contents ditched.

Peter, on arriving to relieve me, burst into fits of laughter as he recalled the scene down below. Sam, after descending from the bridge, took his usual look at the chart before settling down in the wardroom. After a few minutes he remembered that he had been admiring his sapphire shortly before we surfaced. Despite a frantic search under the table and into the corners of the wardroom and much opening and slamming of drawers the match box could not be found. The wardroom messman was summoned and remembered clearing up rubbish and dropping an old match box in the gash bucket. Hence, Sam's agonised shout of, "Stop ditching gash".

Five full buckets ready for ditching beside the three already empty lay at the bottom of the conning tower ladder. Eagerly plunging a hand deep into disgusting bucket contents of stale food, cigarette packets and other rubbish floating in dirty water, our Captain eventually discovered which one was the wardroom bucket from below whose slopping surface he succeeded in fishing out a soggy match box complete with a month's pay worth of sapphire within: end of panic. A tactful silence on the matter was maintained but we were spared any further gloating sessions.

When we were back off the coast of Java, at last, at long last, the masts of a ship were sighted through the periscope. After coming up to twenty-eight feet for a good look in the high power periscope, the Captain, identifying it as a sizeable merchant ship steering south, brought tubes to the ready, closed up diving stations and started an attack.

As the ship approached it became clear she was following a violent and irregular zigzag pattern, sometimes up to sixty degrees either side of her main course. With such large course alterations it would be important to reach a firing position as close as possible to reduce torpedo travelling time. This, however, involved a greater risk of an unexpected zig towards which could drive us deep and foil any attack. So it turned out. Approaching the firing angle, instead of turning away as hoped, she turned towards to pass close by before altering away to allow us to turn and fire three torpedoes "up the kilt"; no luck, however, as she altered course again to sail away, probably totally unaware she had even been under attack.

In the hope of repeating the successful chase from Penang to Puket, we continued to plot the ship's erratic and complicated zigzag diagram till it was safe to surface and give chase. The port of Cheribon lay seventy miles ahead of her and, should she continue on, she would still have to alter to the east and follow the coast to Semarang. While reloading the three empty tubes, we tried, without getting too close, to manoeuvre ahead, carefully plotting the change of bearing every half-hour. Slowly we were able to draw on to her beam till, when off Cheribon, she turned away to enter the port. This was guarded by extensive sandbanks which prevented any repetition of our Puket harbour attack. The smoke of the town could just be seen, dominated by the conical 10,000-foot volcano Mount Chiremai in the background.

We settled down to wait, charging batteries and patrolling offshore. During the night several signals to and from American submarines were deciphered, including a report from *Dace* and *Darter* on patrol in the Sulu Sea south of the Philippines that they had sunk two cruisers and damaged a third during the passage of a Japanese fleet before *Darter* had run aground to be blown up once *Dace* had rescued her crew. We envied the oceanic American submarines whose superior range, speed and comfort enabled them to operate far from base while we were limited to the Malacca Strait or Java Sea where possible targets were mostly limited to coasters and junks.

A thousand miles away, where these two were operating, there had begun the Battle of Leyte Gulf, the largest naval battle in history, involving no fewer than 282 ships and over 2,000 aircraft, where the Japanese were to lose 4 carriers, 3 battleships, 6 heavy and 3 light cruisers and 3 destroyers against the American loss of only 3 carriers and 3 destroyers. It marked the end of Japanese naval might.

We had no need of a long wait off Cheribon for, after breakfast next morning, smoke on the horizon inshore was soon identified as our ship emerging from her night in harbour. It soon became clear that she had resumed the wild zigzag which had frustrated our torpedo attack the day before. Once more the Captain manoeuvred to try to reach a good torpedo attacking position, only once more to be frustrated by an unexpected turn towards us which forced us deep for a three minute burst of speed; there was a slim chance that a shot from our external stern tube might be successful, but this torpedo track she also avoided.

After Sam had abandoned the periscope in disgust, I pleaded to be given a chance to achieve with my gun what his best torpedo endeavours had failed to do and, against his better judgement I suspect, he agreed. Back on the surface in bright sunshine, only 3,000 yards off on the port bow, there lay a 10,000-ton cargo vessel of modern design with single funnel, gantry type masts and a Japanese flag drooping from the gaff. Our first round, fired less than half a minute after breaking surface, fell short but, following a range correction, the third hit fair and square on her deck below the funnel. Continuing to fire and score hits, I became aware of other flashes separate from our shell bursts.

However, such was my concentration on the task in hand, peering through binoculars, that I was almost completely unaware what else was going on around me. I did notice a turn towards our target to allow us to fire two torpedoes which, by a sharp alteration of course, she managed to evade, causing them to pass close down one side. It also became apparent from cordite smell and blurring of my vision by drifting gun smoke, that we were no longer firing ahead but now abaft the beam.

The target was getting closer and when shells started to miss as I tried to correct the gun's range, I kept having to reduce it and the deflection. Then I heard Sam order the Oerlikon on the gun platform behind the periscope standards to rake her bridge. Following the rattle of its firing, pinpoints of a line of bursting shots peppered her.

Sam yelled an order to cease fire and dive. No longer the hunter, we seemed to have turned into the hunted. While the gun's crew abandoned their gun to pile below, the first one down the conning tower pressed the klaxon as the other five of us followed, leaving the Captain to clip the hatch tight as water gurgled over the top.

"Sixty feet; shut off for depth charging," he shouted down before descending. We had only reached fifty feet before the enemy passed close over the top, its propeller thumping, to be followed shortly after by a mighty explosion, a whoosh of water against the hull, a clang as the bar of the lower lid thumped down, a rattle of crockery, shower of dropping cork and a failure of several lights: not what might be expected from an unarmed and defenceless merchant ship and most unfriendly. I was told that before we dived, while I was concentrating on gun control, shells from its two guns were exploding in the water around us. We appeared to have taken on an armed merchant ship and got the worst of it. Worse was to follow.

When the relief for the PO LTO in the motor room failed to arrive on watch, a messenger was sent to wake him. I rang through from the control room to the fore ends to be told he was not there and must be aft. A careful search failed to find him. As he was the gun trainer, the gun layer was sent for. He thought the trainer had dropped below ahead of him down the gun tower but had noticed the hatch had seemed heavier than usual as he pulled it down. It became clear the gun trainer had been left up top. A shell had burst alongside a few seconds before the order to dive, which might have wounded or stunned him; if not, the exploding depth charge would have destroyed any hope of his survival. When we later surfaced, the open sights of the gun were shattered and a lookout posted at the rear of the bridge discovered the trainer's telescope lying there. Gloom descended with the feeling that everything was going wrong as we followed our ship eastwards.

It was seen from examining the chart that it would not be possible to attack any ship in Semarang harbour due to extensive sandbanks to seaward of the narrow inshore channel. We sailed east seeking easier prey off Mandalika Island, past which in any case our recent adversary would pass, were it to be bound for Surabaya. Patrolling on the surface before dawn, after the officer of the watch had sighted a dark shape, the Asdic operator reported fast revving HE ahead. We turned away and dived, suspecting another submarine. We transmitted in her direction on Asdics and received an answer. Then we both surfaced for a shouted conversation. *Tantalus*, newly arrived, after being told of our troubles over the last two days, informed us she was going west to wait off the route from Singapore.

At last we seemed to have discovered a focal point for Javanese coastal shipping, because that afternoon two small coasting vessels steering westward were seen close inshore. Now under American overall command, we were using American signalling nomenclature. In place of our usual Apple, Beer, Don etc. we now used Able, Bravo, Dog. Destroyers were Dog Dogs and coasters Sugar Dogs. After tea, another report of a Sugar Dog in sight made an unwelcome interruption at a crucial stage in the hectic uckers contest round the wardroom table.

However, this time it proved to be a more substantial Sugar Dog, a long tanker with stumpy bridge aft and a short funnel from which rose a series of puffs and occasional rings of smoke. Lying deep in the water she appeared to be fully loaded as she hugged the coast in shallow water.

Because of the shallow banks we kept the sounding machine running, which showed four fathoms under our bottom as we closed the shore at diving stations. I soon found the bow beginning to rise, the depth gauge showing thirty-one feet and both planes hard a dive without effect. The sounding machine still recorded four fathoms as I flooded water in the forward tank but we continued to rise and I warned Sam he'd have to lower the periscope further. At twenty-eight feet he ordered, "Whatever you do, Number One, don't break surface." In desperation I flooded in a further ton forward then five tons into Q. Still we came up and Sam suddenly realised just before the periscope standards broke surface that we must be sliding along the bottom. "Surface gun action" was ordered with the ucker game spilling on the deck as the table was removed to fit the gun tower ladder.

There up above, 5,000 yards off, between us and the shore, lay our Sugar Dog seeming quite unaware of our presence. Sam, unhappy at our inability to dive in the shallow water, urged me to get on with it and be quick. After two shots falling short, the third hit fair and square amidships. We estimated we were firing at a modern 700-ton diesel tanker which surprisingly maintained course and speed while we continued to pound her.

Even after her crew had been seen to abandon ship, she continued to steam on. We brought down her mast, holed her bridge, peppered her hull with a score of hits and still she continued. Sam was getting impatient. Oh, for the 4-inch gun fitted to later built S-class submarines; our 3-inch appeared sadly ineffective. Then a hit on the deck just forward of her bridge produced a mighty flash from which soon leapt flames forty feet high: we must at last have hit a deck fuel hose connection. A cheer rose from the gun's crew as we ceased fire, to turn and make for deeper water. Dense clouds of black smoke rose high into the sky as we steered clear of the area and even after dark the reflection of flames below the horizon continued to flicker on the smoke cloud astern.

After discovering Bawean Island anchorage fifty miles north to be empty, we returned to the Javanese coast at Awar Awar which the Pilot stated could easily be distinguished by bearing on the distinctive hill Kalak Willis four miles inshore. This area was plagued by small fishing praus and sampans which proved a considerable nuisance to navigation and where one afternoon Prosper claimed to count seventy-five in sight. He further claimed to have distinguished in the high power periscope a front tooth stopping in the open mouth of one sleeping occupant. Anti-submarine patrols disturbed our nights once the fishermen had returned to the beach. Dived for one darkened ship, Jock had picked up his HE till, it having grown faint, we surfaced again only to be immediately forced down after sighting up moon two destroyers within three miles. Most of that night was spent bobbing up and down like a yo-yo as the following entries in the officer of the watch's notebook records:

0526	Dived for a Dog Dog
0547	Surfaced: Nice dog
0548	Dived: Bad Dog
0602	Surfaced: Dog departing to perhaps look for another bone

Tired of being pestered by these persistent DDs we shifted to watch the channel between Java and Madura which led to the Surabaya naval base, where we were able to patrol undisturbed till a mast was at last sighted to the north of us. This turned out to be a large cargo vessel with a two destroyer escort, which a study of Jane's Fighting Ships revealed to be of the Shidri Class. This time we were ideally positioned ahead and even the zigzag was kind to us. After evading one of the destroyers, Sam reached a position a mile off the ship at which he loosed a salvo of four magnetic headed torpedoes set to run deep. Not even were she to alter course should she be able to avoid them. However, the other destroyer approached to drive *Stoic* deep thus unable to remain up to observe the result. When two loud metallic explosions rang out after two minutes we felt it safe to claim a successful sinking.

We had reached 190 feet in our descent before the first depth charge exploded some distance away, followed later by others as we settled gently on the sandy bottom at 240 feet, listening to our hunters milling around above apparently unable to find us. Several hours later unable to detect any propeller noises, we rose gingerly for a look. What would we find? Could one of the DDs be waiting for us, engines stopped? But no, only a distant junk was to be seen. No trace of floating wreckage could be found, so our three remaining torpedoes were loaded before making a night passage on the surface down the narrow Sapudi Strait between the islands of Madura and Sapudi. In its narrowest part the shore each side loomed menacingly close but nothing impeded our passage to prevent us reaching to within a few miles of Panarukan by dawn.

There, soon after breakfast, the happy cry from Peter at the periscope rang out, "Sugar Dog in sight." With the magazine almost empty, despite our hundred extra shells, Sam decided to approach within a mile before surfacing when, to our consternation as we prepared to open fire, a machine-gun mounted on the bridge of this ramshackle 150-ton coaster peppered us, though fortunately without causing any casualties before, we were able to silence it with a direct hit. Unlike our earlier tanker, this vessel sank after less than a dozen hits on her waterline.

All the ammunition remaining now was twenty high explosive, twelve fused anti-aircraft and six star shells so, our patrol being almost complete and our position betrayed, Sam decided we might as well bombard the harbour warehouses and molasses tanks of the sugar factory in sight. Unfortunately, our hope of setting the molasses alight failed because the tanks were surrounded by bricks, though we were able to knock a few holes in the walls and asbestos roofs of the warehouses before all our HE was exhausted.

The submarine chaser which eventually arrived, put us down for a couple of hours before we were able to surface and set off eastwards towards Bali.

While still off Java, yet another small ship came into view to be revealed as what the Americans described as a "G" type landing craft complete with the number 31 painted on her bow.

To avoid wasting any of our few remaining anti-aircraft shells, which had been re-fused to explode on impact, we moved in close before opening fire. After the fourth shell had cracked home, her crew wisely leapt overboard leaving us to fire the remainder at leisure. Still she remained afloat when all we had left were a few star shells designed to release a parachute flare in the air to illuminate any target at night. These were hoisted up and fired, each one puncturing a neat round hole in her waterline. Following a shout from below, "All ammunition expended" the landing craft at last slowly turned turtle to slip below the surface with barely a ripple. Moving towards the bobbing heads of her crew the rope thrown over the saddle tanks allowed six very black natives to climb up to the casing but, surprisingly, a seventh man continued to swim away from us only to sink gently under water and not reappear as we approached.

This, we discovered, was the Japanese skipper achieving the remarkable feat of committing suicide by drowning, honour thereby preserved.

Prisoners safely below, we dived. For watchkeeping, our crew were divided into three watches, Red, White and Blue and they soon nominated our visitors the Black Watch. Making use of a Malay phrase book, the TI with much patience succeeded in establishing communication of a kind to discover them to be Timor boys press-ganged into service. They seemed quite happy to be set to work in the fore ends scrubbing out, peeling potatoes, washing up and carrying out any other suggested chore.

On watch during the night as we were making towards the Lombok Strait along the north coast of Bali, I was able to watch flames leaping from the cone of an erupting volcano above which a dense smoke cloud reflected flickerings from deep down in the crater. Along the mountain below, a thin straggling line of fire marked the passage of lava down the slope, burning all before it. With its reflection in the surface of the sea it made a dramatic and unforgettable scene. Aided by the outflowing current, our exit from the Java Sea through the Lombok Strait, unlike our entrance a month earlier, proved simple, uneventful and devoid of anxiety despite observing patrolling submarine chasers in the distance. Surfacing outside at nightfall, we set course for Exmouth Gulf, once more to fuel from the diesel barge and to grill in midday heat.

Soon after getting underway following an anti-shark charge, hands were piped to bathe and cool off. Given permission to join in, the Black Watch leapt off the bow with cries of delight. The TI, their mentor and friend, noticed that they always leapt in feet first and decided he would teach them to dive head first. His attempts, greeted with mirth by the Timor boys, were to no avail. Always at the last moment their resolve would falter, resulting in some resounding belly flops but never in a proper dive.

We resumed passage to Fremantle, entering harbour with our ensign sadly at half mast for the third LTO, to whose next of kin I had later to write enclosing a cheque for the sum realised from generous purchasers of his kit at the customary sale. Our thirty-five day patrol, at that time longer than that of any other S-class, proved to be not entirely without success.

CHAPTER 19

Sunda Strait

LIMITED FRESH WATER SUPPLIES during our thirty-five day patrol precluded a daily shave so I had decided to allow my beard to grow. Though not dissatisfied with a luxuriant black moustache, the patchy, scraggy, reddish Ho Chi Minh beard lacked charm, so that I willingly agreed to accept Joe's test that it should be shaved off next morning were I to fail to secure an acceptable farewell kiss on departure from the nurses' dance which we visited on our first run ashore: the beard remained.

Joe and I together spent our five-day leave with a local GP/Surgeon in the small grain port of Bunbury, 100 miles south of Fremantle. There we bathed, caught crabs in meat-baited net rings; shot with a rifle rabbits so numerous that missing one's aim would usually fell its neighbour alongside; chased kangaroos in a jeep, later to enjoy the resulting steaks and rich kangaroo-tail soup; rode borrowed nags across miles of empty bush to picnic and swim in a gum-tree sheltered creek; and even attended surgical operations as suggested by our host when told that I, as First Lieutenant, acted as submarine doctor. Refreshed, we returned to relieve the other three.

A priority air passage allowed Peter to fly to stay with friends in Sydney, while Sam, a keen and experienced horseman, spent his five days inland on and about an extensive sheep station near Koolgardie, from which he returned with an arm in a sling due to a broken collarbone. There he heard that our successful Java Sea approach to the escorted cargo ship had proved abortive when the magnetic heads on the torpedoes had exploded prematurely fifty yards on the beam; he made sure the replacement torpedoes loaded were fitted with contact heads to explode on impact.

In his absence I had been allowed to take *Stoic* across the harbour to be slipped in a cradle for Asdic repair and bottom scraping. It had been decided that we would not carry out any second Java Sea trip but, instead, would spend three weeks in the Sunda Strait between Java and Sumatra on our passage back to Trinco and refit in Britain.

After a St Andrew's Day farewell party for friends, in which our guests overflowed to the next door submarine, we left *Maidstone* and the happy 8th Submarine Flotilla for home.

Sailing south of Bali and Java from Exmouth Gulf, our chart and Pilot study showed a triangular strait leading up to the narrow entrance to the Java Sea between Java and Sumatra. It seemed dominated by the remains of Krakatoa Island, whose violent eruption in 1883, heard in both Perth and Ceylon, both 2,000 miles away, had killed by tidal wave over 36,000 people, with ashes landing in Singapore 300 miles distant. The arc of that cone left remained active, one amongst many other volcanoes fuelled by lava rising from the meeting place of two of the earth's major faults.

Following several fruitless days off Java Head, we made a night passage to the western entrance off Sumatra where we spent most of each day surfaced on what proved to be a butterfly migration route. Once, when a strong westerly breeze had raised a short sharp sea, a stream of many thousands of butterflies, mostly white but some of startlingly bright colours, drifted across for several hours from Sumatra to Java.

We felt happier on the surface in this area for, when dived, we were often disturbed by rumbling, creaks and groans in the sea bed: in no circumstances did this seem an area in which to bottom for fear of being swallowed up while we awaited the arrival of some ship to attack. Occasionally driven below by patrolling aircraft, we were otherwise without disturbance to the even tenor of our ways.

Following two weeks of dull routine patrolling, a mere four days before we were due to depart for Trincomalee and home, Prosper, in a state of excitement, rushed from control room to wardroom to announce: "Smoke in sight" Sam, seated at the wardroom table, put down his broken-hammered shotgun which he had spent much time examining, taking apart and cleaning. It had cost him a fiver in Perth and seemed to have replaced sapphire-study as an occupation to take his mind off his responsibilities.

Reaching the control room Sam quietly ordered, "twenty-eight feet; Number One take over the trim"; then, when we were at the ordered depth, "Up periscope" and after swinging it round and pausing on the bearing ordered, "Diving stations". Shutting up the handles and motioning the leading stoker to lower it, he announced, "There's a ship in sight; sixty feet," then "Group up, full ahead together; Port 30; Steer 250." We heard the motor switches click out then clomp home again till, as the rheostat was turned, the propeller thump increased, the boat began to vibrate and the compass card which had been slowly clicking round began to turn faster as speed increased. "Stand by all tubes; set ten feet." Soon six lights glowed "READY".

Up to thirty feet once more, after a five minute burst of speed deep, Sam steadied on the target: "The bearing is *that*."

"Bearing Green 85," read off the signalman from the periscope bearing line.

"Range in high power is *that*."

"Eight," came the reply.

"Set a masthead height of sixty feet."

"Range 18,000 yards," announced Joe from the fruit machine.

"Start a plot, I am forty degrees on his port bow."

Then, after taking three bearings of the shore to fix our position, "Set enemy speed at 12 knots; down periscope," The range had decreased at each subsequent look, then Jock reported, "HE bearing Red 30; reciprocating," and later, "Fast revving HE bearing Green 80; diesel." Our target was being escorted by a submarine chaser. At each look, bearing, range and angle on the bow were noted and plotted with possible re-adjustment of the latter as a result of suggestions from the Plot.

Once the range had fallen to three miles, use of the big periscope with its binocular vision and high magnification could no longer be chanced, for fear of the feather from its 4-inch head breaking surface being observed. Now it was safe only to use the small attack periscope. Then the close relationship developed over time between Captain and leading stoker at the periscope's hydraulic control became vital. As the heavy brass cylinder rose from its well, the Captain, squatting down, pulled out the handles, pressed his face to the eye piece to rise with it slowly till, by the merest movement of a finger, he could control its height to allow only a few inches to break the unrippled mirror of the sea's surface. In a few seconds he had just time to note range and bearing before ordering it to be lowered again. Our ship seemed to be coast crawling without any unpredictable zigzag.

Everyone in the boat seemed keyed up, planes men busy controlling depth and angle with small plane movements; I added a few gallons amidships, tapping the depth gauge carefully to check its effect: all seemed well with both planes nearly level.

"Up periscope:" Sam swung rapidly round with it: "Down periscope."

"You should be seventy-five degrees on the port bow," from Fruit Machine.

"No, set 80," came his reply.

"Eighty set, Sir, new DA 14."

"Stand by; up periscope; bearing *that*; down periscope."

"Ten degrees to go," from Plot.

"Up periscope; Signalman put me on my DA."

The signalman from opposite turned the periscope a few degrees on to the firing angle.

"Fire One; down periscope a little," Sam ordered quietly but sharply.

"On by Asdics," announced Jock.

"Fire Three; down periscope."

"Up periscope; fire Five."

"Down periscope; sixty feet; shut off for depth charging."

"Torpedoes running," from Jock then, in answer to a request for a bearing of the escort, "Red 45."

"Torpedoes running seventy seconds," from the stop-watch worker; they should arrive any time now. All waited tensely. Then two loud explosions rang out in quick succession. Jock took off his earphones to rub his ears ruefully. We had hit.

Stoic down at sixty feet altered course away to try to avoid any retribution. The two depth charges eight minutes later exploded some distance away, followed at intervals by a further fourteen. We had already heard a couple of thumps followed by a distant metallic rattle, almost certainly breaking up noises caused by the collapse of the ship's bulkheads under pressure during its descent to the bottom, sounds quite distinct from the volcanic rumbling to which we had become accustomed in the Sunda area.

Later, back at periscope depth with the submarine chaser some distance away, Sam reverted to watch diving and, while the officer of the watch kept an eye on her, rum was issued and cheerful hands went to dinner as we steered south for the open ocean. Peter watched the dropping of two further depth charges five miles off as the chaser circled round till, before sunset, she disappeared north. Despite being only 100 miles from the main Japanese air base in Batavia, no plane troubled our surfacing. Before it was even dark, we sailed out of American command after receiving a final congratulatory signal from their admiral. Back once more to British ciphers and signals under SEAC to berth alongside *Wolfe*, depot ship of the 2nd Submarine Flotilla, which had replaced *Maidstone*, allowing a reunion with the Temple Cottage VADs.

In Aden we again met Mr Briggs before making a brief call in Alexandria, then on to Malta where we were detained several days for security reasons. Ashore in Valetta one afternoon I walked past Field Marshal Sir Alan Brooke in the street, confirming the rumour that Churchill and Roosevelt and their staffs were in the island for, as it turned out, preparatory discussions before their later meeting with Stalin at Yalta. In Gibraltar, where an earlier returning submarine had discovered that sherry was unaffected if filled into a bitumen-lined tank, we emptied the distilled water from our 240-gallon tank used to top up batteries, to refill it with Fino la Ina for later bottling in *Dolphin*, the Fort blockhouse submarine base in Gosport, and for use in their wardroom mess. The established reward for this bulk sherry transport was a month's free wine bill.

Following a distant sighting of Lizard Head lit through the haze by a setting sun, making our way up the Channel overnight, we entered patches of thick fog till visibility was so reduced that the only sign that we were passing the Needles at daylight lay in the nasal grunt of its foghorn groaning to starboard. For safety should we ground, *Stoic* was trimmed down to increase the draught by three extra feet while we felt our way forward at reduced speed, aided only by inadequate radar bearings, sounding machine, the hearing of bridge watch-keepers and a flood tide on our tail. Our whistle emitted a five-second blast every two minutes and the occasional clanging bell of an unseen anchored vessel rang out.

Eventually the stress of such progress, uncertain of our position, became too great, so the casing party were ordered on deck to get ready to anchor. Then, as they prepared, out of the fog ahead loomed a buoy. After reading the name painted on its side it became clear that, aided by a greater tidal set on our tail than expected, we were off Egypt Point on the Isle of Wight, leaving the Spit Bank as the only serious remaining hazard to our progress to the entrance of Portsmouth harbour. Dismissing the anchor party, the Captain continued east when, after feeling our way past the clanging bells of more anchored vessels, with the dim shape of one liberty ship briefly sighted, his persistence was

Stoic's crew on return from the Far East, February 1945.

rewarded by a clearing of the fog to reveal the skeleton-like remains of Mulberry Harbour pontoons now moored off the Isle of Wight and, ahead, West Spit Buoy allowing safe passage past Spit Bank to Fort Blockhouse.

While hands changed into clean white submarine sweaters below to make a proper show on the fore casing on entering harbour, the signalman was told to flash up the signal tower at Fort Blockhouse. Taken by surprise by our flashing signal numbers, there was some delay before they answered "Welcome Home" followed by a granting of permission to enter Haslar Creek despite the tide being unfavourable. Descending the conning tower ladder, Bunts returned up to secure to the periscope standards both our paying off pennant, a narrow streamer of bunting stretching to beyond the stern, its end supported by an inflated condom, and the Jolly Roger, a skull and crossbones surmounting three white bars, nine stars under crossed guns, a dagger, a factory and a Popski bomb, all we had to show for a year's work, limited as it had been by a lack of targets.

The depot had piped "Clear lower deck" so that the sea wall and jetty were lined by her officers, men and a few Wrens in greeting to a returning submarine on completion of her commission.

Amongst our first visitors after securing alongside, were officers of HM Customs and Excise out to collect a suitable sum of duty but keen to be helpful to sailors returning from a long spell overseas. Discovering a large quantity of dutiable goods and souvenirs aboard they agreed, once their dues were paid, to send over the customs launch next day to land those going on leave alongside Portsmouth Harbour station, now back in use after its severe blitz damage, outside the customs controlled area. Thus were a pair of rugs bought by me from an Aden trader in Crater City safely landed.

Before *Stoic* had sailed for home, Sam was asked by Captain S/M of the 8th Flotilla to do his utmost to discover a way to fit into an S-class submarine a more satisfactory radar set, a task Naval Constructors had claimed to be impossible. To this purpose he sacrificed his first week's foreign service leave, spending many hours, tape measure and signal pad in hand, working with an RNVR radar expert from Admiral Submarines' staff to try to solve the problem, eventually successfully persuading a high powered conference of Admiralty and Submarine experts that a proper plan-presentation radar could and should be fitted into each new and refitting S-class boat, beginning with *Stoic*. I later had cause to bless him when I commanded *Sturdy* so fitted.

There followed three happy leisurely months while *Stoic* refitted in Portsmouth dockyard, allowed ample weekend leave, a chance of spring chalk-stream fishing, and the achievement of reasonable proficiency at snooker table and on squash court.

In mid April 1945, with the war in Europe drawing to a close, I joined a party to prepare for U-boat surrender, having been ordered to instruct them on the differences between their interior and handling compared with those of one of our submarines. Thus we were ready for the eventual announcement that 8th May would be VE day.

CHAPTER 20

By U-boat to Westminster

RECOVERING FROM A VE NIGHT HANGOVER, following wild and happy Portsmouth celebratory revels among cheering crowds thronging the streets ending up with fireworks and uninhibited dancing round a huge bonfire on Southsea Common, and a frantic dash by our party of submariners and Wrens to catch the last boat across the harbour to *Dolphin*, an unwelcome tannoy blared out a pipe ordering the U-boat surrender party to muster. This left just sufficient time to splice the main brace, an extra tot for each rating and the only authorised rum issue to officers as well, before boarding a bus for Portland. The Captain's Secretary had promised to postpone my arranged Buckingham Palace attendance with Sam and four of *Stoic's* crew to collect DSCs and DSMs due a week later.

Each U-boat at sea had been ordered to surface, signal its position and hoist the black flag they were known to carry, while awaiting instructions. *U248* had already surfaced off the Lizard and been ordered to steer to arrive off Portland Bill the next morning. There an MTB carrying a Polish boarding party and our three officers met her. The German invasion of Poland having started World War Two, it was most appropriate it should be Poles who accepted the first U-boat surrender at its end, travelling in her to berth alongside a trawler loaded with press photographers and newsreel men anchored outside the breakwater in Portland Bay.

Only then did our party board, go below and search likely sites for demolition charges, of which I was aware from earlier trials in *Graph*.

Once these had been checked clear, our party were asked by the assembled press to enact the charade of pretending to capture *U248*, already several hours in Allied hands. How much more graphic would it have been had only *Stoic*'s piratical bearded Leading Seaman Robinson wielding his own chosen weapons been available to demonstrate his own stylish technique for junk boarding and capture. Instead, feeling and looking both self conscious and absurd, we had several times to repeat for the assembled cameras leaps, revolver in hand, on to her casing beneath the disdainful gaze of assembled Poles and German officers looking down on us from her bridge. It was only after a boat had borne the press ashore to meet their deadlines that there was time to make a more thorough examination of our captive.

Outside, instead of *Graph*'s 88-millimetre gun forward, she mounted abaft her bridge an elongated platform with a pair of twin 20-millimetre machine-guns ahead of a 40-millimetre anti-aircraft cannon next to the Schnorkel tube, allowing use of the diesel engines whilst remaining dived, with only its top showing above the surface: all clear proof of how effective our radar fitted anti-submarine aircraft had proved.

The interior appeared very similar to that of *Graph* captured four years earlier. On reaching the crew accommodation forward, however, our nostrils were assaulted by a nauseous stench of rotting food and stale urine resulting from their method of gash disposal by gathering it to load into an empty torpedo tube and waiting till it was fully loaded before firing out the contents with a charge of compressed air. The crew appeared to have made little effort to clean up the inevitable spillage which had been left to rot. By the last year of the war, U-boat crews were often required to suffer the ordeal of seven weeks at sea in the conditions of severe discomfort which, in *Graph*, we had discovered reduced our carefully selected crew's efficiency after a mere three weeks at sea: no wonder their losses had mounted.

When *U248* had secured to a jetty inside the breakwater within Portland Harbour, we sent away to prisoner of war camps all her officers and most of her junior ratings, leaving us just a skeleton crew to stay aboard and carry out essential maintenance work. As our party was to be accommodated two miles away in *Osprey*, the anti-submarine school, we were lent two motor cycles and a lorry for transport to and fro. *Osprey* also provided sentries to mount guard at the end of the jetty, to keep out onlookers and permit access only to those we authorised.

As *U248* was soon joined by two more U-boats escorted in by a destroyer from the Channel, we were to become a tourist attraction. Once more all their officers and most of their crews were despatched to prisoner of war camps, leaving us a day working party of thirty experienced ratings to maintain all three boats, later to be joined by a fourth. Despite some language difficulties, once they became aware that our officers and ratings were all experienced submariners, our captives seemed happy to accept our orders.

It was to take two days and many gallons of Jeyes Fluid before the mess had been disinfected and cleanliness restored. By this time visiting torpedo experts from *Vernon* had found two torpedo heads of especial interest and worthy of detailed examination. As our next planned task was to disembark all torpedoes and ammunition, we were able to meet their request to have them just as soon as they could despatch a collection lorry from Portsmouth. A host of other specialist officers kept arriving to examine sound detection, wireless, radar, anti-radar, signal and much other equipment and we tried to meet their demands.

One of our earliest concerns was the avoidance of any theft or looting of equipment or German possessions still aboard. While obviously valuable items such as binoculars, sextants and chronometers had been landed to be put under lock and key ashore, there was much of value left aboard, a temptation to the less honest. The coxswain was given responsibility only to authorise removal by crew members to *Osprey* of such items as a souvenir tin helmet, one of the excellent rubber one-man-escape dinghies or the odd food tin.

Our anxieties were to prove well founded. A few days after arrival, Chief and I were motor cycling back to the mess in *Osprey* for lunch when we were waylaid by an indignant coxswain stating that he wished to make a complaint. While everyone was down working with the Germans in the boats, our ratings' private lockers had been opened, searched and all their authorised souvenirs and even a sum of money from an AB's belt had been removed. The discovery of this invasion of their privacy left them in a state of seething discontent bordering on mutiny. The coxswain made clear that, had the reason for it been explained, no one would have objected to a search of his locker in his presence by his own officer.

Our CO discovered from the ever helpful Commander of *Osprey* that his suggestion that this was the proper procedure had been brushed aside by his Captain, who had all along appeared to disapprove of our party and resent their independence. It was only after a stormy meeting in the office of Flag Officer Portland that the property was returned but the episode left behind a feeling of indignation.

When the *Illustrated London News* published pictures of the atrocities discovered in Buchenwald and Belsen, I took a copy borrowed from *Osprey*'s mess down to show to our German captives. It was "Stand Easy", and they were up on deck enjoying the bright sunshine when I called them over to look. With one exception, they did appear shocked and one with broken English explained that, while everyone knew there were concentration camps, they had no idea what went on therein. The one exception seemed uncaring, with even the vestige of a sneer on his lips. With a message to the Army guards to keep an eye on him, we made sure he was kept locked up and did not return.

That evening we were told that it was planned to sail two U-boats with British crews, open to the public at each port of call, one eastward and the other westward round the coast. The next day, who should arrive but Sam Marriott who had succeeded in gathering several more ex *Graph* hands, including Subby Pratt, who had taken over from me as her third hand and was now

'Joe' Perowne, 'Sam' Marriott and the author on *Stoic's* return, February 1945.

recovered from the skin complaint that had caused him to be invalided from *Stoic*, her splendid stalwart Coxswain Brigham Young and Petty Officer Teague, her second coxswain. He had also arranged for me once more to join him as First Lieutenant.

With this nucleus of U-boat experience we were soon ready to make a trial trip round the harbour in *U776*, the best of our four captured boats. Down in the motor room, attended by German ratings, I worked one motor and the PO LTO the other without any problems. On our return, Sam reported *U776* would be ready, British-manned, to sail on Monday 21 May, only twelve days from *U248*'s surrender. By then one of *Stoic*'s ERAs appointed to join us had returned from the investiture to say that the King, noting the absence of Sam and me, had enquired where we were. Unusually, submariners had the privilege that officers and men would receive their decorations together rather than separately and it seemed the Lord Chamberlain's office had not been told of our inability to be present, or why.

The day of departure dawned fine as we set forth for the Thames, glad to be no longer dependent on the hospitality of the unfriendly Captain of *Osprey* but appreciating the gesture, perhaps to make amends, by the Commander and several other officers in taking time to travel down to the jetty to see us off. Bright sunlight shone on the white Dorset cliffs and, pleased to be at sea in a captured U-boat once more, we soon reached St. Catherine's Head where a Cunarder, westbound after rounding the Isle of Wight, steamed close by, dipping her ensign to us as she passed. Once within the well-buoyed mineswept channel through the Dover Strait, at sunset we slowed down to reach Nore Light Vessel at dawn, embark a pilot and reach Tilbury to await the flood tide. After breakfast, the ship's company cleaned into running rig, their freshly laundered submarine sweaters gleaming white.

Setting forth with a new pilot up the Thames, our progress was triumphant: cotton wool clouds floated in a blue sky and shipping docked either side of the river hooted in greeting, some of their crews lining their decks to cheer; one or two cranes ashore even dipped low in salute. A boat load of photographers had joined our escort of two tugs before we passed below Tower Bridge. Two bridges later, as we shot a central arch of the new Waterloo Bridge, crowded with onlookers, a small boy spitting down over its side scored a direct hit on PO Teague in charge of the forecastle party to his intense and loudly expressed irritation.

After piping HMS *President*, berthed ahead of Scott's *Discovery* beside the Embankment, ahead lay Westminster Bridge so thick with sightseers that they had blocked the progress of crossing trams and overflowed to line the Embankment. Sam, refusing proffered assistance from tugs, stopped in midstream short of Westminster Bridge to move astern at an angle stemming the flood tide till we were able to pass over wires to two waiting Thames watermen and gently secure alongside Westminster Pier.

A staff officer from the Admiralty waited to greet Sam and explain their rejection of his protest that he believed it unsafe to berth a round hulled vessel drawing sixteen feet on an outside river bend in water drying out to ten feet at low water; their claim that the U-boat would settle into the muddy bottom contradicted all experience that, on an outside bend, any mud present would long have been washed away to leave a bare gravel bottom. With Sam unconvinced and fearing the worst, I was ordered to double up wires of far larger diameter than usual. Unfortunately the pontoon afforded just two substantial bollards on which both breast and spring wires had to be attached, the smaller boat cleats being of no help.

Above us Big Ben boomed out the hours and quarters. Sam left to lunch ashore, soon followed by most of the rest of the ship's company travelling in a lorry to the mess in *President*, leaving just me, the Second Coxswain and five

Sailing the captured *U776* up to Westminister Pier, May 1945.

others as duty watch aboard. By the time the captain returned *U776*, with a further three hours of ebb tide left to surge past till low water, was already aground. Quite unaware of our growing anxiety, the milling crowds looking on from the Embankment remained packed solid.

Taut wires started to sing at the strain and, after the gangway had been put back on the pontoon as a precaution, I went below to discover the outward list was already nearly five degrees. Returning up top for a shouted discussion across to Sam anxiously fingering his tie, a sure sign of concern, he told me to clear men from the casing, suggesting that we shelter in the comparative safety of the far side of the conning tower. Soon after, a 2½-inch wire spring parted with a sharp twang, then a second wire followed with a crack causing the whole submarine to judder.

It seemed impossible that, as the falling tide exposed more and more of the hull, the remaining breasts, quivering at the stress of taking the full strain, would continue to hold; the onlookers were likely to witness the dramatic spectacle of a capsizing U-boat.

When it finally happened, the forward wire broke with a rending thump while those aft held, but instead wrenched from the pontoon the bollard to which they were tied, catapulting it out to splash into the Thames. With a mighty lurch *U776* rolled over on its side till its roll was arrested with a jerk when the drowned hydroplane hit the bottom; as a wave spread across the Thames towards County Hall, our small party, desperately hanging on to the conning tower hand rail, had narrowly avoided an involuntary swim. Crawling round the conning tower out on to the sloping deck, I was able to shout to our anxious Captain that we were none the worse, before setting off on to the bridge to get down below and find out if the two remaining seamen were safe, check whether a whiff of chlorine would indicate battery pollution and investigate the damage.

Descending a ladder leaning over fifty-eight degrees proved surprisingly difficult. Awkwardly hanging half upside down like a lemur, it was necessary to hook a toe round each rung of the steel ladder in turn. At the bottom, after slithering down the slippery steel deck till stopped by the side of the chart table, now more horizontal than the deck itself, I crawled forward, then up again to negotiate the round hatch before finally collapsing heavily into the Captain's bunk on the far side. From there a loud shout brought a reassuring reply that the two others were unhurt.

Piles of furniture, heaters, mattresses and bedding lay in disarray beneath the assorted contents of starboard side drawers in the angle between deck and bunk. Heaving up, in and out of wardroom, galley and petty officers' mess, I was able to survey through the bulkhead the chaos in the fore ends. There, below a ladder hanging drunkenly by one hook, was littered a pile of hammocks, kit bags, upturned lockers and other debris amid which the two men were vainly trying to rescue some of their shipmates' possessions.

After they had abandoned this hopeless task, the three of us helped each other to crawl back through the control room to reach the ERA's mess and peer into an engine room showing little sign of damage, switch on the battery fans at full blast and return. Climbing up the conning tower ladder seemed even more difficult, each of us in turn losing footing to be left hanging in mid air like drunken trapeze artists. Three hours would elapse before the flooding tide would refloat the boat and, till then, there seemed little useful for our party to do but stare back at the watching crowds ashore.

When afloat once more, *U776* was ignominiously towed to a buoy beside Blackfriars Bridge in the Pool of London where, in preparation for next forenoon's visit from the Prime Minister, we worked half the night to clear up the chaos and restore order and cleanliness. Apart from one battery cell polluted with salt water, which was cut out of the battery, we discovered that salt water had also entered the armature of the port main motor through a missing inspection plate out of sight. While checking circuits, the PO LTO and I were rewarded, when we put in its starting switch, by a violent bang, purple flash and a smell of burning. It was never again possible to achieve a safe insulation reading, which meant that motor could no longer safely be used. Fortunately, U-boat diesel engines, unlike those in our submarines, were reversible so the port screw was still available for shiphandling.

Towed back to Westminster Pier and showing no visible sign of the misadventure of the day before, we were ready to receive Mr Churchill and other distinguished visitors; it had even been rumoured that we might receive a visit from the King. Sadly it was not to be. That forenoon the Coalition War Government had fallen, the Prime Minister had tendered his resignation to the King and agreed to continue with a caretaker government until a general election could be held. The visit was cancelled.

Disappointed, we still showed round assorted MPs and senior civil servants, our most distinguished guests being the First Sea Lord, Admiral Sir Andrew Cunningham, the Chief of the Imperial General Staff, Field Marshal Sir Alan Brooke, both accompanied by wives, and Mr A.V. Alexander spending his last day as First Lord of the Admiralty.

Sam had to show round the politician, whose interest seemed minimal apart from constant queries on the whereabouts of press photographers.

I was fortunate to accompany the two Service Chiefs. They behaved like a pair of small boys enjoying a special half holiday from school, asking numerous questions and keen to miss nothing. Patiently their wives followed them round. After I had taken Sir Andrew half way up the conning tower to the kiosk, he perched in the saddle of the attack periscope, driving it round, peering through the eyepiece and clicking from high to low power before shouting down, "Here, Alan, come and look at this." Only the impatient message from Mr Alexander that photographers were waiting, cut short their visit. Photographs once taken on the fore casing, the politician, with curt acknowledgement, returned ashore while, in contrast, both Service Chiefs had the courtesy to thank and shake hands with each of us before being piped ashore.

Westminster Pier having proved unsuitable, it was decided we should next day enter Shadwell Basin and berth in Western Dock opposite the Crescent Wine Vaults just downstream from Tower Bridge.

Safely docked in the basin, we had to decide how to give a look at their captured U-boat to as many visitors as possible. Following the arrival of the Chief Superintendent of the Port of London Police, it became clear we were to be involved in crowd control as well. We agreed that, once past the dock security gate, visitors would be shepherded by police in an orderly line, weaving past two ancient red brick warehouses to reach our berth; we further accepted the suggestion that the whole policing operation be placed under the overall control of our duty officer.

Once aboard over the forward of two gangways, visitors would cross the fore casing, descend through the hatch, move through the boat, taking a quick look through the periscope, to emerge up the steep after hatch before passing a Wren presiding over a large open box collecting donations to King George's Fund for Sailors on their way back to Tower Street, The duty petty officer on the fore casing would welcome visitors and show them below, where they would first look at the torpedo tubes, with a rating to answer questions, before passing other crew members posted in accommodation space, control room, galley, engine room and finally motor room before emerging after being helped up by the last seaman and a plain clothes detective.

People began to queue outside the gates next day a full hour before they were due to open. We soon discovered that we could only manage four visitors a minute through the boat which would allow between 9 am and 6 pm only 2,000 daily visits. When, on that first morning's opening, over 9,000 were waiting in a long patient queue by eleven, it became obvious some change of plan was essential. By lowering the periscope, we discovered throughput could be increased to six a minute, thus increasing daily capacity to just over 3,000, which would still be totally inadequate for those patiently waiting. After discussion with our police colleagues, it was decided to form two queues, one for those willing to face a long wait to go inside the boat, while the remainder would be able to flow slowly past on the jetty without undue delay. Once this arrangement had been made known, most of those waiting opted just to walk past, so reducing the wait to not more than a couple of hours for those determined to come aboard.

Our sailor commissionaires were encouraged to answer questions briefly before repeating, "Would you please move on now; there are many more waiting behind." On the fore casing, the welcoming PO had been instructed to push six a minute down below when sheer limit of space should ensure emergence of a similar number aft. For the remainder of our London stay we coped with over 3,000 aboard daily while between 15,000 and 20,000 walked past, shepherded by a squad of fifty police, some lent by the Metropolitan force working watches like us. In this, their first very own exhibition of the war, it seemed half the East-Enders who had suffered such grievous damage in the blitz came from Limehouse, Stepney and Shadwell to look.

On the first day, we laid out as souvenirs a pile of German novels and a sack of rusty nuts and bolts discovered aboard and these soon disappeared. Some of our visitors, avid for some memento of their visit, were utterly unscrupulous in trying to remove and steal tally plates, valve wheels or any other portable item to be seen, so we acquired locally large sacks loaded with scrap nuts and bolts in self protection and these were made available as souvenirs. Above the after hatch the sharp witted cockney detective sergeant who, in addition to helping old ladies negotiate the awkward after hatch, adding any assurance needed that little Alfie still below would soon be retrieved and returned, had a remarkable instinct for spotting a petty thief: his occasional request to see contents of pocket or handbag almost invariably produced some looted object.

One afternoon a very rotund lady jammed firmly in the 22-inch diameter after hatch. On duty at the time, a message reached me and, on descending from the bridge, I discovered her stuck with one arm grasping a loaded shopping bag up top with the other jammed down below. After relieving her of the bag, the detective and I vainly attempted to free her by tugging her one available arm.

"I'll have to go down again," she gasped.

"Lidy, yer can't do that, there's solid people down there," replied the detective, which reminded me to ask the PO at the other hatch to cease pushing six more down below every minute, which must already have caused a tightly packed crush in the limited space.

Our heavily breathing visitor readily agreed to the stoker down below applying a shoulder to her ample rear. Anxious in case the strain might rip her clothing we waited in apprehension, still ready to heave on her one available arm. However, with little help from us, the heave from below unjammed her and, popping out like a champagne cork, she rose to land clear on the dock above, allowing those below to bubble forth. Breathing heavily, her only comment, bless her heart, was that she'd need to give up fish and chips before joining submarines. Once she had her breath back, I escorted her ashore and was touched when she contributed what surely must have been to her the princely sum of half a crown in the Wren's collecting box. The constant good-natured humour of our cockney visitors never ceased to amaze.

When we were told of an impending visit to *U776* by the Lord Mayor of London, Sam raised a nice protocol problem. By ancient custom the Lord Mayor is also Lord Admiral of the Port of London and, as such, would be entitled to be piped aboard. Were we, or were we not, to pipe him? Some official delving deep in dusty Admiralty archives discovered that a special ceremonial uniform existed for the Lord Admiral. Because he would visit in plain clothes he was not entitled to a pipe.

Despite being denied this courtesy, the Lord Mayor took a lively interest when shown round and, two days later, entertained three of us to dinner in the Mansion House, to which we travelled in a chauffeured Rolls supplied by the Admiralty, to be greeted by a liveried footman on arrival. After an informal dinner with his wife and daughter, Sir Frank Alexander returned the compliment by personally showing us round the Egyptian Hall and, down in the vaults, allowing us to wield the pearl sword of the City, which is always proffered to the Sovereign on the city boundary. Also, we were allowed to examine the gold and silver trophies. We proudly entered *U776* as our address in the visitors' book.

Resulting from a visit by Sir George Abyss, Assistant Commissioner at Scotland Yard, we also enjoyed a trip to the Black Museum with its gruesome relics of famous crimes – weapons, murderers' death masks and the ropes that had hanged the murderers, before watching activity in the map room where moving counters on four flat maps of the Metropolitan area marked the movements of patrol cars and the positions of crimes reported on 999.

Officers off duty would often make a pre-lunch call down in the nearby Crescent Wine Vault, which held in bond rows and rows of sherry casks set in cradles on an earthen floor in part of the honeycomb of cellars underneath dockside buildings. Within its gloomy interior, above which pillars arched to support the roof, regular brandy fortification of each cask was supervised by skilled warehousemen who, every few months, would extract a sample of each cask's content to estimate the amount of brandy required. These samples of amber liquid, usually spilled onto the earthen floor, were available to any

Sceptre, commanded by the author, and *Taciturn* leaving Portland for exercises, May 1946.

fortunate visitor admitted below. Steadiness of foot after half an hour's sampling was liable to be reduced, but fortunately the police canteen lay nearby to provide much needed blotting paper. Not only our officers were offered hospitality and entertainment. The ship's company enjoyed a party arranged by the Mayor of Westminster and received free theatre tickets and many other perquisites.

I was not too disappointed when, soon before *U776* was due to sail north calling at assorted ports all the way up the east coast till she reached Lerwick, I was relieved as First Lieutenant by Pratt, the third hand, to return to *Dolphin* and await my "perisher", the Submarine Commanding Officers' Qualifying Course. Before leaving I joined in the party given to thank our police colleagues for all their help and willing co-operation. Sam made a brief speech and, once beer from the barrel tapped in the fore ends began to flow, our visitors relaxed, undid their uniform collars, and soon snatches of song wafted to the wardroom where we entertained the Super and his four inspectors with the confiscated contents of the bottles of spirit discovered in the German CO's locker at the time of surrender. My farewell memory of *U776* is of the Super, supported by a sergeant on either side, weaving ashore assured in a broad Irish brogue that, "Don't you be worrying, sorr, we'll see you safely home." No breathalyser in those days.

Ahead for a few months lay the opportunity to wind down in *Dolphin* while waiting for the "perisher", which would qualify me for my own submarine command, to begin. Social life was full and varied, with sailing in the Solent, while near at hand were wary trout in a friend's chalk-stream beat to be tempted by a well placed dry fly. Although the struggle in the Far East had several weeks to run, my war had come to an end. In the words of Psalm 107:

> They that go down to the sea in ships, that do their business in great waters;
> These see the works of the LORD and his wonders in the deep.

Seeing the works of the Lord and his wonders in the deep during the Second World War had not proved unenjoyable while it lasted.

Glossary

AA	Anti Aircraft.
AB	Able Seaman.
AMC	Armed Merchant Cruiser.
A/S	Anti Submarine.
Aldis lamp	A hand searchlight for flashing morse.
Angle on the Bow	The number of degrees that an attacking submarine finds herself lying to port or starboard of the enemy's bow.
Asdic	A transmitting device for detecting dived submarines by receiving an echo off their hulls, now known as Sonar.
BLO	Bombardment Liaison Officer.
Ballast Tank	These tanks are used for surfacing and diving the submarine. She dives when they are flooded and surfaces when they are blown.
Boat	Slang for submarine. Perhaps connected with the early submarine or Holland boats.
Bow Cap	The door which shuts out the sea from a submarine torpedo tube and which has to be opened before a torpedo can be fired.
Broach to	Turn beam on to a heavy sea.
Bunts	Slang for Signalman, literally "Bunting Tosser".
CB	Confidential Book.
COPP	Combined Operations Pilotage Party.
Captain (S/M)	The Captain in command of a submarine flotilla. If a number is added, it indicated the number of the flotilla.
Captain (D)	The Captain in command of a Destroyer flotilla. With a number added, as above.
Carley float or raft	An oval life saving raft.
Casing	The steel deck of a submarine.
The Charge	Used in connection with battery charging in a submarine, i.e. Start the charge. Break the charge. Start a running charge port side, etc., etc.
Chef	The cook.

Chief	The engineer officer. Also used sometimes when addressing a chief petty officer.
To clean	To clean into any rig is sailor's language for changing into it.
Commander (S/M)	The second in command of a submarine flotilla, who is in charge of submarine administration.
Coston Gun	A method of firing a light line by rifle from one ship to another.
Cyphers	Naval messages in secret cypher, as opposed to confidential code.
"D"	Captain (D)
"D19"	Captain (D), 19th Destroyer Flotilla.
DF	Destroyer Flotilla.
D/F	Direction Finding.
Dan Buoy	A light metal buoy with a wooden pole through it, which is easily handled.
Davits	Steel arms from which boats are lowered and hoisted.
Degaussing	A treatment to neutralise a ship's magnetic field and so protect her from magnetic mines.
Director	A steel encased turret which controls and fires the guns.
Dogs	See Watches.
Doppler	A phenomenon whereby the pitch of an echo indicates whether the object off which the echo is received is advancing or retiring.
EA	Electrical Artificer.
ERA	Engine Room Artificer.
Engines	In a submarine, engines always refers to the diesels, as distinct from motors, which are the electric motors.
FAA	Fleet Air Arm.
FOO	Forward Observation Officer, who is ashore with own forces to spot the fall of shot in any bombardment carried out from ships supporting a landing.
First	See Watches.
Fix	A navigational position.
Flags	The signals officer.
Folboat	A collapsible canvas canoe.
Forecastle	The forward part of a ship (pronounced "fokesle" and "forrard').
Fore-ends	The sailors living quarters, and the stowage space for reload torpedoes.
Fore-endman	A rating who lives in the fore-ends.
Fore planes	The forward hydroplanes.

Freeboard Height of the deck above the waterline.

Fruit Machine The Submarine Torpedo Attack Instrument, so called because its face resembles a gambling fruit machine.

GCO Gunnery Control Officer.

Group up A submarine term for "motors in parallel", i.e. high speed.

Guns The gunnery officer, or gunner (T).

Gunwale The top edge of a boat's side.

HA High angle, i.e. anti-aircraft.

HE High explosive, or Hydrophone Effect which is the noise that a ship's propellers make under water.

Harbour Stations Stations for entering and leaving harbour (in a submarine).

Heads W.C.

Heave-to To lie head to the seas maintaining steerage way while waiting for the weather to moderate.

Hook rope A wire with a hook spliced on one end.

HSD Higher Submarine Detector on Asdics

Hydroplanes Horizontal rudders, one pair forward, and one pair aft.

Kai Slang term for Navy cocoa – hot, thick, containing arrowroot, and most sustaining.

Khamseen Pronounced "hamseen". A hot sand-laden wind which blows off the land.

Kingston A valve at the foot of a tank either to let in or keep out the sea as required.

Klaxon The diving hooter.

LA Low angle.

Liar Dice A popular form of gambling with five dice.

Long Stay A ship riding at long stay has a long length of cable between the bow and the buoy, so that she rides more comfortably in rough weather.

LST Tank Landing Ship.

LTO One of the three ratings in a submarine responsible for working and maintaining motors, batteries and electrical machinery.

Main Line A pipe running the length of the submarine with connections to various tanks, and to the pump.

Make and Mend Half holiday.

Middle See Watches.

Motors The electric motors in a submarine, as opposed to the diesel engines.

Number One The first lieutenant, who is second in command of a destroyer or submarine.

OA Ordinance Artificer.

OD Ordinary Seaman.

OOD Officer of the Day.

OOW Officer of the Watch.

Outside ERA The ERA who is responsible for machinery outside the engine room, and for controlling the blowing panel and telemotor system when dived.

PO Petty officer.

PO LTO The senior LTO in a submarine.

Pay off A ship pays off when her commission is completed and she returns for refit.

Periscope depth A convenient depth under water for using the periscope.

Perisher Slang for COQC (Submarine Commanding Officers' Qualifying Course).

Ping (i) The Asdic officer. (ii) The actual Asdic echo. (iii) To transmit on Asdics.

Pilot The navigating officer.

Plane Hydroplane in a submarine.

Pooped A ship is pooped when a stern sea breaks over her stern and carries it under, the water racing forward over the deck and pushing the whole ship under.

"Q" A tank used for making a submarine bodily heavy rapidly, and for quick diving.

Quarterdeck The after part of a ship.

RT Radio telephone.

Radar A wireless method of using short waves to detect ships, aircraft, and land by means of echoes.

Rate Officer The man responsible for estimating enemy course and speed and for watching for alterations thereof.

SAP Semi armour piercing.

SEAC South East Asia Command.

Schoolie The instructor officer.

Schnorkel An air pipe which, when raised above the surface, allows a submarine to use its engines, draw in air, and thus remain dived for weeks.

Scratch The secretary.

Screen A number of destroyers positioned round a fleet, convoy, or valuable ship to give protection from submarine or air attack.

Smoke Candle A container fired by a dived submarine which gives off smoke on the surface, and thus marks her position when she fired it.

Snotties Nurse The officer responsible for midshipmen.

SouWesPac American abbreviation for South West Pacific Command.

Stoker PO The petty officer in charge of tanks, fuel, and trimming in a submarine.

Sub Sub-lieutenant, or substitute, but never, please, oh never, for a submarine!

TS Transmitting station. This contains the tables, and instruments, which use information passed from the director and, after correcting it, pass it on to the guns.

Telemotor System A hydraulic method of working equipment by oil pressure.

Tiddly ship A smart polished clean efficient ship.

Tiddly suit A sailor's best uniform, reserved for shore going and divisions.

Torps The torpedo officer.

Trailer Pump A mobile pump for supplying water, which was extensively used to fight fires during air raids.

Trim Dive The first dive after leaving harbour which adjusts and corrects the calculated trim put in the tanks before sailing.

Trot A trot of submarines is one or more lying alongside a depot ship or each other. A movement of submarines to alter the trot is known as a trot fob.

Tube Torpedo tube.

Uckers A popular naval variation of ludo. It is much faster, and more exciting and hazardous than the rather staid ludo.

Voice pipe A tube between two compartments for shouting messages from one to the other.

WT Wireless/telegraphy.

Waist The deck of a destroyer either side of the funnel amidships.

Watches Middle: Midnight to 4 am. Morning: 4 to 8 am. Forenoon: 8 am to noon. Afternoon: Noon to 4 pm. Dogs: First Dog: 4 to 6 pm. Last Dog: 6 to 8 pm. First: 8 pm to midnight.

Watchkeeping Ticket The watchkeeping certificate which is granted to sub-lieutenants considered competent to keep a watch alone at sea.

Yeoman A signal petty officer.